ARLINGTON

ALSO BY JAMES GINDLESPERGER

So You Think You Know Gettysburg? (with Suzanne Gindlesperger)
So You Think You Know Gettysburg? Volume 2 (with Suzanne Gindlesperger)
So You Think You Know Antietam? (with Suzanne Gindlesperger)
Escape from Libby Prison
Fire on the Water
Seed Corn of the Confederacy

John F. Blair, Publisher
Winston-Salem, North Carolina

HERE RESTS IN
HONORED GLORY
AN AMERICAN
SOLDIER
KNOWN BUT TO GOD

ARLINGTON
A Color Guide to America's Most Famous Cemetery

by James Gindlesperger

Published by

John F. Blair,
Publisher
1406 Plaza Drive
Winston-Salem, North Carolina 27103
blairpub.com

PRINTED IN CHINA

COVER IMAGE: *Autumn colors the trees throughout Arlington National Cemetery*

MAPS: Courtesy of Arlington National Cemetery

Library of Congress Cataloging-in-Publication Data

Names: Gindlesperger, James, 1941- author.
Title: Arlington : a color guide to America's most famous cemetery / by James
   Gindlesperger.
Other titles: Color guide to America's most famous cemetery
Description: Winston-Salem, North Carolina : John F. Blair, Publisher, [2016]
   | Includes index.
Identifiers: LCCN 2016037877 | ISBN 9780895876775 (pbk. : alk. paper)
Subjects: LCSH: Arlington National Cemetery (Arlington, Va.)—Guidebooks. |
   Arlington National Cemetery (Arlington, Va.)—Pictorial works. | Soldiers'
   monuments—Virginia—Arlington—Pictorial works. | Sepulchral
   monuments—Virginia—Arlington—Pictorial works. | Generals—United
   States—Biography. | Soldiers—United States—Biography. | United States.

Armed Forces—Biography.
Classification: LCC F234.A7 G55 2016 | DDC 975.5/295—dc23 LC record available at https://lccn.loc.gov/2016037877

10 9 8 7 6 5 4 3 2 1

To the men and women who have served our country— a grateful nation thanks you!

Contents

Preface

They are at peace now, these four hundred thousand souls resting in Arlington National Cemetery. But such was not always the case. Some died horrific deaths, some were prisoners of war, and some received Medals of Honor. Others paid the ultimate price before they were out of their teens, never fully enjoying the fruits of the freedom they fought for. Many are listed as unknown, nameless defenders of freedom whose families never learned what happened to their loved ones. But all now repose in honored glory in America's most famous cemetery.

Those interred here are unable to see the more than three million visitors who come each year to pay them tribute. They are unaware of the reverence and respect they are accorded and the tears shed on their behalf, often by people who never knew them. Conversely, those who visit often have no idea what stories the honored dead could tell if they had the opportunity.

Many visitors come just to see the Tomb of the Unknowns or the changing of the honor guard. Others come with no other destination in mind but the burial place of President John F. Kennedy. Many see both, then visit other sites in the cemetery. But few take the time to go to the outermost sections of the 640-acre shrine unless they have a loved one there. For the most part, those who rest in the outlying sections are unknown, their stories untold. Even the achievements of those in oft-visited sections are rarely discussed. And when they are, it is usually by families and friends.

This book seeks to make some of those stories known. The stories will answer questions and refresh memories. For example, how many people know how the unknown soldiers were selected, or who selected them? Or how many recipients of the Medal of Honor

are buried in Arlington? Or what Somervell's Folly was? Or who the first burial was? Or why so many graves are marked simply "Citizen"? Or how Arlington National Cemetery came about in the first place? Or how one man got two graves? Or what makes Richard McKinley's grave so unique? Or why Admiral Robert E. Peary was removed from his original grave and relocated to another section of the cemetery? Or the identity of the American pilot who was recorded as missing in action because he was erroneously listed as an unknown German soldier, and how the mystery was solved? Or why Section 15 has so many children, and how three enemy prisoners of war came to be buried in that same section? These and other questions are answered in these pages. I make no discrimination by rank, including the lowest with the generals and admirals.

I provide photos of the headstones. To accommodate readers who wish to visit the graves, each chapter is fronted by a map of the area. That map includes a separate number for each grave discussed. For example, the map for Chapter 2 includes nineteen scattered numbers. Each of those numbers indicates an individual grave or memorial and corresponds to a number in the text that follows. In other words, the number 3 on the map for Chapter 2 indicates the third site discussed in that chapter. It is designated in the text as 2-3, or Chapter 2, site 3. The grave in question happens to be that of Michael Castura, who earned two Distinguished Service Crosses in a span of twenty-six days. He is buried in Section 43, Grave 4519. Because the section numbers in the older portions of the cemetery are not in any particular order, and because the grave-numbering system is often difficult to understand, I also provide GPS coordinates to aid in locating each site.

Readers will note that the sites do not always follow the sections in numerical order. While the sections are generally numbered sequentially in the eastern sector of the cemetery (below Eisenhower Drive), the older sections are not numbered in any particular order. As a result, Chapter 2 contains sites in Sections 27, 28, 36, 38, 40, 41, 42, 43, 51, 52, and 53. Other chapters also follow what may appear to be random selections of sections. I have set up the sites to allow relatively efficient routes, should readers wish to use this guide for walking tours. In some cases, this results in leaving particular sections in favor of others, only to return again to the earlier sections. Readers, of course, are free to deviate from this pattern at their discretion.

Each grave in Arlington has a story. No single body of work can discuss every one. Although I present more than 225 individual stories in these pages, they represent only a small fraction of those interred. However, for those few who are included, their stories are no longer buried with them.

My hope is that these stories are sufficient in number to provide an idea of what those who went before us have done, and that they will pique readers' interest enough to allow reflection and respect for the others interred here as well.

Arlington National Cemetery is a microcosm of our nation's history. We owe it to those who shaped that history, and to ourselves, to learn more about it.

Acknowledgments

Most nonfiction works require the services of many people behind the scenes. Without them, this book would have existed only in the mind of the author.

Out of respect for those about whom it is written, I felt obligated to seek permission from officials at both Arlington National Cemetery and the Department of the Army. I am indebted to John D. Manley, director of U.S. Army Public Affairs for the Northeast, and to both Jack Lechner, superintendent of Arlington, and Jennifer Lynch, public affairs officer for the cemetery, for their assurances.

I would be remiss if I didn't acknowledge the help of my family. My wife, Suzanne, our daughter, Cheryl, and our son, Mike, were supportive of this project from the beginning. They spent many hours with me as we searched for veterans' graves, accompanying me on visit after visit and walking miles to help me gather the information in this book. I couldn't have done it without them! And even though I never met him, I have to acknowledge my ancestor Albert Barnitz, Civil War hero and author in his own right. He is buried in Section 1, and it was my visit to his grave that prompted this project. Thank you, Uncle Albert!

I also could not have completed this work without the help of the Arlington National Cemetery records.

The grave-numbering system at the cemetery can be confusing, and the staff members were always eager to help. I am especially grateful to those who keep the cemetery looking so beautiful. Not only do they do an outstanding job in maintaining the cemetery's appearance, but more than once they saved me time and confusion by pointing me in the right direction when I was baffled by the grave-numbering quirks.

I thank the Medal of Honor Historical Society of the United States and the Congressional Medal of Honor Society, both of which provided invaluable assistance when I was gathering information on the Medal of Honor recipients discussed in the book.

Thanks also to the Library of Congress for making available the period photos included in the opening chapter and to NASA for information on the various astronauts whose stories are presented here.

I appreciate the information provided by the *Baseball Almanac* and the Negro League Baseball Players Association regarding Spottswood Poles and Ernest Wilson. The *Baseball Almanac* also provided information on Luzerne Blue and John Lavan. And I thank the Detroit Tigers organization for valuable insight on Luzerne Blue.

I found many news organizations to be extremely helpful in providing information—namely, the *Washington Post* (for information on Pan Am Flight 103 and background on Thomas Selfridge, Brehon B. Somervell, Jeremiah Denton, Michael Blassie, and Donald Alexander), the *Washington Evening Star* (for its obituary of General Robert Sink), the *Greensburg* (Pa.) *Tribune-Review* (for the story about Joseph Snock), the *Sydney Morning Herald* (for information on the *Georgia* explosion), the *New York Times* (for its obituary of Lee Marvin and information on Paul Bates), NBC News (for the history of Exercise Tiger), the *Chicago Tribune* (for information on the Bonus Marchers), *Smithsonian* magazine (for information on Henry Johnson), the *Longview* (Tex.) *News-Journal* (for information on George Turner), the *Oakland Tribune* (for its story on Bruno Forsterer), *USA Today* (for information on Cecil Harris), *U.S. News & World Report* (for information on Eddie Carter), the *Gloucester City* (Pa.) *News* (for information on Robert Fenstermacher), the *Los Angeles Times* (for information on Robert White), the *St. Augustine Record* (for its story on Ronald Owens), *Armchair General* magazine (for information on the Mauldin-Patton encounter), the *Spencer* (Iowa) *Daily Reporter* (for information on Merlyn Dethlefsen), *Military Times* (for its story about William Maddox), *Stars and Stripes* (for information on Robert Hopkins), and the *Fort Worth Star-Telegram* and *Army Live* (for the story of Miguel Vera).

Likewise, many private and public organizations provided information: Together We Served (information on Robert Fenstermacher), the Maryland State Archives (details on the death of James Lingan), the National Aviation Hall of Fame (information on Thomas Selfridge's ill-fated flight), the National Security Agency (biography of William Friedman), the National Park Service (information on George Washington Custis), Donald Wise (information on the original land grant to Robert Howson), the Department of State (details on the embassy bombings in Africa), and the History Channel (details of the distribution of Lincoln assassination reward money).

It stands to reason that the military would provide much of the information related to stories about a military cemetery, and it came through with flying colors. The Department of Defense provided information on Richard Byrd and Floyd Bennett; the Department of the Army provided information on the children and foreign POWs in Section 15, the Nakashima brothers, and Charles Durning; the U.S. Air Force provided information on Benjamin Davis Jr. and Sr., the Tuskegee Airmen, Jimmy Doolittle, and Juanita Hipps; the U.S. Marine Corps provided information on John Lejeune; the Department of the Navy provided assistance on John McCloy, Allen Buchanan, and the USS *Tallapoosa*; and the U.S. Coast Guard provided information on the USS *Serpens* explosion.

Details on the requirements to become a tomb sentinel came from the Society of the Honor Guard. The U.S. Army Center for Military History provided information on Omar Bradley, Bernard Pious Bell, and the 372nd Infantry. Several naval sources came through, including the Naval History and Heritage Command (David McCampbell), the U.S. Navy Memorial (Jackie Cooper), and the U.S. Submarine Veterans Incorporated (the *Thresher* disaster).

I thank my agent, Rita Rosenkranz, whose advice and guidance have proven invaluable on many occasions and is deeply appreciated. Thank you, Rita!

The people at John F. Blair, Publisher, have always made the challenges of getting a book published far less daunting than they could be. Their hard work and friendly demeanor have always impressed me, and I have enjoyed working with them on every one of my books they have published.

And finally, a nod of appreciation goes to the men and women whose stories appear in these pages. They represent the best America has to offer, and we owe them a debt of gratitude. I thank them for all they did!

They shall grow not old, as we that are left grow old:
Age shall not weary them, nor the years condemn.
At the going down of the sun and in the morning
We will remember them.

From "For the Fallen"
by Laurence Binyon, 1914

Courtesy of Arlington National Cemetery

Today, Arlington National Cemetery encompasses 624 acres. However, at one time, it was much larger, and it wasn't always a cemetery.

On October 21, 1669, Governor William Berkeley of the colony of Virginia granted a parcel of land to Welsh sea captain Robert Howson. Howson had transported 116 passengers to the colony on his ship, earning him the land under the formula of fifty acres for each person. As the captain, Howson himself was counted as four people under the bonus system in existence at the time, thus garnering him a total of six thousand acres.

Over the years, that property was subdivided numerous times and the parcels sold. In 1778, John Parke Custis purchased eleven hundred acres that had been part of the original six thousand. Custis, the son of Martha Washington through her first marriage to Daniel Parke Custis, and now the adopted son of George Washington, planned to clear the land and build an estate.

Custis did not live to see his dream become reality. He died in 1781 of swamp fever—a catch-all name for a wide range of health problems—leaving his widow and four young children. Now without a husband and unable to support her family, Custis's wife agreed to allow George and Martha Washington to adopt two of her children, George Washington Parke Custis and Eleanor Parke Custis. The two went to Mount Vernon to live with George and Martha.

George Washington died in 1799, followed by Martha in 1802. Washington's nephew Bushrod Washington inherited Mount Vernon. Young George Washington Parke Custis offered to purchase it from his cousin, who had no interest in selling. Custis had another option, however. Upon turning twenty-one, he had assumed ownership of the properties formerly held by his natural father, including the eleven hundred acres from Robert Howson's original plot. Custis decided that if Mount Vernon was unavailable, the land he had inherited from his father would suit his purpose for a home and a shrine to George Washington.

As a start to honoring the first president, Custis called the estate Mount Washington. He planned to follow that by filling the home he would build there with items owned by or associated with Washington. Many of those he had inherited, others he would purchase. He eventually abandoned the plan to name the estate Mount Washington in favor of Arlington House, after the family's original estate, given to Custis's father by the Earl of Arlington.

Custis chose English architect George Hadfield, who had helped in the construction of the Capitol, to design the home, which was built in stages. The first section—what is now called the North Wing—was built in 1802. A second section, the South Wing, followed in 1804.

Following completion of the South Wing, Custis married sixteen-year-old Mary Fitzhugh in 1807. The two lived in the North Wing and used the South Wing as an office for the estate and a storage place for Custis's growing collection of George Washington memorabilia. The space between the two wings provided a home for Custis's chickens and geese. Part of the land around the mansion was used to grow crops, with another portion devoted to the breeding of mules and sheep.

In 1808, Mary Anna Randolph was born, the only one of the Custises' four children to survive to adulthood. Upon her would fall the responsibility of continuing the Washington legacy. She did so until she was forced to leave the property when the Civil War began.

In 1818, a third section was constructed between the two wings, connecting them and forming one structure. The completed mansion featured a portico with eight Doric columns. Custis now had a suitable showcase in which to display his collection of Washington artifacts. The home became a popular destination for visitors—not only locals but also famous personages from around the world. Custis had achieved his dream.

In 1831, Mary Anna Randolph Custis married a childhood friend and distant cousin. The wedding, a lavish affair befitting the Custis family, took place in Arlington House. The groom was Robert E. Lee, a young army lieutenant who had graduated second in his class at West Point two years earlier. Lee, an admirer of George Washington, took to the task of assisting on the estate and preserving Washington's memory.

Lee served in the Army Corps of Engineers and spent the next six years in the Washington area. However, in 1837, he was reassigned to St. Louis, where he supervised waterfront construction. His wife and children accompanied him, leaving the Arlington estate back in the hands of Custis. Custis, unable or unwilling to keep up the property, saw the condition of the estate and the mansion deteriorate.

Lee went on to serve with distinction in the war with Mexico and in 1852 was appointed superintendent at West Point. Mrs. Lee returned to Arlington House to care for her mother, who died in 1853 and was buried in the family plot on the estate, now part of Section 13 of the cemetery.

Custis devoted his time on the estate to perpetuating Washington's legacy, breeding mules and sheep, and becoming a modestly accomplished artist; some of his paintings are displayed in Arlington House today. He died in 1857, leaving the estate to his daughter. Lee was named the executor.

Lee requested and received permission from the army to return to Arlington House, which he found to be in much poorer condition than the last time he was there. Using the slaves that came with the estate, he began the arduous task of bringing it back to what it had once been. A stipulation in the will called for the slaves to be freed within five years, so the undertaking was made even more difficult by the limited time frame.

One of Lee's first tasks was the repair of the mansion. He and Mary then furnished it with items accumulated in Lee's travels with the army; many of those pieces can be seen in Arlington House today. He also brought the grounds back to their earlier condition. Slowly, the estate returned to profitability. Then fate intervened.

In October 1859, the federal arsenal and armory at Harpers Ferry, Virginia (now West Virginia), were captured by a fanatical abolitionist named John Brown and his group of five black men and sixteen white men, a group he called his "Provisional Army." His goal was to use the captured weapons to arm slaves and initiate a slave revolt. Lee, by now a lieutenant colonel, was given command of the troops assigned to capture Brown, an assignment he completed successfully. The incident is considered one of the major events that led to the Civil War.

Robert E. Lee
Courtesy of Library of Congress,
Reproduction Number LC-DIG-cwpb-04402

In April 1861, Lee was offered command of a new army that was in its initial stages of organization. He knew it meant he would be called upon to take up arms against the South, including his home state of Virginia, should a secession vote be successful. He returned to Arlington House to wrestle with his decision. When Virginia seceded, he knew he could not accept the position that had been offered to him, and he resigned his commission in the U.S. Army.

On April 22, Lee left Arlington House for Richmond, where he offered his services to his native state. When he was offered command of Virginia's military troops and a rank of major general, he immediately accepted. He would never return to Arlington House.

Back home, Mary Custis Lee took temporary shelter at the home of her aunt in Fairfax County, Virginia. There, she penned letters to both General-in-Chief Winfield Scott and Brigadier General Irvin McDowell, who commanded the Federal troops already beginning to take up positions in the vicinity of Arlington House. Her letters asked that the estate be protected. McDowell gave her his assurance that the home of George Washington's family would come to no harm. However, that was not to be the case.

When many of Lee's personal items began to disappear, McDowell ordered that what remained should be crated and moved to the Patent Office in Washington, the crates to be marked "Captured at Arlington."

Since Arlington House sat on a strategically critical hill that placed the nation's capital within artillery range, more Union troops quickly occupied the estate, which became General McDowell's headquarters. Fort Whipple (now Joint Base Myer–Henderson Hall) was constructed northwest of the house. Fort McPherson was set up on what is now Section 11 of the cemetery.

In June 1862, Congress passed a law providing for the taxing of all "insurrectionary properties." The law further required that the taxes be paid in person by the properties' owners. This was a thinly veiled method of ensuring that those properties could be confiscated, since most of the owners were Confederate sympathizers who feared arrest if they came in person to pay their taxes.

By now, Mary Custis Lee was in poor health, confined to a wheelchair, and unable to make the trip behind Union lines to pay her $92.07 tax bill on the estate. Her cousin Philip R. Fendall was dispatched to Alexandria to make the payment. When he arrived, his payment was refused because he was not the property owner, and the tax was declared in arrears.

The property was put up for auction in January 1864. The only bidders were the tax commissioners, who were awarded the estate—including eleven hundred acres plus the house and all outbuildings—for its assessed value of $26,810. The Federal government now held the deed to Robert E. Lee's estate.

As the government took ownership of the property, the war dragged into its third year. Heavy fighting around northern Virginia and Washington brought wounded soldiers into Washington hospitals. Churches and government buildings took in large numbers of them. As many died, every available cemetery rapidly reached capacity. It was apparent that something had to be done quickly, not just for humanitarian reasons but also for sanitation purposes. Secretary of War Edwin Stanton directed the quartermaster general, Montgomery C. Meigs, to find a location for a new cemetery.

Meigs had served with Robert E. Lee in the Army Corps of Engineers and considered him a traitor for having gone over to the Confederacy. He didn't look far for a location for a cemetery, recommending the former Lee estate on June 15, 1864.

Stanton quickly approved the recommendation,

making that portion of the property around Arlington House the newest military cemetery. It was fortunate for Meigs that Stanton agreed to his recommendation, since several soldiers had already been buried on the grounds. Stanton's agreement saved Meigs from a potentially embarrassing situation.

In fact, the first burial, that of Private William Christman of the Sixty-seventh Pennsylvania Infantry, had taken place a full month before Meigs even submitted his recommendation. Christman had died of peritonitis and was buried in what is now Section 27 on May 13, 1864. That area was chosen because it was sufficiently far from the house that it raised no objections from the soldiers quartered there. A few hours after Christman's burial, Private

Montgomery Meigs
Courtesy of Library of Congress,
Reproduction Number LC-BB13-6417A

William H. McKinney of the Seventeenth Pennsylvania Cavalry, who had died of pneumonia, was also buried in Section 27. That same day, Private William Blatt of the Forty-ninth Pennsylvania Volunteers was mortally wounded in the fighting at Spotsylvania Court House. He was buried on May 14 immediately beside Christman. Blatt was the first battle casualty buried in Arlington. By the end of June, some twenty-six hundred bodies had been interred on Robert E. Lee's former estate.

Meanwhile, many black refugees fleeing the war-torn South found themselves in Washington with no skills and no place to live. They set up makeshift camps around the city. Soon, overcrowding led to the spread of diseases. The government responded by establishing a small village on the Arlington estate to house freed blacks, now referred to as "contrabands." Called Freedman's Village, the community included churches, schools, a fifty-bed hospital, an industrial training building, and houses divided into sections to accommodate two to four families. Although the exact location of the village is unknown, it is thought that it originally sat in a swampy area in what are now Sections 8, 47, and 25 of the cemetery, along what is now Eisenhower Drive. It eventually was relocated to Section 4 to avoid the diseases brought on by the swampy conditions. Set up as a temporary shelter, it would last for nearly thirty years.

Those who could work were put on construction projects, including the Capitol. Others were assigned farming tasks. Workers received a small stipend, half of that to be paid back to village authorities to cover costs associated with operating the camp. Residents came under military discipline and were given military rations. Those who died were buried in what is now Section 27 of Arlington National Cemetery. Nearly thirty-eight hundred former slaves or free blacks occupy graves there, many of their headstones

simply inscribed with the designation "Citizen" or "Civilian."

Slave owners often came looking for fugitive slaves during that time. At one point, the U.S. Colored Troops were called in to protect the inhabitants of the village from those who wanted to return them to the South.

Among those who lived in Freedman's Village was Sojourner Truth, famous for smuggling slaves out of the South on the Underground Railroad. Also, the 107th U.S. Colored Troops were recruited from the village.

After the war, enthusiasm to help the freed slaves lessened until it was nearly nonexistent. Neighbors surrounding the village complained about crime, as well as the cost of keeping the village open. Finally, in 1882, the Supreme Court ruled that Freedman's

Village be closed. On December 7, 1887, the people at the village were given ninety days to leave. Freedman's Village closed completely in 1900.

Meigs's intent to use Lee's estate as a cemetery was to make the property so undesirable as a home that Lee would never want to return. However, when Meigs first visited the cemetery, he found that the burials were so far from the house that they couldn't even be seen. He immediately ordered that the next burials be in the Lee rose garden, adjacent to the house. Today, those graves surround the garden's perimeter.

To add to the insult, Meigs ordered that remains be gathered from the battlefield at Bull Run and the route to the Rappahannock River. The remains of 2,111 casualties were brought to Arlington and interred in a common vault along the rear edge of the garden. The vault containing those remains, all unknown and presumably including both Union and Confederate soldiers, constitute the memorial to the Civil War's unknown dead.

In April 1865, Robert E. Lee surrendered his Confederate army at Appomattox Court House. The Civil War was effectively over, although pockets of fighting would continue for two more months. What would become of the Arlington estate now? Would Lee try to reclaim it?

In 1867, Congress enacted legislation requiring that all military cemeteries be surrounded by a fence. Meigs ordered that the wall around the cemetery at Arlington be constructed of red Seneca sandstone. Included in the wall were gates honoring Major General George B. McClellan, Major General Edward Ord, Major General Godfrey Wetzel, and General Philip Sheridan. When the cemetery was extended from what is now Eisenhower Drive to its present boundary of Jefferson Davis Highway, the Ord-Wetzel and Sheridan Gates were dismantled. Only

Early graves on perimeter of Mrs. Lee's rose garden

the McClellan Gate remains of the original three. It sits in Section 33 of the cemetery.

On Christmas Day 1868, President Andrew Johnson issued a general amnesty for all former Confederates, removing any opportunity to try Lee for treason. Seeing the softening stance of the nation toward former Confederates, Mrs. Lee penned a letter to President Johnson requesting the return of the estate to her family.

Her request was granted. Johnson directed the secretary of the interior to arrange for the return of not only the house and grounds but also any items still in possession of the government. Before the transfer of the property could be completed, however, a rumor arose stating that Lee intended to invade the property and remove all items owned by George Washington. The Radical Republicans in Congress, who had already failed in their attempt to impeach Johnson, saw this as another opportunity to defame the president. Accusing Johnson of conspiring with Lee to turn over George Washington's property, Congress hurriedly passed a resolution the night before Johnson was to leave office, reaffirming that the property belonged to the government and that Johnson had no right to dispose of it.

Lee thus lost his opportunity to regain ownership of Arlington House. He died in 1870 while president of Washington College, now Washington and Lee University, in Lexington, Virginia.

Although Lee never returned to Arlington, his widow did. In 1873, Mary Custis Lee came to see the estate and visit her parents' graves. The condition of the abandoned home broke her heart. One of her former slaves recognized her and brought her a drink of water, but Mrs. Lee was so ill by now that she was physically unable to go into the house. She died three months after her visit.

Upon her death, the title to the property fell to her son, George Washington Custis Lee, in accordance with the wishes laid out in the will of Mrs. Lee's father, George Washington Parke Custis. George Washington Custis Lee—or Custis Lee, as he was known—had graduated first in his West Point class of 1854 and had served as aide-de-camp to Confederate president Jefferson Davis. He was named the successor to his father as president of what by then was Washington and Lee University.

While president at Washington and Lee, Custis Lee explored his options with respect to regaining ownership of the Arlington estate. In April 1874, he filed a legal claim with the U.S. government for recovery of the property. With the emotional wounds of the Civil War still festering, Lee's request met with considerable opposition from the Radical Republicans, who stood firm in their position that the property was now owned by the government and would remain so.

After three years of unsuccessful negotiation, Lee filed a lawsuit to have the property returned to his family. This raised deep concerns in the halls of government, whose members feared that the seven-teen thousand bodies buried on the grounds would have to be removed if Lee won his case. Representatives at all levels of the federal government did everything in their power to persuade Lee to withdraw his suit. Unsuccessful, they then turned to placing as many impediments in his path as they could.

Finally, in January 1879, the case came before a jury. The arguments from both sides lasted six days, at the end of which the jury announced its verdict in Lee's favor. The government immediately appealed the decision to the Supreme Court, which deliberated two months before announcing that, by a five-four decision, it agreed with the lower court's verdict. The Court ruled that Mary Custis Lee had been denied due process when her tax payment was refused.

Faced with the fact that Custis Lee now had the legal right to demand the disinterment of every grave, the government began negotiations in earnest. Fortunately for those who had long opposed the return of the property, Lee was willing to accept financial compensation for what he believed was his. The government quickly accepted Lee's offer, and on March 3, 1883, Congress authorized a payment of $150,000 (estimated to be worth about $3,500,000 in 2017 dollars), to be paid to Lee in return for ownership of the property.

While the controversy with Custis Lee raged on, an amphitheater was constructed not far from Arlington House, to be used for ceremonies and patriotic gatherings. Dedication of the structure took place in 1874. It was used until a larger facility, the Memorial Amphitheater, was constructed in 1915 and dedicated in 1920. From that time on, the original amphitheater was informally identified as the Old Amphitheater until 2014, when it was officially renamed the James Tanner Amphitheater, in honor of the Civil War soldier who compiled the official records of President Abraham Lincoln's death and the trial of his assassination conspirators.

Old Amphitheater

Temple of Fame
Courtesy of Library of Congress,
Reproduction Number LC-DIG-det-4a10980

In 1884, Meigs had work crews construct the Temple of Fame not far from the Civil War Memorial in one final attempt to insult the memory of Robert E. Lee. It is an open-air domed structure with eight columns, each containing the name of a Union general: Thomas, Garfield, Meade, McPherson, Sedgwick, Reynolds, Humphreys, and Mansfield. On the entablature above the columns were inscribed the names of Washington, Lincoln, Grant, and Farragut. The Temple of Fame was demolished in 1967.

In 1868, plans had been announced that volunteers would place flowers on the graves of the Union dead. Surviving Confederate widows arrived with a request that they be permitted to provide the same honor to the relatively small number of Southern soldiers buried at Arlington. With the war having ended just three years earlier, feelings were still strong, however, and they were denied. That action led to many Southern families removing the remains of their loved ones over the next several years. It was not until 1900 that animosity between the North and South subsided sufficiently for Southerners to con-

sider burial in Arlington, and for Northerners to accept them.

After the Spanish-American War, feelings had tempered enough that those who fought for the Confederacy would be welcome in Arlington. In 1900, Congress authorized the erection of a Confederate statue in what is now Section 16. Confederate dead from the U.S. Soldiers' Home National Cemetery, as well as many who had already been interred in Arlington, were moved and reinterred in the circular section. On June 4, 1914, a bronze sculpture created by Moses Ezekiel, one of the cadets from Virginia Military Institute who had fought at the Battle of New Market, was dedicated. President Woodrow Wilson, in his dedication speech, declared that the opening of the Confederate section of the cemetery represented an end of sectional differences in America.

Confederates who died in Washington during the war had originally been buried in scattered sections of the cemetery. The headstones marking their graves were the same as those used for civilians. The 1900 legislation that authorized the burial of Southern soldiers also required that "proper headstones" be used to distinguish the Confederate veterans' graves from civilians'. The headstones selected are

Confederate Monument

Graves of Confederate soldiers surround Confederate Monument

nearly identical to those used for Union soldiers, the only difference being the tops of the stones, which are rounded for Union soldiers and pointed for Confederates. Pointed headstones are now the standard for Confederates in all national cemeteries. A legend has since evolved that the tops are pointed to keep Yankees from sitting on them.

In 1921, one of the most memorable ceremonies in Arlington's long and storied history took place when an unknown soldier from World War I was brought from a cemetery in France and laid to rest in a special tomb. That ceremony would be repeated in 1958, when another unknown soldier, this one representing those who had fought in World War II and Korea, was buried adjacent to the unknown soldier from World War I. In 1981, a third tomb was built to hold the remains of a soldier who had died in Vietnam. In 1998, that soldier was removed from the tomb and identified through mitochondrial DNA testing as First Lieutenant Michael Blassie of the air force. Blassie was reinterred at Jefferson Barracks National Cemetery near St. Louis, and his crypt at Arlington was left empty. (For a detailed treatment of the selection process, see Chapter 7, site 7-2.)

In 1925, Arlington House became a permanent memorial to Robert E. Lee, and the mansion was restored to its appearance prior to the Civil War. The house was opened to the public in 1929. In 1933, the mansion and the grounds immediately surrounding it were transferred from the army to the National Park Service. The rest of the cemetery remains under the management of the army.

In 1963, the burial of assassinated president John F. Kennedy catapulted Arlington into the international spotlight (see Chapter 3, site 3-8). That ceremony precipitated an outpouring of requests for burials in the cemetery, making it necessary for a change in policies to avoid running out of space. The current criteria for burial are summarized in Appendix B.

On September 11, 2001, the United States came under attack by terrorists who flew planes into the World Trade Center towers in New York City and the Pentagon, adjacent to Arlington. A fourth plane crashed in a field in Shanksville, Pennsylvania, when passengers fought back against the hijackers. A memorial to the victims at the Pentagon was placed in Section 64, many of whom were buried around the monument.

The latest activity at Arlington is a major expansion project that will provide an additional thirty thousand burial and niche spaces. Known as the Millennium Project, this endeavor began in 2014 and is expected to take about five years, including final landscaping. Covering twenty-seven acres, the development will include stream restoration, niche space in the Columbarium, two committal service shelters, and in-ground burial space. Many of the in-ground spaces will contain concrete crypts, which will be buried during initial construction, rather than at the time of a burial. This is expected to improve the quality and consistency of burials while reducing the time and labor involved. After construction is completed and landscaping has become established, burials are expected to begin in mid-2019.

Today, an average of twenty-eight burials take place each day at Arlington. Thirty minutes before the first funeral of the day, flags in front of Arlington House and at the Memorial Amphitheater are low-

ered to half-staff. They remain in that position until thirty minutes after the last funeral of the day.

More than four hundred recipients of the Medal of Honor rest in Arlington, as do the remains of five five-star officers: Admiral William D. Leahy, General George C. Marshall, General Henry F. Arnold, Admiral William F. Halsey, and General Omar N. Bradley.

Only two presidents are buried in Arlington: John F. Kennedy, near Section 5, and William Howard Taft, in Section 30. Also interred in Arlington are the remains of twelve Supreme Court justices and nineteen astronauts.

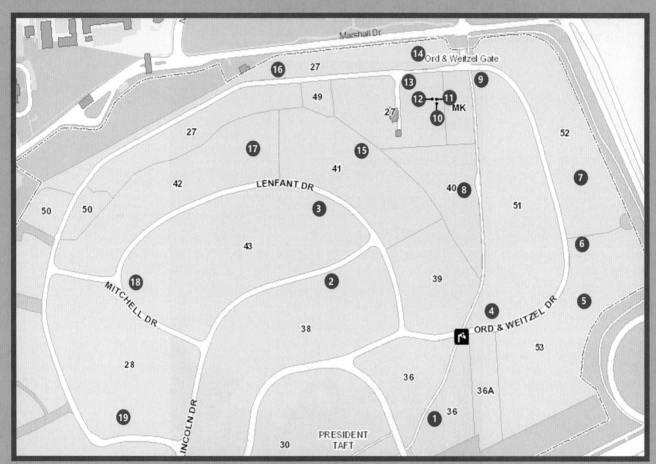

Courtesy of Arlington National Cemetery

2-1: Medgar W. Evers, Section 36, Grave 1431
38° 53.041' N, 77° 4.095' W

Medgar Wiley Evers was born in Decatur, Mississippi, on July 2, 1925. He served in the army during World War II and took part in the invasion of Normandy. After his discharge, he returned to Mississippi, earning a degree from Alcorn College in 1952.

Following graduation, he became active in the National Association for the Advancement of Colored People and its civil-rights work in his home state. In late 1954, he was named the first field secretary for the NAACP in Mississippi, organizing boycotts and setting up new local chapters.

His efforts to win equal rights for blacks in the once deeply segregated Southern states made him a target of white supremacists. He faced attempts to burn his home and to run him down with a car. Both were unsuccessful.

On June 12, 1963, however, a white supremacist lay in wait for him as he returned from an NAACP meeting. Evers pulled his car into his driveway. As he got out, he was shot in the back by the assassin's bullet. He was rushed to a hospital, where he died a short time later.

His assassin escaped justice for thirty-one years, as two all-white juries were unable to reach verdicts even though the assassin's fingerprints were found on the rifle used to kill Evers. The white supremacist was arrested again in December 1990 after new evidence was found, including numerous errors that had occurred in the first two trials. The third time, a jury of eight blacks and four whites found the man guilty of murder after

a two-week trial. He was sentenced to life in prison, where he died at age eighty.

In October 2009, Evers was honored by the navy when the USNS *Medgar Evers*, a Lewis and Clark–class dry cargo ship, was launched.

2-2: Calvin Bouknight, Section 38, Grave 240
38° 53.127' N, 77° 4.177' W

Specialist Calvin Bouknight was twenty-four years old and in the Ia Drang Valley of Vietnam on November 16, 1965. Bouknight was a conscientious objector who refused to carry a weapon despite his plan to become a career soldier. But on that day, he was immersed in one of the fiercest firefights of the Vietnam War. The battle at Landing Zone X-Ray would

become famous through then–lieutenant colonel Harold Moore and Joe Galloway's book, *We Were Soldiers Once . . . and Young.*

A medic for B Company, First Battalion, Seventh Cavalry, Bouknight lay pinned down by fire. His company had been forced back by a large concentration of enemy troops, and he knew more than a dozen of his comrades lay dead or wounded. Despite the intensity of the battle, he rose and dashed through a hail of bullets to reach the casualties. Miraculously, he arrived unharmed and began administering aid. Witnesses said he kept his own body between the enemy and the men he was treating, protecting them as best he could.

After successfully treating several soldiers, Bouknight was mortally wounded by a bullet that struck him in the back, paralyzing him instantly from the waist down. He was recovered by others in his company during a lull in the fighting. Morphine had no effect on his excruciating pain. In a matter of minutes, Calvin Bouknight lay dead on the jungle floor.

Bouknight was awarded the Purple Heart for his wound and a Silver Star for his bravery under fire. Several officers in the Seventh Cavalry tried unsuccessfully to get his Silver Star elevated to the Medal of Honor. He was held in such high esteem by the men he served with that the enlisted men's club at the unit's base camp was named Bouknight Hall in his honor.

2-3: Michael Castura, Section 43, Grave 4519
38° 53.167' N, 77° 4.188' W

Michael Castura was born September 22, 1893, in Eckley, Pennsylvania. When the United States entered World War I, he enlisted in the army and was assigned to Company C, 125th Infantry, Thirty-second Division, attaining the rank of sergeant before mustering out at war's end.

Castura is remembered for the unusual feat of being awarded two Distinguished Service Crosses for

actions in France that occurred only twenty-six days apart. In the first incident, he led his platoon through heavy enemy fire to accomplish the mission objective, then disregarded his own safety to carry a wounded man to shelter. His citation for this action reads,

> The Distinguished Service Cross is presented to Michael Castura, Sergeant, U.S. Army, for extraordinary heroism in action at Cierges and Mont St. Martin, northeast of Château-Thierry, France, August 1 and 3, 1918. During the attack on Cierges, Sergeant Castura took command of his platoon when the commanding officer had been evacuated and led it successfully through the barrage to its objective. On August 3, when one of his men had been left wounded on the field and no first aid men were present, this soldier dashed through a terrific barrage and carried the wounded man to shelter.

He duplicated his heroic feat less than four weeks later by leading another attack until he was wounded. He refused to leave the field until a replacement arrived and orders were transferred. That citation reads,

> The Distinguished Service Cross is presented to Michael Castura, First Sergeant, U.S. Army, for extraordinary heroism in action east of Juvigny, France, August 29, 1918. While leading his company in the advance in the direction of Juvigny, Sergeant Castura was severely wounded but refused to be evacuated until he had directed one of his platoon commanders to assume command of the company. He remained at his post despite his wounds until the new commander had arrived and was given the necessary orders and instructions. By his bravery, coolness under fire, and devotion to duty, Sergeant Castura was a great inspiration to the men of his command.

Castura was the only man in the entire Thirty-second Division to receive two Distinguished Service Crosses. He also was awarded a Purple Heart for the wound he received near Juvigny. Castura died June 23, 1967, at the VA hospital in Philadelphia.

2-4: African Embassy Bombings Memorial, Section 51
38° 53.106′ N, 77° 4.033′ W

On August 7, 1998, terrorist bombings took place almost simultaneously at American embassies in Nairobi, Kenya, and Dar es Salaam, Tanzania.

In the Nairobi bombing, a loud explosion rocked the five-story embassy at 10:37 A.M., followed by a second blast a short time later. Outside, in the rear parking lot, terrorists had detonated a vehicle packed with hundreds of pounds of explosives. The embassy was badly damaged, and an adjacent building collapsed. Many of the victims were in this second building. Twelve Americans and thirty-four local employees were killed and dozens more wounded. Outside, the toll was even worse; more than two hundred Kenyans lay dead, and five thousand more were wounded. Alert guards had denied the terrorists access to the embassy's underground parking garage, preventing many more casualties.

Two minutes after the Nairobi bombing, a similar attack took place at the embassy in Dar es Salaam. There, a huge vehicle bomb detonated on a public street

outside a gate to the embassy. Since the embassy in Dar es Salaam was located in a less populated area, casualties were lower than those in Nairobi. No Americans died, though some were wounded. Seven foreign nationals were killed, and another was declared missing.

Although the attacks were directed at American facilities, most of the casualties were local citizens of the two African countries. Between the two attacks, twelve Americans lost their lives. An investigation led to charges against twenty-one people, including Osama bin Laden. Of those, eighteen have been either captured or killed.

This plaque and a tulip tree were dedicated to those who lost their lives in the attacks.

2-5: Keith Allen Campbell, Section 53, Grave 2862

38° 53.112' N, 77° 3.953' W

Keith Campbell was born in Long Beach, California, on March 3, 1946. After graduating from high school, he enlisted in the army, going to parachute school at Fort Benning and then to Fort Bragg, where he served with the Eighty-second Airborne Division. In April 1964, he began medic training, the first leg of his dream to become an army doctor. Following completion of his training, he spent the next year in the Dominican Republic in his first combat tour. He was discharged in 1966.

Wishing to continue to serve, he reenlisted with the Special Forces Reserve and enrolled in a premed program, still planning to become an army doctor. However, with the fighting in Asia heating up, Campbell left college and signed up to go to Vietnam with the 173rd Airborne Brigade, Headquarters Company, First Battalion, 503rd Infantry.

He encountered combat conditions immediately on his arrival in Vietnam. In a firefight in Bien Hoa on February 8, 1967, he volunteered to move up to the front line to assist in treating the wounded. While there, he observed a wounded soldier lying fifty meters in front of the American lines, next to an enemy bunker. Campbell raced under fire to the man, killing an enemy sniper along the way. Reaching the wounded soldier, he dragged him behind a nearby tree for treatment. Before he could do anything to help, however, he was struck by enemy fire, suffering fatal wounds. He had been in Vietnam only nineteen days.

He was posthumously awarded the Distinguished Service Cross for his actions. His citation includes a statement that Campbell's "unimpeachable valor and selfless sacrifice against insurmountable odds succeeded in saving a fellow soldier's life."

Keith Campbell was buried in Arlington on February 15, 1967, at the age of twenty-one.

2-6: Bruno A. Forsterer, Section 53, Grave 2757

38° 53.147' N, 77° 3.960' W

Bruno Albert Forsterer was born at Königsberg, Germany, on July 14, 1869. After coming to the United States, he enlisted in the Marine Corps in November 1896, serving honorably for thirteen years before his discharge as a gunnery sergeant on November 2, 1909.

On April 1, 1899, Forsterer was assigned to the USS *Philadelphia* in the Philippines when a dispute erupted between two tribal leaders over who had the right of succession to the Samoan throne. The marines, including Forsterer, were sent ashore to intervene. Royal Marines from two British ships also participated as part of a joint operation.

Once ashore, the marines were ambushed. In the ensuing fight, Forsterer performed heroically, enabling a successful withdrawal. Forsterer, two other marines

(Private Henry Hulbert and Sergeant Michael McNally), and a navy gunner's mate (Frederick Fisher) earned Medals of Honor for their actions that day. Forsterer's Medal of Honor was awarded by President Theodore Roosevelt by General Order No. 55, dated July 19, 1901. The accompanying citation reads, "The President of the United States of America, in the name of Congress, takes pleasure in presenting the Medal of Honor to Sergeant Bruno Albert Forsterer, United States Marine Corps, for distinguished conduct in the presence of the enemy while serving with the Marine Guard, U.S.S. *Philadelphia* in action at Samoa, Philippine Islands, 1 April 1899."

When he returned to civilian life, Forsterer got a job with the *Oakland Tribune* in California, assuming the position of publisher and general manager in 1911. He died June 13, 1957.

2-7: Laszlo Rabel, Section 52, Grave 1326

38° 53.182' N, 77° 3.968' W

Born in Budapest, Hungary, on September 21, 1939, Laszlo Rabel fled to the United States with his family following the 1956 revolution in his home country, settling in Minneapolis. He entered the army in 1965 and rose to the rank of staff sergeant.

On November 13, 1968, he was with the Seventy-fourth Infantry Detachment (Long Range Patrol), 173rd Airborne Brigade, in Binh Dinh Province in Vietnam. Rabel and his men were on a patrol when they detected enemy movement ahead. Within seconds, a grenade landed in the midst of the patrol. Reacting immediately, Rabel threw himself onto it, absorbing the explosion with his body. The blast killed Rabel but saved the lives of several others in the immediate area. For his heroism, Rabel was awarded the Medal of Honor. His citation reads,

For conspicuous gallantry and intrepidity in action at the risk of his life above and beyond the call of duty. S/Sgt. Rabel distinguished himself while serving as leader of Team Delta, 74th Infantry Detachment. At 1000 hours on this date, Team Delta was in a defensive perimeter conducting reconnaissance of enemy trail networks when a member of the team detected enemy movement to the front. As S/Sgt. Rabel and a comrade prepared to clear the area, he heard an incoming grenade as it landed in the midst of the team's perimeter. With complete disregard for his life, S/Sgt. Rabel threw himself on the grenade and, covering it with his body, received the complete impact of the immediate explosion. Through his indomitable courage, complete disregard for his safety and profound concern for his fellow soldiers, S/Sgt. Rabel averted the loss of life and injury to the other members of Team Delta. By his gallantry at the cost of his life in the highest traditions of the military service, S/Sgt. Rabel has reflected great credit upon himself, his unit, and the U.S. Army.

His remains were returned to the United States. His burial took place in Arlington on November 25,

1968. In addition to the Medal of Honor, he earned a Bronze Star with oak leaf cluster, an Air Medal with oak leaf cluster, an Army Commendation Medal with oak leaf cluster, and the Purple Heart. These awards are engraved on the rear surface of his headstone.

2-8: Cornelius H. Charlton, Section 40, Grave 300

38° 53.180' N, 77° 4.060' W

Born in West Virginia on July 24, 1929, Cornelius "Connie" Charlton moved with his family to New York in 1944. After graduating from high school, Charlton in 1946 enlisted in the army, where he was assigned to an engineering unit. He served with the occupying forces in Germany after World War II, then was sent to Korea. Preferring something more exciting than an office position, he asked for a transfer to an infantry unit and was placed in Company C of the Twenty-fourth Infantry

Regiment, Twenty-fifth Infantry Division. Long known as the Buffalo Soldiers, the regiment was the last all-black regiment in the army.

On June 2, 1951, his platoon encountered heavy resistance while attempting to take Hill 543 near the village of Chipo-ri. When his platoon leader suffered a serious wound, Charlton took command. Reorganizing his men, he led a second assault against the hill. In that assault, Charlton eliminated two hostile positions and killed six enemy soldiers. As his own casualties mounted and his men became pinned down, he raced from man to man to offer encouragement and to get them reorganized. He then led another assault, only to be pushed back again by a shower of grenades, one of which inflicted a chest wound on Charlton. The severely wounded sergeant refused medical attention and launched a third charge that took him to the crest of the ridge. Peering over the contested ground, he saw that his advance was challenged by one remaining gun emplacement. This time, he raced forward alone and single-handedly attacked the enemy position. Although he successfully disabled the gun, he suffered another grenade wound. A short time later, Charlton succumbed to his wounds at the age of twenty-one.

His body was returned to the United States and buried in Pocahontas, Virginia. The cemetery eventually fell into disrepair, however, and Charlton was reinterred in the American Legion cemetery in Beckley, West Virginia. In 2008, he was reinterred at Arlington.

For his actions during the battle, he was awarded the Medal of Honor in 1952. In addition, Charlton was accorded several civilian honors. In 1952, a park in his old neighborhood in the Bronx was named the Sergeant Cornelius H. Charlton Playground. It later became Charlton Garden. He also had a ferryboat named in his honor, as well as a bridge on Interstate 77 in West Virginia and an army barracks complex in South Korea. In 1958, trees were planted in Van Cortlandt Park in the Bronx in his honor. In 1999, the navy christened a cargo transport ship the USNS *Charlton*.

2-9: Rene A. Gagnon, Section 51, Grave 543
38° 53.249' N, 77° 4.040' W

Rene Arthur Gagnon was born at Manchester, New Hampshire, on March 7, 1926, and completed two years of high school before dropping out to work in a local textile mill. He was inducted into the Marine Corps Reserve on May 6, 1943. Over the next eighteen months, he served in three outfits: the Marine Guard Company at Charleston, South Carolina, the Military Police Company of the Fifth Marine Division at Camp Pendleton, California, and Company E, Second Battalion, Twenty-eighth Marines.

It was with this last unit that he landed on Iwo Jima on February 19, 1945. The island, boasting two Japanese-controlled airfields and a third under construction, was a strategic location that could serve as a staging area for future attacks on the Japanese main islands.

The five-week battle that took place was some of the fiercest fighting of the entire war in the Pacific. After American forces prevailed, the airstrips were used for emergency landings for B-29 bombers.

The Japanese had constructed an extensive network of fortified bunkers and underground tunnels, all protected by minefields. The strongly entrenched defenders, numbering approximately twenty-one thousand, waited for the marines to launch their assault.

The assault was relatively unchallenged at first but became bloody when the marines reached the first line of concealed bunkers. Advancing slowly and taking heavy casualties, they reached Mount Suribachi, the highest point on the island, on February 23, 1945. Colonel Chandler Johnson dispatched a patrol of marines to capture the summit, sending a small American flag for them to raise if they were successful. The Japanese offered minimal resistance to the climb up Suribachi. In a short time, the flag appeared, to the cheers of the marines below.

Naval officials decided the flag was not large enough to be seen by the troops on the eastern end of the island, and Gagnon was dispatched with a larger one. Before he reached the summit, he encountered Sergeant Michael Strank (see Chapter 12, site 12-8), Corporal Harlon Block, Private First Class Ira Hayes (see Chapter 9, site 9-15), and Private First Class Franklin Sousley, who were in the process of running communication wire up the mountain. When the five reached the summit, they were joined by a sixth man, believed for many years to have been navy corpsman John Bradley. In 2014, however, two amateur historians offered evidence that it may have been Private First Class Harold Schultz, rather than Bradley, who assisted the other five; they believed Bradley participated in the first flag raising but not the second.

As the six men raised the second flag, Associated Press photographer Joe Rosenthal took the famous photo that would win the Pulitzer Prize that year. Gagnon is difficult to see in the iconic photo but is easily viewed in Felix de Weldon's sculpture based on it. That famous sculpture, now known as the *Marine Corps War Memorial*, sits just outside the north end of the cemetery.

Six weeks later, Gagnon, Bradley, and Hayes returned to the United States to make personal appearances on behalf of the war-bond drive. (The capture of Mount Suribachi and Gagnon's participation in the war-bond drive are discussed in detail in James Bradley's book *Flags of Our Fathers* and the movie of the same name.) By then, Strank, Brock, and Sousley had all been killed on Iwo Jima. At the end of the war-bond drive, Gagnon was sent to China, where he joined Company E, Second Battalion, Twenty-ninth Marines, Sixth Marine Division. He eventually transferred to the Third Battalion, serving with U.S. occupation forces in China.

Gagnon

On April 27, 1946, Gagnon was promoted to corporal and discharged. He found civilian life difficult and, unable to hold a steady job, drifted into alcoholism. He died at Hooksett, New Hampshire, on October 12, 1979, and was buried in Mount Calvary Cemetery in Manchester. On July 7, 1981, he was reinterred in Arlington. The rear of his headstone shows a replica of the flag raising and bears the inscription,

> For God and His Country
> He raised our flag in
> Battle and showed a
> Measure of his pride at
> A place called Iwo Jima
> Where courage never died.

During his time in the Marine Corps, Gagnon earned the Presidential Unit Citation with one star (for Iwo Jima), the American Campaign Medal, the Asiatic-Pacific Campaign Medal with one star (for Iwo Jima), the World War II Victory Medal, and the China Service Medal.

2-10: William Christman, Section 27, Grave 19
38° 53.241' N, 77° 4.082' W

The dubious distinction of being the first military burial in Arlington belongs to William Christman, who became a part of history when his interment took place on May 13, 1864, a month before Arlington

board with his name in black paint. It was the late nineteenth century before he received a more permanent headstone.

Not well known outside his family, and with a limited military career, Christman could easily have faded into obscurity. However, Company D of the army's Third Infantry made sure that didn't happen. Company D took on a project to document each grave site in Arlington through records and photographs. That project was dubbed Task Force Christman.

2-11: William (W. B.) Blatt, Section 27, Grave 18
38° 53.242' N, 77° 4.082' W

On May 14, 1864, Arlington truly became a military cemetery with the burial of Private William Blatt. Although William Christman was the first military burial in the cemetery, he died of illness. Blatt was the first actual battle casualty to be laid to rest here.

was officially recognized as a national cemetery. Private Christman, of Lehigh County, Pennsylvania, was twenty-one and serving in the Sixty-seventh Pennsylvania Infantry at the time of his death.

Christman was born October 1, 1844. As many youths did in that era, he began working at an early age to help his family financially. Spurred by the death of his brother, Barnabas, at the Battle of Glendale on June 30, 1862, Christman enlisted in the Union army on March 25, 1864. He is believed to have seen army life as a way to help his family, thanks to a sixty-dollar cash bounty and a three-hundred-dollar promissory note he received from the government for enlisting. He sent his bounty and advance pay home.

Three weeks after enlisting, however, Christman was hospitalized with measles in Lincoln General Hospital in Washington. On May 11, 1864, he died of peritonitis, a toxic inflammation of the membrane lining the abdominal cavity. He never had a chance to see combat. His grave was marked with a simple pine

Blatt enlisted at age nineteen as a private with Company K of the Forty-ninth Pennsylvania Volunteers on August 18, 1861. On January 1, 1863, he transferred to Company B. He was badly wounded during the Spotsylvania Court House campaign on May 13, 1864, but the fighting was so intense he could not be removed from the field immediately. Transported by boat to Washington, he died before reaching a hospital. Blatt was buried Saturday, May 14, 1864, thus becoming the third military burial, but the first battle casualty, interred at Arlington. His stone lists his name as W. B. Blatt.

2-12: William H. McKinney, Section 27, Grave 98
38° 53.242' N, 77° 4.084' W

This well-weathered stone marks the final resting place of William H. McKinney of the Seventeenth Pennsylvania Cavalry. McKinney joined the cavalry on March 16, 1864, as a private in Company F. From Adams County, Pennsylvania, he was seventeen at the time of his enlistment. When he signed on with the regiment, he left a job at a local sawmill behind.

Only a short time after entering military service, McKinney fell ill from pneumonia. He died May 12, 1864, with his father at his bedside. He had been in the army only fifty-seven days.

He was buried in Arlington on May 13, 1864, a few hours after William Christman, making him the second soldier interred here. Since his father was in attendance, McKinney became the first U.S. soldier to have family present at his funeral service at Arlington.

2-13: Thomas Shaw, Section 27, Grave 952
38° 53.249' N, 77° 4.108' W

Thomas Shaw is one of four Medal of Honor recipients buried in Section 27. Shaw earned his as a sergeant

in Company K of the Ninth United States Cavalry.

Born in Covington, Kentucky, Shaw entered the service at Pike County, Missouri. The Ninth was a segregated African-American regiment tasked with providing security to the early Western settlers and protecting the border against Indians. It was one of the regiments known as the Buffalo Soldiers.

On August 12, 1881, Sergeant Shaw and his men were surprised by a band of Indians in Carrizo Canyon, New Mexico. After a short fight, they drove off the Indians. Shaw distinguished himself during the fight by stubbornly holding his ground in an extremely exposed position, preventing his command from being surrounded.

On December 7, 1890, more than nine years after the battle, Shaw was awarded the Medal of Honor for his bravery at Carrizo Canyon. He died June 23, 1895.

2-14: William H. Brown, Section 27, Grave 565-A
38° 53.260' N, 77° 4.100' W

William Brown was born in Baltimore, Maryland, in 1836. When the Civil War broke out, he enlisted in the navy, serving as a landsman on the USS *Brooklyn*.

On the morning of August 5, 1864, the *Brooklyn* entered Mobile Bay with seventeen other ships under Admiral David Farragut. The *Brooklyn* led the second column, which consisted of seven smaller wooden ships lashed to the port sides of larger wooden screw steamers.

Shortly before seven o'clock, the fleet opened fire on Fort Morgan. During the attack, the Union monitor *Tecumseh* struck a torpedo, known today as a mine. The violent explosion caused the ship to sink in less than a minute. The *Brooklyn* was to the *Tecumseh*'s port side. When the *Brooklyn* stopped and backed up to clear a row of suspicious-looking buoys under its bow, Farra-

gut issued his famous order, "Damn the torpedoes, full speed ahead."

As the battle continued, the Confederate ironclad *Tennessee* tried to ram the *Brooklyn*, meeting with no success. As the remaining Confederate ships were taken out of the battle one by one, the *Tennessee* was the last Southern ship still fighting. After a fierce battle, it surrendered, resulting in a Union victory.

The battle lasted more than three hours. The *Brooklyn* suffered fifty-four men killed and forty-three wounded while firing 183 projectiles. For the entire time, Brown remained at his position in the powder division and performed heroically despite the bursting of shells so close that many of his crew were forced to clear the area on two separate occasions. Brown was credited with being a major factor in the surrender of the *Tennessee*, as well as in the damaging and destruction of batteries at Fort Morgan.

Brown and twenty-two other sailors and marines

of the *Brooklyn* were awarded the Medal of Honor for their actions in the battle. Brown died November 5, 1896, and was interred in Arlington a few days later.

2-15: George B. Turner, Section 41, Grave 589
38° 53.202' N, 77° 4.147' W

George Benton Turner was born in Longview, Texas, on June 27, 1899. He attended what would become Wentworth Military Academy and College at Lexington, Missouri, then enlisted in the marines in 1918. Although the United States was involved in World War I, a disappointed Turner never left the country and was mustered out without seeing action. He entered civilian life and moved to California, where he got married and lived quietly.

When the country entered World War II, however, Turner once again felt the call to serve. He enlisted in the army at forty-three, fearing his age would once again keep him from combat. Such was not the case. He was deployed with Battery C of the 499th Armored Field Artillery Battalion, part of the famous Fourteenth Armored Division. The men of the Fourteenth became known as "the Liberators" for their role in freeing large numbers of American and Allied prisoners and civilians from Nazi forced-labor and concentration camps.

In January 1945, Turner was serving as a forward observer for the artillery near Philippsbourg, France. Cut off from his unit by an enemy armored infantry attack, he linked up with a group of withdrawing American troops. He observed two enemy tanks and a large force of German soldiers. Seizing a rocket launcher, he rushed under heavy fire toward the enemy position. Standing in the middle of the road, he fired at the tanks, destroying one and disabling the second. He then removed a machine gun from a nearby half-track and fired into the enemy infantrymen, killing or wounding a great number and breaking up the attack.

When Allied troops launched a counterattack, an enemy antitank gun disabled two American tanks. Turner held off the enemy by firing a light machine gun from the hip, allowing the crews of the disabled tanks to extricate themselves. He then ran through a hail of fire to one of the burning tanks to rescue a man who was unable to escape, suffering painful wounds himself when the tank's ammunition exploded. Refusing to be evacuated, he remained with the infantry until the following day, driving off an enemy patrol, assisting in capturing a hostile strong point, and volunteering to drive a truck through heavy enemy fire to deliver wounded men to the rear aid station.

The forty-five-year-old Turner was awarded the Medal of Honor for his actions, making him one of the oldest recipients in all of World War II. His citation states, "The great courage displayed by Pfc. Turner and his magnificently heroic initiative contributed materially to the defense of the French town and inspired the troops about him."

Initially, his battery feared he had been killed or taken prisoner. When Turner returned several days later, his canteen had a bullet hole through it. But except for his injuries received in the tank explosion, he was unharmed.

Turner died June 29, 1963, at the age of sixty-four.

2-16: Slave and Freedmen Burials, Section 27
38° 53.254' N, 77° 4.216' W

Many are unaware that Arlington contains the final resting places of slaves and freedmen. In truth, nearly four thousand former slaves are buried here, most in Section 27. Some were slaves who lived and worked on the Arlington estate. Others were freed or fugitive slaves who lived in Freedman's Village, a model community set up by the government inside the confines of the cemetery. Since record keeping was sketchy at best at that time, many of the headstones say, simply, "Unknown." A fortunate few have their full names inscribed on their headstones, but many are identified simply as "Citizen" or "Civilian." And as seen in the graves of

"Buck—Civilian" and "Thomas—Citizen" above, first names or nicknames were often used.

In some cases, only a small concrete post suggests a burial site, with no name or other form of identification engraved on it.

This section, the oldest part of the cemetery, contains graves placed before the government took over the property. It is also one of the least-visited areas of Arlington.

2-17: Spottswood Poles, Section 42, Grave 2324

38° 53.202' N, 77° 4.243' W

Born December 9, 1887, in Winchester, Virginia, future Negro League baseball star Spottswood Poles showed athletic prowess at an early age. In 1906, he played his first organized baseball game with the Harrisburg Colored Giants. In 1909, he signed a professional contract with the Philadelphia Giants. Perhaps showing some favoritism to teams named the Giants, he signed with the New York Lincoln Giants two years later; he compiled batting averages of .440, .398, .414, and .487 in his four years with New York. Showing outstanding speed, he stole forty-one bases in sixty games his first season. In the 1915 championship, despite having a sub-par batting average of .205, he scored eleven runs in ten games. Over the next three years, Poles played for three Negro League teams: the New York Lincoln Stars, the Brooklyn Royal Giants, and the Hilldale Daisies.

In 1917, he left professional baseball to enlist in the 369th Infantry, also known as the Harlem Hellfighters. Sergeant Poles fought in World War I with the 369th, earning five battle stars and a Purple Heart while serving under the French Army.

At the close of the war, he came home and resumed his baseball career, signing again with the Lincoln Giants. He played until 1923 and was considered one of the fastest players of his time. Always a good hitter, he was dubbed "the black Ty Cobb." His lifetime batting average for fifteen years in the Negro League was .400, and he managed a .319 batting average over four years in the highly regarded Cuban League. Since he lived in an era when blacks had no chance to play in the major leagues, there is no way to know how he would have done at that level, but it is known that he hit .610 against major-league teams in exhibition games. He once got three hits in three at-bats against Hall of

Fame pitcher Grover Cleveland Alexander. Poles is considered one of the best outfielders ever to play professional baseball at any level.

After his retirement at age thirty-six, he started his own taxi service. Poles later worked at Olmsted Air Force Base. He died September 12, 1962.

2-18: Ernest Judson Wilson, Section 43, Grave 1114

38° 53.119' N, 77° 4.175' W

Born February 28, 1894, in Remington, Virginia, Ernest Wilson served in World War I as a corporal in

gro League career, he also played in the Cuban Winter League in the 1920s.

Baseball great Josh Gibson claimed Wilson was a much better hitter than he himself ever was. Satchel Paige said Wilson was one of the two toughest hitters he ever faced, the other being Negro League legend Chino Smith. Even after retirement, Wilson was a formidable batter, hitting two triples in one game at the age of forty-nine. He died in Washington, D.C., on June 24, 1963, and was posthumously elected to the National Baseball Hall of Fame in 2006.

2-19: Loren D. Hagen, Section 28, Grave 1204

38° 53.050' N, 77° 4.357' W

Born February 25, 1946, in Fargo, North Dakota, Loren Douglas Hagen joined the army in 1967. On August 7, 1971, he was serving as a Special Forces first lieutenant in command of a special reconnaissance team in the A Shau Valley of Vietnam. Early that morning, his team came under attack by a much larger enemy force using heavy small arms, automatic weapons, and mortar and rocket fire. Lieutenant Hagan successfully led the team in repelling the attack and then quickly deployed the men into a better defensive location.

In a short time, the enemy struck again. Hagen repeatedly exposed himself to enemy fire as he moved from one team member to the next, directing fire and resupplying the men with ammunition. When an enemy rocket made a direct hit on one of the team's bunkers, he moved in that direction in search of his men, ignoring the fact that enemy troops had already overrun the bunker area. Returning small-arms fire as he crawled through enemy fire toward the destroyed bunker, he advanced until he was fatally wounded.

Hagen was awarded the Medal of Honor for his

Company D, 417th Service Battalion, Quartermaster Corps. But much like Spottswood Poles, it was as a Hall of Fame baseball player that he is remembered.

Wilson became known as "Boojum" after Hall of Fame pitcher Satchel Paige said that was the sound the ball made when one of Wilson's hits bounced off the outfield wall. A hard-hitting infielder from 1922 to 1945 in the Negro League, he played both first base and third base. He played for the Baltimore Black Sox from 1922 to 1930, twice for the Homestead Grays, from 1931 through 1932 and again from 1940 to 1945, and for the Philadelphia Stars from 1933 to 1939. His career batting average of .351 ranks him among the top five players in Negro League history. In addition to his Ne-

courageous actions. The medal was presented to his father by President Gerald Ford at the White House on August 8, 1974. The last sentence of his citation reads, "With complete disregard for his personal safety, 1st Lt. Hagen's courageous gallantry, extraordinary heroism, and intrepidity above and beyond the call of duty, at the cost of his own life, were in keeping with the highest traditions of the military service and reflect great credit upon him and the U.S. Army."

Hagen was buried in Arlington on August 21, 1971. He was twenty-five years old.

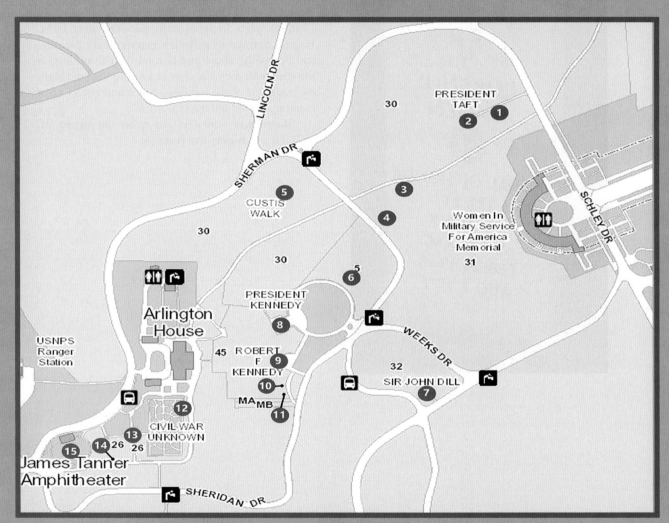

Courtesy of Arlington National Cemetery

3-1: Omar Nelson Bradley, Section 30, Grave 428-1-2

38° 53.024' N, 77° 4.137' W

Known as "the soldier's general," Omar Bradley was born in poverty in Missouri on February 12, 1893. Raised in a log cabin, he was an outstanding athlete in high school and was awarded an appointment to West Point, where he lettered in football and baseball. He graduated in 1915, ranking 44th in a class of 164.

World War I ended with a disappointed and frustrated Bradley never leaving the United States. He then took a position at South Dakota State College, followed by a four-year tour of duty as an instructor of mathematics at West Point under Superintendent Douglas MacArthur.

Over the next few years, he attended the advanced course at the Infantry School at Fort Benning (graduating second in his class), the prestigious Command and General Staff School at Fort Leavenworth, and the Army War College. After a stint as assistant secretary of the general staff in the Office of the Army Chief of Staff, he was promoted in February 1941 from lieutenant colonel to brigadier general, skipping the rank of colonel, and was assigned to Fort Benning to command the Infantry School.

In February 1942, Bradley took command of the Eighty-second Infantry Division and quickly improved its performance. Just as it seemed he would finally lead men in battle in World War II, he received orders from General George C. Marshall to take command of the Twenty-eighth Infantry Division, a National Guard unit that Marshall believed needed help badly. There,

Bradley implemented organizational and training changes that turned the Twenty-eighth into a well-trained, battle-ready combat division.

In February 1943, Bradley was sent to North Africa to work for his classmate Dwight D. Eisenhower. There, he assumed command of the Second Corps. Under Bradley's command, the Second Corps forged toward Bizerte, Tunisia, in April and May. Attacking with infantry followed by armor, Bradley's troops entered Bizerte on May 7, capturing more than forty thousand German troops.

Bradley followed that success by proceeding to Algiers, Algeria, to help plan the invasion of Sicily. That invasion was marked by thirty-eight days of hard fighting. By August 16, 1943, British and American forces held Sicily, forcing Italy to withdraw from the war.

In October 1943, Bradley took on the dual roles of First Army commander and acting commander of the skeletal First U.S. Army Group (subsequently redesignated the Twelfth Army Group). When Eisenhower, now the supreme Allied commander for the invasion of Europe, arrived in England in January 1944, he placed Bradley in command of the American army group when it was activated.

As plans for the invasion of France unfolded, it was Bradley who successfully fought to have the 82nd and 101st Airborne Divisions dropped behind Utah Beach on D-Day. During the months before the invasion, Bradley supervised the refinement of assault plans and troop training.

On the morning of D-Day, June 6, 1944, Bradley had his headquarters aboard the cruiser USS *Augusta*. The men assaulting Utah Beach met relatively light resistance, but Omaha Beach became such a nightmare that Bradley considered evacuating the troops and launching assaults on one of the other invasion beaches. By evening, however, the Allies established themselves firmly on the Normandy coast.

Over the following month, Bradley sent the Seventh Corps to capture the port of Cherbourg and expanded the beachhead into the hedgerow country behind the coast. He then conceived a plan for a one-corps attack centering on Saint-Lô. In a thirty-five-mile advance, American armor reached Avranches and began a rout of the Germans.

Bradley then turned the First Army over to General Courtney Hodges and activated the Twelfth Army Group, assuming command of twenty-one divisions comprised of 903,000 men. When Hitler ordered his commanders to attack, rather than withdraw, Bradley reinforced the Seventh Corps sector at Mortain, where the German attack seemed aimed. Bradley's plan worked, the Thirtieth Infantry Division, supported by tactical air power, decimating the assaulting force. The battle effectively ended the fighting in Normandy, the Allied forces destroying two German armies.

In December 1944, the Germans attacked in the Ardennes in what would become known as the Battle of the Bulge. Bradley directed General George Patton to reorient his attack to the north, hoping to relieve American forces besieged in Belgium. Patton's divisions moved nearly one hundred miles in bad weather in two days to attack the German left flank and link up with the 101st Airborne Division at Bastogne.

In January 1945, Bradley began a series of continuous offensives that smashed through the Siegfried Line, crossed the Rhine, and finally met the Soviets on the Elbe River. Along the way, Bradley's troops captured more than 315,000 prisoners.

At the end of operations in Europe, Bradley's Twelfth Army Group was the largest ever commanded by an American general, encompassing twelve corps, forty-eight divisions, and 1.3 million men. Eisenhower considered Bradley the master tactician of American forces and at the end of the war predicted he would eventually be recognized as America's foremost battle leader.

Following the war, Bradley directed the Veterans Administration, rebuilding the organization on a regional basis. He completely overhauled a medical-care system that had been described as medieval, revised and extended the educational benefits of the G.I. Bill, arranged for jobs and job training, established a program of loans for veterans, and administered the growing veterans' insurance and disability pension programs.

On February 7, 1948, Bradley succeeded Eisenhower as army chief of staff and in August 1949 became the first chairman of the Joint Chiefs of Staff. On September 22, 1950, Congress officially promoted him to general of the army with five stars, making him the last officer to hold that rank.

Bradley served two terms as chairman of the Joint Chiefs. He became directly involved in the creation of the North Atlantic Treaty Organization and the rearming of Western Europe, serving as the first chairman of the Military Committee of NATO. On August 15, 1953, Bradley left active service after being an advisor to President Harry S. Truman during the Korean War.

Among Bradley's many military honors and awards were the Defense Distinguished Service Medal, the Army Distinguished Service Medal with three oak leaf clusters, the Navy Distinguished Service Medal, the Silver Star, the Legion of Merit with oak leaf cluster, the Bronze Star, and the Presidential Medal of Freedom. He also was decorated by numerous foreign nations, including Mexico, France, Luxembourg, Poland, Russia/Soviet Union, and Great Britain. Bradley died April 8, 1981, just a few minutes after receiving an award from the National Institute of Social Sciences. He was buried in Arlington on April 14, 1981.

3-2: William Howard Taft, Section 30, Grave S-14
38° 53.020' N, 77° 4.159' W

William Howard Taft is one of only two presidents interred in Arlington, the other being John F. Kennedy (see site 3-8). Taft served as the nation's twenty-seventh president and tenth chief justice, the only man in history to hold both offices.

He was born September 15, 1857, in Cincinnati and attended Yale University, graduating second in his class of 121 in 1878. He immediately began the study of law. From 1887 to 1890, he was a judge of the Superior Court of Ohio, leaving that position when President Benjamin Harrison appointed him solicitor general of the United States. In 1892, he was appointed a judge of the newly created Circuit Court of Appeals, Sixth Circuit.

From 1896 to 1900, he served as dean and professor of law at the University of Cincinnati while remaining a circuit-court judge. In 1900, Taft resigned those positions to become the chairman of a commission to institute civil government in the Philippines. It was not long before he became governor of the Philippines.

In 1904, despite never serving in the military, Taft succeeded Elihu Root as secretary of war in President Theodore Roosevelt's cabinet. In 1908, he was elected to the presidency by a huge majority, both popular and electoral. However, he met overwhelming defeat four years later, winning only eight electoral votes in an unusual four-person race. Taft did achieve some firsts in his one-term presidency, however. He was the first president to throw out the first pitch to begin the professional baseball season, and he was the first president to own a car at the White House.

In 1921, he was appointed chief justice by President Warren Harding, marking an unprecedented political comeback. He retired from the Supreme Court on February 3, 1930, due to ill health and died five weeks later on March 8, 1930, at age seventy-three.

3-3: Robert Todd Lincoln, Section 31, Grave S-13

38° 52.983' N, 77° 4.181' W

Robert Todd Lincoln was born in 1843, graduated from Harvard, and served on the staff of General Ulysses Grant during the Civil War. He was the only child of President Abraham Lincoln to live to adulthood, although he came dangerously close to missing that milestone. While a youth, he was rescued from falling from a platform into the path of a slowly moving train by actor Edwin Booth. In a touch of irony, Edwin Booth was the older brother of John Wilkes Booth, the assassin of President Lincoln.

In addition to being at his father's bedside when he died, Robert Lincoln was in the crowd at the Washington, D.C., railroad station when President James Garfield was shot. He was also at the Buffalo Pan-American Exposition when President William McKinley was shot. Lincoln eventually refused to attend presidential functions, fearing his presence brought bad luck. The exception was his last public appearance at age seventy-eight at the dedication of the Lincoln Memorial in 1922, when he appeared with President Warren G. Harding.

He served as the last minister (now known as ambassador) to Great Britain. He also served as secretary of war from 1881 to 1885 under President Garfield and as president of the Pullman Company from 1897 to 1922. He and his wife had three children, but his only son, Abraham Lincoln II, died of an infection in France while Lincoln was serving as minister in London. Known as Jack, the young Lincoln is buried with his father. Lincoln's wife, Mary, is also buried in the tomb.

Lincoln is known for having his mother, Mary Todd Lincoln, committed to an institution in 1875 when her mental health began to deteriorate. He died of a cerebral hemorrhage on July 16, 1926, at his Vermont estate and was temporarily buried in Manchester, Vermont. He was interred in Arlington nearly two years later, on March 14, 1928. Robert and his son Jack are the only members of President Lincoln's immediate family not resting in the Lincoln family grave in Springfield, Illinois.

3-4: Richard Leroy McKinley, Section 31, Grave 472

38° 52.956' N, 77° 4.212' W

Richard McKinley was born in Ohio on December 22, 1933, and served with the army in Korea. On January 3, 1961, he was working with two other technicians at the National Reactor Testing Station in Idaho Falls, Idaho, when a violent explosion tore through the building, killing all three. An investigation of the incident led to the conclusion that a control rod was manually withdrawn by about fifty centimeters (forty centimeters would have been enough to make the reactor critical), increasing the reactivity and creating a power surge of twenty thousand megawatts in about .01 second, causing the fuel to melt. When the molten

fuel interacted with the water in the vessel, it produced explosive steam that caused the water above the core to rise with such force that it hit the lid of the pressure vessel and pushed the vessel itself more than nine feet into the air before it dropped back down. The incident was the first fatal nuclear accident in the United States. The investigation suggested it was the result of a suicide by one of the two operators working with McKinley.

The three technicians were so heavily contaminated by radiation that their burials followed strict guidelines established by the Atomic Energy Commission (later replaced by the Nuclear Regulatory Commission and the Department of Energy). Each man was buried in a lead-lined casket, which was then sealed in concrete and placed in a metal vault. The vaults were buried approximately ten feet in the ground. Concrete was then poured on top, ensuring that visitors could safely visit the graves.

McKinley was the only one of the three buried in Arlington. His records at the cemetery contain the following warning: "Victim of nuclear accident. Body is contaminated with long-life radio-active isotopes. Un-

der no circumstances will the body be moved from this location without prior approval of the Atomic Energy Commission in consultation with this headquarters."

3-5: Edward A. Silk, Section 30, Grave 1045-C
38° 52.965' N, 77° 4.299' W

Born June 8, 1916, in Johnstown, Pennsylvania, Edward Silk enlisted in the army and was serving as a first lieutenant in Company E, 398th Infantry, 100th Infantry Division, on November 23, 1944, near Pravel, France. He was in command of the weapons platoon when the end battalion was assigned the mission of seizing high ground overlooking Moyenmoutier prior to an attack on the city itself. By noon, he reached the edge of a woods in the vicinity of Pravel, where scouts saw an enemy sentry standing guard before a farmhouse in the valley below. One squad was immediately

pinned down by intense machine-gun and automatic-weapons fire from within the house. Silk quickly had his men return fire, but when fifteen minutes elapsed with no slackening of resistance, he decided to launch a one-man attack.

His Medal of Honor citation describes what followed:

> Running 100 yards across an open field to the shelter of a low stone wall directly in front of the farmhouse, he fired into the door and windows with his carbine; then, in full view of the enemy, vaulted the wall and dashed 50 yards through a hail of bullets to the left side of the house, where he hurled a grenade through a window, silencing a machinegun and killing 2 gunners. In attempting to move to the right side of the house he drew fire from a second machinegun emplaced in the woodshed. With magnificent courage he rushed this position in the face of direct fire and succeeded in neutralizing the weapon and killing the 2 gunners by throwing grenades into the structure. His supply of grenades was by now exhausted, but undaunted, he dashed back to the side of the farmhouse and began to throw rocks through a window, demanding the surrender of the remaining enemy. Twelve Germans, overcome by his relentless assault and confused by his unorthodox methods, gave up to the lone American. By his gallant willingness to assume the full burden of the attack and the intrepidity with which he carried out his extremely hazardous mission, 1st Lt. Silk enabled his battalion to continue its advance and seize its objective.

A year later, on November 1, 1945, Silk received his Medal of Honor from President Harry S. Truman. Silk rose to the rank of lieutenant colonel before leaving the service. He died November 18, 1955, at the age of thirty-nine. The Edward Silk Memorial Bridge in his hometown is named in his honor.

3-6: H. G. Rickover, Section 5, Grave 7000-NH
38° 52.920' N, 77° 4.243' W

Hyman Rickover was born Chaim Godalia Rickover in 1900 in a section of Russia that is now part of Poland. He and his family emigrated to the United States in 1906. Looking toward a naval career, he attended the U.S. Naval Academy and earned a master's degree in electrical engineering from Columbia University.

After serving in various capacities in the navy, Rickover was assigned to the forerunner of the Atomic Energy Commission's Oak Ridge laboratory in 1946. When he was named chief of the Nuclear Power Division in the Bureau of Ships, he began the design of a pressurized water reactor that he envisioned could be used for submarine propulsion. That work led to the development of the first nuclear-powered submarine, the *Nautilus*.

He was featured on the January 11, 1954, cover of *Time* and in 1958 was promoted to vice admiral. He

became a four-star admiral in 1973. Having directed the development of naval nuclear propulsion and controlled its operations for three decades as director of naval reactors, Rickover is often referred to as "the father of the nuclear navy."

For his work, Rickover received many military honors and awards, including the Distinguished Service Medal, the Legion of Merit, the Navy Commendation Medal, and the World War II Victory Medal. Great Britain saw fit to name him honorary commander of the Military Division of the Most Excellent Order of the British Empire. Among his many civilian awards were the Enrico Fermi Award, the Congressional Gold Medal for exceptional public service (awarded twice), and the Presidential Medal of Freedom, the nation's highest nonmilitary honor.

Rickover served on active duty with the navy for more than sixty-three years, becoming the longest-serving naval officer in American history. He died at home in Arlington, Virginia, on July 8, 1986.

3-7: John Dill, Section 32, Grave S-29
38° 52.849' N, 77° 4.191' W

Born in Ireland on September 25, 1881, John Dill served in the British army during the South African and 1914–18 wars. He commanded British forces in Palestine in 1936 and 1937, when he was knight commander of the Order of the Bath. He then served as commander of the First Army Corps in France in 1939 and part of 1940, when he became vice chief of the Imperial General Staff for King George VI.

In the early stages of World War II, he served as chief of the Imperial General Staff until Prime Minister Winston Churchill, fearing Dill was too cautious, had

Equestrian statue of John Dill's grave

him replaced by advancing him to knight grand cross of the Order of the Bath and assigning him as the senior representative to Washington for the remainder of the war. There, he became chief of the British Joint Staff Mission and senior British representative on the Combined Chiefs of Staff. He became a close personal friend of the U.S. Army chief of staff, General George C. Marshall, whose influence made it possible for Dill to be buried in Arlington after his death on November 4, 1944, from aplastic anemia.

Dill was posthumously awarded an American Distinguished Service Medal in 1944 and received an unprecedented joint resolution of Congress in appreciation of his services. The equestrian statue on Dill's grave was dedicated in 1950. President Harry S. Truman gave the main address. It is one of only two equestrian statues in the cemetery, the other being Major General Philip Kearny's in Section 2.

3-8: John F. Kennedy, Section 45, Grave S-45
38° 52.892' N, 77° 4.287' W

John Fitzgerald Kennedy, thirty-fifth president of the United States, served as a naval officer in the South Pacific during World War II. In August 1943, he was in command of patrol torpedo boat PT-109, sent with fourteen other PT boats to intercept a convoy of Japanese destroyers. During that mission, Kennedy's boat was rammed by the Japanese destroyer *Amagiri*, which cut the PT boat in two and killed a pair of sailors. Kennedy was credited with saving the lives of the survivors.

On his return home at the close of the war, he ran successfully for the U.S. House of Representatives from Massachusetts. He later served as a U.S. senator and in 1960 defeated Vice President Richard Nixon for the presidency.

On November 22, 1963, Kennedy was assassinated as he rode through Dallas, Texas, in an open motorcade.

His body was returned to Andrews Air Force Base and transported from there to the White House, where it lay in state in the East Room. On November 24, his remains were borne to the Capitol on a horse-drawn caisson, where thousands of mourners passed his bier. The next day, his remains were moved in a formal procession to St. Matthew's Cathedral for his funeral. From St. Matthew's, his body was taken to Arlington.

The site chosen for his grave was selected from three proposed. The first, near the mast of the USS *Maine*, was deemed inappropriate by Attorney General Robert F. Kennedy, the president's brother. A second one, at Dewey Circle, was determined to be too inaccessible. The third was on the slope below Arlington House. Robert Kennedy liked this location but left the final decision to Mrs. Kennedy. When she saw the third site, she immediately gave her approval. President Kennedy himself had inadvertently aided in the selection when, eight months earlier, he made an impromptu Sunday visit to the Custis-Lee mansion and remarked that the view of Washington from there was so magnificent that he could stay forever.

Dignitaries from around the world attended the state funeral. Fifty navy and air force jets flew past the

Section of Kennedy Memorial wall engraved with the president's famous "Ask not what your country can do for you . . ." speech

grave site in three V formations, the last in the missing-man formation. They were followed by Air Force One, which dipped its wings in final tribute.

Remembering the eternal flame gracing the Tomb of the Unknown Soldier in Paris, Mrs. Kennedy requested that a similar flame be installed at the president's grave. A temporary torch was implemented for the funeral and a more permanent flame installed later. On the day of the funeral, Mrs. Kennedy and Robert lit the temporary flame. The permanent flame sits in the center of a five-foot circular, flat granite stone at the head of the grave. A constantly flashing electric spark near the tip of the nozzle relights the gas, should the flame be extinguished by rain, wind, or accident.

On December 4, 1963, just ten days after the president's burial, the remains of his two deceased children were relocated from their original burial sites and reinterred at the presidential grave site. His unnamed infant daughter, who died August 23, 1956, was transferred from Newport, Rhode Island, while his infant son, Patrick Bouvier Kennedy, who was born prematurely and lived only two days, was moved from Brookline, Massachusetts, where many had assumed the president would also be buried.

The original grave was twenty feet by thirty feet, surrounded by a white picket fence. Over the next year, more than 3,000 people an hour visited the site. On weekends, an estimated 50,000 visited. Within three years of Kennedy's death, more than 16 million people had come to visit the grave. The crowds overwhelmed the grave site, and a decision was made to construct a larger one. The president and his two deceased children were moved to what became the permanent grave, just a few feet away. The new site was completed July 20, 1967.

On May 23, 1994, President Kennedy's widow, Jacqueline Bouvier Kennedy Onassis, was buried next to her husband, after her death from cancer.

In December 1997, intruders made an unsuccessful attempt to dig up the granite paving stones at the grave site. The guilty parties have never been identified.

Kennedy is one of only two presidents buried at Arlington. The other is William Howard Taft, who died in 1930 and rests in Section 30 (see site 3-2).

3-9: Robert Kennedy, Section 45, Grave S-45A
38° 52.871' N, 77° 4.289' W

Robert "Bobby" Francis Kennedy was born in Boston on November 20, 1925, the seventh in a family of nine children. Six weeks before his eighteenth birthday, Kennedy enlisted in the Naval Reserve as a seaman apprentice. In 1944, he was a Harvard sophomore when he received the news that his older brother Joseph Jr. had been killed when his navy plane went down over the English Channel. A few months later, in an effort to deal with his grief, he requested and received assignment to a destroyer newly named for his brother. At the end of his military service, he returned to Harvard. After graduating, he went on to obtain his law degree from the University of Virginia, then began his career in the Department of Justice, rising to chief counsel for the Senate Select Committee on Improper Activities in the Labor or Management Field. In this positon from 1957 to 1959, he investigated the role of organized crime in the labor movement, clashing so often with Teamsters president Jimmy Hoffa that Hoffa claimed Kennedy was engaged in a vendetta.

In 1959, he resigned to serve as campaign manager for his brother John's bid for the presidency. When John F. Kennedy was elected, he chose Bobby, only thirty-six, for the position of attorney general. On his acceptance, Bobby became the youngest person ever to hold that office. Active in the civil-rights movement, he led the government effort that permitted James H. Meredith, a black student, to enroll in the University of Mississippi in 1962. He also continued his pressure on organized crime until his resignation on September 3, 1964.

Later that year, he moved to New York, where he was elected to the U.S. Senate, taking office in early 1965. In 1968, he became a candidate for president. On June 4 of that year, he won the California primary, placing him in a strong positon for the Democratic nomination. That evening, he was shot by an assassin in the kitchen of the Ambassador Hotel in Los Angeles as he shook hands with a seventeen-year-old busboy. Shortly afterward, Kennedy died at Good Samaritan Hospital. It was less than five years since the assassination of President Kennedy and only two months since the assassination of Martin Luther King Jr.

The funeral for Senator Robert F. Kennedy took place four days later at St. Patrick's Cathedral in New York City. The remains were transported on a slow-moving train to Washington, passing through Newark, Trenton, Philadelphia, and Baltimore. Large crowds lined the tracks, delaying the procession. The train did not arrive until 9:10 P.M., prompting Arlington officials to allow the burial that same evening.

The procession moved from Union Station to Arlington, stopping briefly at the Lincoln Memorial, where the Marine Corps Band played "The Battle Hymn of the Republic." The motorcade arrived at the cemetery at 10:30. Floodlights had been erected at the grave site, and service members provided fifteen hundred candles for the mourners, providing illumination for a brief service conducted by Terence Cardinal Cooke, archbishop of New York. A simple white cross adorned the grave. Kennedy's funeral was the only one ever to take place at night at Arlington.

In 1971, the Kennedy family requested a more elaborate grave site, which added a granite plaza to blend better with the adjoining plaza for President Kennedy's grave. The plaza contains two well-known inscriptions from Robert Kennedy's speeches. The unassuming cross was retained as the grave marker.

In November 2001, President George W. Bush renamed the Justice Department Building in Washington the Robert F. Kennedy Department of Justice Building.

Long before President Kennedy's grave was vandalized, Robert Kennedy's grave was the target of similar attacks. On January 4, 1970, the white cross at the head of his grave was pulled out. Arlington officials placed it back into position the same day without fanfare. In 1981, the cross was stolen, along with the footstone that marked the grave. They were never recovered and had to be replaced.

3-10: Edward Kennedy, Section 45, Grave S-45B
38° 52.858' N, 77° 4.287' W

The youngest of the Kennedy brothers, Edward "Ted" Kennedy was born February 22, 1932, in Boston. By the time he died in 2009, he had become the third-longest-serving member in U.S. Senate history.

Kennedy entered the Senate in 1962 after winning a special election to fill his brother John's seat, vacated when John became president. Over the next forty-seven years, Ted Kennedy was a leader in liberal causes including civil rights, health care, and immigration, but was also known to work well with those on the opposite side of the political spectrum. Some historians have called Kennedy, known as "the Liberal Lion," one of the most effective legislators in the history of the Senate. During his time on Capitol Hill, he was responsible for some twenty-five hundred bills, over three hundred of which became law.

In November 1979, Kennedy announced he would run against incumbent president Jimmy Carter for the 1980 Democratic presidential nomination. Kennedy won primaries in ten states, but his campaign was doomed by an incident that had occurred on July 18, 1969, when he drove his car off a bridge on Chappaquiddick Island, Massachusetts, killing his passenger, Mary Jo Kopechne. Kennedy failed to report the incident to the authorities for nearly ten hours, claiming the delay was the result of a concussion he suffered in the accident and that he was exhausted from attempting to rescue Kopechne. Kennedy pled guilty to leaving the scene of an accident and received a two-month suspended sentence, enraging his political opponents. When the incident came up repeatedly on the campaign trail, he recognized it was destined to follow him throughout his political career. At the 1980 Democratic National Convention, he withdrew his bid for the presidency.

In May 2008, Kennedy was diagnosed with a malignant brain tumor. He succumbed to the disease at his home in Hyannis Port, Massachusetts, on August 25, 2009, at the age of seventy-seven. His body was transported to Boston, where it lay in repose at the John F. Kennedy Library. Thousands came to pay their respects. Following a funeral mass at Our Lady of Perpetual Help Basilica in Roxbury, Massachusetts, Kennedy was transported to Washington. A motorcade proceeded toward the Capitol, where thousands of people, including legislators and congressional staffers, stood to view the procession. From the Capitol, the cortege continued to Arlington, following the same route of President Kennedy's 1963 funeral procession.

Kennedy qualified for burial in Arlington as a result of his two years of service in the U.S. Army, combined with his time as senator. He was laid to rest on the same slope as his brothers, just a hundred feet from Robert Kennedy. A simple oak cross, painted white, marks his grave, and a flat marble footstone bears the modest inscription, "Edward Moore Kennedy, 1932–2009."

3-11: Joseph P. Kennedy Jr., Section 45, Grave S-45C

38° 52.847' N, 77° 4.285' W

Joseph Patrick Kennedy Jr. was the oldest son of Kennedy family patriarch Joseph Patrick Kennedy Sr. and his wife, Rose Fitzgerald, and the brother of John Fitzgerald, Robert Francis, and Edward "Ted" Kennedy. Born July 25, 1915, he was destined to serve in the highest reaches of government, if his father had anything to do with it. He graduated from Harvard College in 1938, followed by a stint at Harvard Law School. He attended the 1940 Democratic National Convention as a delegate at the age of twenty-five.

Eschewing his final year of law school, he entered the navy not long before America's entry into World

War II. He also became engaged to Athalia Ponsell, an aspiring actress and model. Never without a plan, Kennedy intended to run for Congress from the Eleventh District of Massachusetts when he left the service.

In May 1942, he earned his wings as a naval aviator and sixteen months later was sent to Britain, where he piloted PB4Y Liberator patrol bombers on antisubmarine details during two tours of duty. Kennedy completed his twenty-five combat missions and was told he was eligible to return home. Instead, he volunteered for a mission known as Operation Aphrodite, which involved flying an old bomber filled with high explosives, to be detonated by a remote-control device, toward the coast of France, where it would be crashed into a predetermined strategic target. These missions were extremely dangerous, the remote controls having questionable reliability. Worse, the explosives were extremely sensitive.

On August 12, 1944, Kennedy and his copilot, Lieutenant Wilford John Willy, took off toward their target, a German V-3 artillery site at Mimoyecques in northern France. Their plan was to turn on the remote control and arm the explosives, then parachute out of the aircraft as it left English airspace. At that point, a second plane was to take over the remote control of the abandoned bomber and crash it into its intended target. But as Kennedy and Willy prepared to abandon the plane near the town of Blythburgh, it exploded. Both men were killed instantly. Their remains were never recovered.

Kennedy and Willy were posthumously awarded the Navy Cross, the Distinguished Flying Cross, the Purple Heart, and an Air Medal.

Kennedy's name is inscribed on the Tablets of the Missing in the Cambridge American Cemetery and Memorial in Cambridge, England. When the new pathway was added for Ted Kennedy's grave at Arlington in 2012, the memorial headstone shown in the photo on page 44 was also placed and dedicated in Joseph Kennedy's honor.

In 1946, the navy named a destroyer the USS *Joseph P. Kennedy Jr.* His younger brother Robert briefly served aboard the ship that bore Joseph's name. Before being decommissioned, the ship took part in the blockade of Cuba during the Cuban Missile Crisis in 1962 and served with the recovery teams for Wally Schirra and Tom Stafford in the Gemini VI and Frank Borman and James Lovell in the Gemini VII manned spaceflights in 1965. It is now a floating museum in Fall River, Massachusetts.

3-12: Albert H. Packard, Section 26, Grave 5203
38° 52.839' N, 77° 4.354' W

Captain Albert Packard was serving with Company A of the Thirty-first Maine Volunteer Infantry at the Battle of the Wilderness when he suffered a severe head wound in early May 1864. He was moved to a Washington hospital, where he died of his wounds ten days later.

As one of more than eighteen thousand Union casualties at that battle, Packard was destined to slip into the shadows of history, unknown to few outside his family. Then his burial site was selected. With several other victims of the war, his remains were transported to a new military cemetery on the outskirts of Washington that would eventually become Arlington National Cemetery.

On May 17, 1864, Packard was interred in a grave on the edge of Mrs. Robert E. Lee's rose garden, becoming the first officer buried in Arlington.

3-13: Unknown Civil War Dead, Section 26
38° 52.826' N, 77° 4.391' W

Tucked away in what once was the rose garden of Arlington House is a monument to the unknown soldiers who died in the Civil War. The monument sits above a masonry vault containing the remains of 2,111 soldiers found scattered across the battlefield or in shallow graves from Bull Run and along the route to

3-14: Amputated Legs, Section 26, Grave 5232
38° 52.811' N, 77° 4.393' W

the Rappahannock River. It is almost certain that Union and Confederate dead are comingled in the vault. The monument was dedicated in September 1866 and was the first at Arlington to honor unidentified soldiers who died in battle.

In a mood of vindictiveness, Quartermaster General Montgomery Meigs ordered that the bodies be gathered and buried on this particular site, knowing they would prevent Robert E. Lee and his family from returning to their home.

The memorial includes this inscription:

Beneath this stone
Repose the bones of two thousand one hundred
and eleven unknown soldiers
Gathered after the war
From the fields of Bull Run, and the route
to the Rappahannock.
Their remains could not be identified, but their
names and deaths are recorded in the archives of
their country, and its grateful citizens
Honor them as of their noble army of martyrs.
May they rest in peace.
September A.D. 1866

In a neat row between the Arlington House rose garden and the James Tanner Amphitheater sits a solitary, worn marker with only the number 5232, indicating the grave site, on it. The grave contains a curious occupant—or, if you prefer, occupants.

The most common treatment of wounds to the limbs during the Civil War, particularly those that involved fractures, was amputation. This grave contains three amputated legs from soldiers treated at Judiciary Square Hospital in May 1864.

The records of one of those soldiers, Arthur Mc-Guinn of the Fourteenth U.S. Infantry, do not indicate what his ultimate fate was. Another, Private James Carey of the 106th Pennsylvania Infantry, survived his amputation and lived until 1913. The third, Sergeant Michael Creighton of the Ninth Massachusetts Infantry's Company B, lived for two weeks after his amputation but died on June 9, 1864. Of the three, Creighton is the only one buried in Arlington. His remains were interred in Section 27, Grave 819, about eight hundred yards from his amputated leg, making him the only person to have two graves here.

3-15: James Tanner Amphitheater (Old Amphitheater), Section 26

38° 52.816' N, 77° 4.433' W

The Old Amphitheater was built in 1873 and dedicated in 1874 for the celebration of the fifth Decoration Day. For many years, it served that purpose, in addition to being the site for other patriotic meetings. But by 1920, it was apparent that more seating was needed for these events, and the larger Memorial Amphitheater was constructed (see Chapter 7, site 7-1), rendering the Old Amphitheater obsolete. However, one group, the Sons of Union Veterans, opted to continue holding its annual Memorial Day ceremonies at the Old Amphitheater.

When the idea arose to give the amphitheater a more formal name, that of James Tanner was suggested. Tanner, a corporal in the Eighty-seventh New York Volunteer Infantry during the Civil War, was wounded in the Second Battle of Bull Run, necessitating the amputation of both legs. After the war, he became a stenographer and served in that capacity both at Lincoln's deathbed and during the trial of the Lincoln conspirators, compiling the official records for the government at both events. Tanner was buried in Section 2 not far from the Old Amphitheater (see Chapter 4, site 4-3).

On May 30, 2014, the Old Amphitheater was officially renamed the James Tanner Amphitheater, in recognition of Tanner's tireless efforts on behalf of veterans.

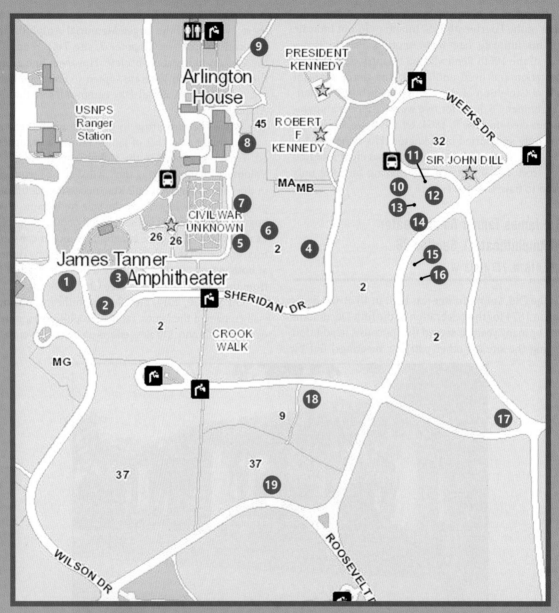

USNPS
Ranger
Station

Arlington
House

9

PRESIDENT
KENNEDY

45 ROBERT
F
KENNEDY

8

32

WEEKS DR

11 SIR JOHN DILL

10 12

13

14

MA MB

7

CIVIL WAR
UNKNOWN

6

5 2 4

2

15

16

26 26

James Tanner
1 Amphitheater
3

2

SHERIDAN DR

2

CROOK
WALK

MG

18

9

17

37

37

19

WILSON DR

ROOSEVELT

Courtesy of Arlington National Cemetery

4-1: Philip Kearny Jr., Section 2, Grave S-8

38° 52.797' N, 77° 4.458' W

Born into a life of privilege, Philip Kearny could have avoided risking his life in military service. But he chose just the opposite, serving heroically in four wars. His fearless nature led to his nickname, "Kearny the Magnificent."

After graduating from West Point, Kearny served on the frontier a short time, then went to France, where he attended the French cavalry school and participated with the cavalry in France's battles in Algiers in 1840.

Back in the United States, Kearny quickly became recognized for his bravery and leadership. General Winfield Scott called him "the bravest man I ever knew, and a perfect soldier." As he led a daring charge in the Mexican War, his left arm was wounded so badly that it had to be amputated. He was breveted a major for his gallantry in that action. When the war ended, Kearny moved to New York City and became an army recruiter.

In 1859, he went to Europe, where he served in Napoleon III's Imperial Guard during the Italian War. In line with his bold reputation, he was said to have taken part in every cavalry charge at Magenta and Solferino with the reins clenched in his teeth.

When the Civil War broke out in 1861, Kearny was appointed a brigadier general despite concerns that his disability would hinder his effectiveness. The

need for experienced combat officers, however, caused those objections to be overruled, and he was assigned to command a brigade of New Jersey regiments. Those who supported his commission were not disappointed. On July 4, 1862, he was promoted to major general. Two months later, he inadvertently rode into the Confederate lines and was shot as he tried to make his escape. He was killed instantly.

Kearny was buried in Trinity Cemetery in New York. In 1914, he was reinterred in Arlington. The statue that marks his grave was a gift from the people of New Jersey and is one of only two equestrian statues in the cemetery, the other being that of British field marshal John Dill in Section 32 (see Chapter 3, site 3-7).

He is credited with developing what became known as "the Kearny patch," a forerunner of the insignia patches later worn by all units in the Union army. The town of Kearny, New Jersey, is named in his honor.

4-2: Arthur MacArthur Jr., Section 2, Grave 856-A

38° 52.782′ N, 77° 4.436′ W

Arthur MacArthur Jr. was the patriarch of a highly decorated military family. He received the Medal of Honor for actions during the Spanish-American War. His son Douglas MacArthur also received the Medal of Honor, making the two the first father-son recipients of that award. Only one other father and son, Theodore Roosevelt and Theodore Roosevelt Jr., have achieved that honor. MacArthur's second son, Arthur III, was awarded the Navy Cross, the second-highest award the navy offers.

Arthur Jr. joined the Twenty-fourth Wisconsin Infantry at the outbreak of the Civil War. At Missionary Ridge, he placed the regimental flag on captured works at the summit. It was this action that gained him his Medal of Honor. His citation reads, "Seized the col-

ors of his regiment at a critical moment and planted them on the captured works on the crest of Missionary Ridge." He also fought at Chickamauga, at Stones River, at Chattanooga, in the Atlanta campaign, and at Franklin.

Except for a brief stint in 1864 and early 1865 when he studied law, MacArthur spent his entire career in the army. He participated in the Indian Wars (during which he fought against Geronimo), the Spanish-American War, and the Philippine-American War. After MacArthur's last war, President William McKinley named him military governor of the Philippines. However, he clashed so often with civilian governor William Howard Taft that he was eventually transferred back to the United States.

In 1906, the position of army chief of staff became available. By that time, however, Taft was president, and he remembered his conflicts with MacArthur. MacArthur was overlooked in favor of Lieutenant General John C. Bates.

MacArthur retired from the army on June 2, 1909, his sixty-fourth birthday. Three years later, he suffered a massive heart attack and died while addressing his old Civil War comrades. He was buried in Milwaukee but was moved to Arlington in 1926.

4-3: James Tanner, Section 2, Grave 877
38° 52.802' N, 77° 4.411' W

James R. Tanner was working as a schoolteacher in 1861 when the Civil War began. He enlisted in the Eighty-seventh New York Infantry as a seventeen-year-old corporal. At the Second Battle of Bull Run, he was wounded so severely by shrapnel that both his legs had to be amputated below the knees. He could not be moved when the Union army retreated and was taken captive. Released ten days later, he went home to New York, where he learned how to walk with artificial legs. When released from the hospital, Tanner began to study stenography, a vocation that plunged him directly into one of America's most historic events.

On April 14, 1865, an assassin's bullet tore into the head of Abraham Lincoln while he was watching a play at Ford's Theatre. Lincoln was taken across the street to the Peterson House, where he died without regaining consciousness. When it became apparent that the president was not going to survive, Secretary of War Edwin Stanton called for a stenographer to record eyewitness statements. It was Tanner who received the assignment. He spent the night recording the events as they took place in the room. Tanner was present when Lincoln was declared deceased the next morning. He

also recorded testimony at the trial of the Lincoln conspirators.

After the war, he became active in the Grand Army of the Republic, serving as the organization's New York State commander, a position in which he became known for his fight for veterans' benefits. In 1889, he was appointed by President Benjamin Harrison to the position of commissioner of pensions. He resigned just six months later to work as an attorney and file numerous claims against the government on behalf of Civil War veterans. In 1906, he became the national commander of the GAR. He died in 1927 and was buried in Arlington.

In 2014, the Old Amphitheater in the cemetery was renamed the James Tanner Amphitheater in his honor (see Chapter 3, site 3-15).

4-4: William Frederick Halsey Jr., Section 2, Grave 1184
38° 52.796' N, 77° 4.300' W

William Frederick Halsey was born October 30, 1882. Known to the world as Bull Halsey, he graduated from the U.S. Naval Academy in 1904 after garnering several honors as fullback on the academy's football team.

Halsey was awarded the Navy Cross for his actions while in command of the USS *Benham* and the USS *Shaw* during convoy escort duties in World War I. In 1934, at the age of fifty-two, he earned his naval aviator wings, becoming the oldest person to do so in the history of the navy.

In February 1942, by now a vice admiral, Halsey led the first counter-strikes of World War II against the Japanese with carrier raids on the Gilbert and Marshall Islands. Two months later, his task force launched the famous Doolittle Raid against targets in the Japanese homeland. That same year, he was placed in command

of the South Pacific Area. Promoted to commander in chief of the Third Fleet in 1944, he provided support for General Douglas MacArthur's invasion of the Philippines. The Japanese surrender took place on Halsey's flagship, the battleship USS *Missouri*, in Tokyo Bay. In December 1945, he was promoted to five-star fleet admiral, one of only five men ever to hold that rank. He retired from the navy in 1947 to become president of International Telecommunications Labs, Inc.

Halsey died of a heart attack on August 16, 1959. Prior to his burial, his body lay in state at Bethlehem Chapel at Washington National Cathedral. He was buried August 20, 1959, next to his father, a former captain in the navy. Among Halsey's awards were the Navy Cross, the Navy Distinguished Service Medal with three gold stars, the Army Distinguished Service Medal, the Presidential Unit Citation, the Mexican Service Medal, the World War I Victory Medal, the World War II Victory Medal, the American Defense Service Medal, the Asiatic-Pacific Campaign Medal, and numerous foreign awards from Brazil, Chile, Colombia, Cuba, Ecuador, Greece, Panama, Peru, the United Kingdom, Venezuela, and Guatemala.

In 2003, the navy announced it was naming a new guided missile destroyer (DDG-97) after Halsey. It became the second ship to carry his name. The first was

CG-23, a cruiser decommissioned in 1994. Halsey Field House at the U.S. Naval Academy bears his name.

4-5: Hiram Berdan, Section 2, Grave 979
38° 52.815' N, 77° 4.344' W

Hiram Berdan was a mechanical engineer and inventor who gained his fame during the Civil War as the colonel of the First U.S. Sharpshooters. Berdan had been recognized as an excellent marksman before the Civil War and through political connections was chosen to head up the first sharpshooter unit. Sharpshooters under Berdan were required to put ten bullets in succession within five inches of the center of a target at a distance of two hundred yards if supported by a rest or a hundred yards if not. The shooters could use their own rifles, but they had to have open sights. If a prospective recruit missed the target, or if his misses averaged more than five inches from the center, he was

disqualified. Berdan's men wore distinctive green uniforms that served as an early version of camouflage. In spite of this, and because they often operated in front of the battle lines, they had a high casualty rate. Confederate newspapers often referred to them as "the Green Coats" or "the Green Demons."

Berdan had enemies in the upper levels of the Union army, many considering him unscrupulous and unfit for command. Nonetheless, he was breveted a brigadier general of U.S. Volunteers for his service at Chancellorsville and was nominated for brevet major general by President Andrew Johnson for his actions at Gettysburg. The second brevet was never confirmed.

On two occasions, Berdan was unsuccessfully court-martialed on charges of cowardice and misconduct. Not long after Gettysburg, he took an unauthorized leave of absence. He never returned to command and resigned from the service on January 2, 1864.

Before the Civil War, Berdan invented a repeating rifle and a patented musket ball. Later, he developed a twin-screw submarine gunboat, a torpedo boat for evading torpedo nets, a long-distance range finder, and a distance fuse for shrapnel. He died March 31, 1893.

4-6: Joseph Wheeler, Section 2, Grave 1089
38° 52.820′ N, 77° 4.321′ W

Joseph "Fighting Joe" Wheeler is best known for his role as a general in the Confederate cavalry during the Civil War. Relatively few are aware, however, that he was also a general in the U.S. Army during both the Spanish-American War and the Philippine-American War. He also saw service in various Indian campaigns in Kansas and New Mexico following his graduation from West Point in 1859.

During the Civil War, Wheeler was wounded three times and had sixteen horses shot from under him while taking part in such battles as Perryville, Murfreesboro,

Chickamauga, Knoxville, and Shiloh. He was appointed cavalry general of the Confederate armies on May 11, 1864, and spent the rest of the war opposing General William T. Sherman's March to the Sea.

Following the war, he practiced law and planted cotton. He was elected to Congress in March 1881 but lost the next election in June 1882. When his successor died a short time after taking office, Wheeler ran successfully for the same seat in January 1883, serving the last two months of the term. He was again elected to Congress in 1884 and served from March 1885 until his resignation in April 1900. He was chairman of the prestigious Ways and Means Committee. He retired as a brigadier general in the regular army in 1900.

Wheeler died at his sister's home in Brooklyn, New York, on January 25, 1906. He is one of only two former Confederate generals in Arlington, the other being Marcus Joseph Wright, who is buried in Section 16 adjacent to the Confederate Memorial.

4-7: John Lincoln Clem, Section 2, Grave 993

38° 52.831' N, 77° 4.343' W

When Fort Sumter was attacked in April 1861, President Abraham Lincoln issued a call for volunteers to put down the rebellion. One of those who answered that call was John Clem, a boy ten years old. He tried to enlist as a drummer in the Third Ohio Infantry but was rejected because of his age. Undeterred, he was adopted as the mascot and drummer for the Twenty-second Michigan Infantry and followed the regiment into battle. He was officially permitted to enlist two years later. Until that happened, the regiment's officers chipped in so he could receive the same pay as the enlisted men, thirteen dollars a month.

At Chickamauga, he carried a scaled-down musket instead of his drum, receiving three bullets through his cap but shooting a Confederate colonel who was about to capture him. As his reward, Clem was promoted to sergeant, making him the youngest noncommissioned officer ever to serve in the U.S. Army. His exploits gave rise to his nickname, "the Drummer Boy of Chickamauga." Clem also fought at Perryville, Murfreesboro, Kennesaw, and Atlanta, where he was wounded twice. In October 1863, he was captured while guarding a train but was released a short time later.

Clem was discharged from the army in 1864, a veteran at the age of thirteen. He rejoined in 1871 when President Ulysses S. Grant offered him a promotion to second lieutenant after he failed the West Point entrance exam several times. Clem rose to the rank of colonel by 1903 and assistant quartermaster general by 1906. The last Civil War veteran actively serving in the U.S. Army, he retired in 1915 with the rank of major general. On May 13, 1937, he died in San Antonio, Texas.

4-8: Pierre Charles L'Enfant, Section 2, Grave S-3

38° 52.865' N, 77° 4.339' W

Pierre Charles L'Enfant was born in France but came to the United States in 1777 at age twenty-three. He joined the Continental Army and, following his recovery from a wound suffered at the siege of Savannah, served on General George Washington's staff as a captain in the U.S. Engineers for the remainder of the Revolutionary War. While at Valley Forge with

Washington, the Marquis de Lafayette commissioned L'Enfant to paint a portrait of the general. L'Enfant was promoted by brevet to major of engineers on May 2, 1783, in recognition of his service.

When Washington became president, he directed L'Enfant to lay out a plan for the new federal city of Washington, D.C. What is believed to be L'Enfant's original plan is now in the Library of Congress. Although it was revised, it became the basis for what is now Washington. The plan called for a seat of government on what is now Capitol Hill and a presidential palace to be situated along a broad avenue connecting the two. An even wider avenue would eventually become today's National Mall. Streets were to be laid out in a grid pattern, periodically broken up by circles and open spaces that could be used to recognize notable American figures.

In 1792, L'Enfant's relationship with the three commissioners to whom he reported became so contentious that they convinced President Washington to dismiss him. L'Enfant spent the next several years trying to convince Congress that he was owed a substantial sum of money for his work. When Congress finally paid him, he received only a portion of what he had requested, and most of that went to his creditors.

L'Enfant died in poverty in 1825 and was buried in Prince George County, Virginia. In 1909, his grave was relocated to Arlington.

4-9: Mary Randolph, Section 2, Grave S-6
38° 52.912' N, 77° 4.334' W

Mary Randolph came from what many might call a pedigreed line. Born August 9, 1762, outside Richmond, Virginia, as one of thirteen children, she enjoyed all the trappings of a wealthy family. She was a direct descendant of Pocahontas; a cousin of Thomas Jefferson; a cousin of Mary Lee Fitzhugh Custis, the wife of

George Washington Parke Custis, who built Arlington House; and a cousin of Robert E. Lee. Her brother Thomas was governor of Virginia and the husband of Thomas Jefferson's daughter, Martha.

Randolph eventually had eight children of her own, only four of whom survived to adulthood. In 1824, she wrote *The Virginia Housewife*, a housekeeping guide and cookbook so popular that it was reprinted and published into the 1860s. It is believed to have been the first cookbook published in America.

She died on January 23, 1828, and was buried a short distance from her cousin's home, Arlington House, making her the first person buried in what eventually would become Arlington National Cemetery.

4-10: William J. Donovan, Section 2, Grave 4874-A
38° 52.841' N, 77° 4.236' W

William Joseph Donovan was better known as "Wild Bill," a sobriquet whose origin is a bit murky.

continued with his unit until it withdrew to a less exposed position.

During World War II, Donovan founded and headed the Office of Strategic Services, which evolved into today's Central Intelligence Agency. He also served as assistant to Robert Jackson, the chief American prosecutor at the Nuremburg war-crimes trials. In 1953, he was appointed United States ambassador to Thailand.

Donovan died February 8, 1959.

4-11: Daniel "Chappie" James Jr., Section 2, Grave 4968-B

38° 52.845' N, 77° 4.209' W

Daniel "Chappie" James was born in Pensacola, Florida, and attended Tuskegee Institute, where he learned to fly under the government-sponsored Civilian Pilot Training Program. In 1943, he received an appointment as a cadet in the Army Air Corps. Six months later, he received his commission, becoming one of the famed Tuskegee Airmen. For the remainder of World War II, he trained pilots for the all-black Ninety-ninth Pursuit Squadron and worked in other assignments.

Trained as a fighter pilot, he flew 101 combat missions in Korea and another 78 in Vietnam. On one of his Vietnam missions, he led a flight in which seven MiG-21s were destroyed, the highest total MiG kill of any mission during the war.

In June 1967, James became vice wing commander of the Eighth Tactical Fighter Wing in Thailand, under the command of Colonel Robin Olds. In 1969, he famously came face to face with future dictator Muammar Gaddafi, then a colonel in the Libyan army. Gaddafi had rushed with his men onto Wheelus Air Base when he was confronted by James. Both men had pistols on their hips, and Gaddafi began to reach for his. James warned

Some say he acquired it as a star football player at Columbia University, while others insist it came from his exploits during World War I. Whatever its origin, Wild Bill Donovan remains the only person to be awarded all four of the nation's highest awards: the Medal of Honor, the Distinguished Service Cross, the Distinguished Service Medal with two oak leaf clusters, and the National Security Medal. He also was awarded a Silver Star and a Purple Heart with two oak leaf clusters.

He earned his Medal of Honor near Landres-et-Saint Georges, France, in October 1918. His citation reads,

> Lt. Col. Donovan personally led the assaulting wave in an attack upon a very strongly organized position, and when our troops were suffering heavy casualties he encouraged all near him by his example, moving among his men in exposed positions, reorganizing decimated platoons, and accompanying them forward in attacks. When he was wounded in the leg by machine-gun bullets, he refused to be evacuated and

One of America's most famous explorers, Richard E. Byrd Jr. was a 1912 graduate of the U.S. Naval Academy. On May 9, 1926, he and Floyd Bennett (see Chapter 8, site 8-8) reported flying over the North Pole, becoming the first to accomplish the feat. Both were awarded the Medal of Honor for their achievement. Since then, evidence has arisen that Roald Amundsen actually had the first verifiable claim to the North Pole, as well as the South.

Byrd's Medal of Honor citation recognizes him "for distinguishing himself conspicuously by courage and intrepidity at the risk of his life, in demonstrating that it is possible for aircraft to travel in continuous flight from a now inhabited portion of the earth over the North Pole and return."

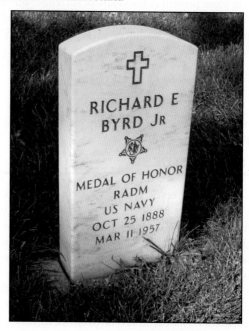

him to move his hand away from his weapon, and the Libyan backed down. Eventually, the United States vacated the base, but James became a legend among his men for the incident.

Following an assignment as vice commander of the Thirty-third Tactical Fighter Wing, he was promoted to brigadier general. In 1970, he was named deputy assistant secretary of defense for public affairs. In 1975, he became the first black officer in the history of the U.S. military to attain four-star general rank. With that came a promotion to commander of the North American Air Defense Command, with responsibility for all aspects of air defense of the United States and Canada.

James died of a heart attack on February 25, 1978, three weeks after his retirement. His many awards are highlighted by the Defense Distinguished Service Medal, the Air Force Distinguished Service Medal, the Legion of Merit with oak leaf cluster, the Distinguished Flying Cross with two oak leaf clusters, and the Air Medal with thirteen oak leaf clusters.

Byrd undertook his first Antarctic expedition in 1928, followed by a second in 1934, when he spent five months alone while operating a meteorological station. He almost lost his life due to carbon monoxide poisoning from a poorly vented stove. Only when his radio reports became incoherent did outsiders suspect something was wrong, and rescuers were dispatched. He made a third expedition in 1939. In 1946, he led a group of forty-seven hundred men to Antarctica in an expedition known as Operation Highjump. His last expedition was in 1955–56 as commander of the navy's Operation Deep Freeze, which resulted in the establishment of permanent U.S. naval bases there.

Byrd was also awarded the Navy Cross, the Navy Distinguished Service Medal, the Distinguished Flying Cross, the Legion of Merit, the Congressional Gold Medal, and the Silver Lifesaving Medal. In addition, he was honored with three ticker-tape parades. Byrd was among those present at the Japanese surrender on September 2, 1945. He died in 1957. The USS *Richard E. Byrd* was named in his honor in 1962 and the USNS *Richard E. Byrd* in 2007.

A memorial to Byrd also stands on Memorial Avenue, the entrance to Arlington National Cemetery.

4-13: Brehon Burke Somervell, Section 2, Grave 4946

38° 52.833' N, 77° 4.229' W

Brehon Somervell graduated sixth in a class of 106 from the U.S. Military Academy in 1914 and was commissioned as a second lieutenant in the Corps of Engineers. In Paris when World War I began, he immediately gained a favorable reputation by efficiently organizing and getting American citizens safely home. He also helped organize the Fifteenth Engineers, the first engineering regiment to go overseas. During World War I, Somervell headed several projects, including an

important ammunition dump near Mehun-sur-Yèvre. All of his projects were completed on schedule despite the challenges brought on by the war. He was awarded the Distinguished Service Medal for his efforts and, in 1918, the Distinguished Service Cross for leading a patrol to inspect damage to a bridge six hundred yards in front of American lines. He was one of only nine American officers to receive both awards in World War I.

Somervell is best known for a project he supervised in his home country. In 1941, the War Department was inefficiently scattered across seventeen separate sites throughout the Washington area. Government officials recognized the need for a central location. As commanding general of the Army Service Forces, Somervell was responsible for the design and construction of a new facility. Initially controversial for its design and even more for its location in rural Virginia, the facility was referred to by many as "Somervell's Folly." Families were evicted from their homes to make room for the building. Some feared that moving so many workers out of the capital to a site "clear down in Virginia" would lead to Washington's becoming a ghost town. Others complained that the site, a swampy piece of property along the Potomac River, would not support the building, which would eventually sink into the muck. Somervell's design called for nearly forty-two thousand pilings to be driven into the mud to alleviate that concern, but naysayers still fought to scuttle the project. The *Washington Post* called it one of the worst blunders of the war period.

Eventually, Somervell prevailed. His concentric and interconnected five-sided structure became the largest office building in the world and was named for its shape: the Pentagon.

4-14: Khe Sanh Memorial Tablet and Tree, Section 2

38° 52.826' N, 77° 4.216' W

The Battle of Khe Sanh took place in Quang Tri Province in South Vietnam from January 21 to July 9, 1968.

The North Vietnamese Army had moved large numbers of troops into the area around Khe Sanh Combat Base in late 1967, causing American leaders to reevaluate their original assessment that the NVA troop movements were routine offensives. A buildup of Marine Corps forces was ordered, which attracted a series of ground, artillery, mortar, and rocket attacks by the NVA. President Lyndon Johnson ordered that Khe Sanh be held at all costs. There would be no withdrawal.

To keep enemy forces from using the hills surrounding the base as observation posts and possibly firebases, the marines continuously defended the positions in what would become known as "the hill fights." Living conditions at the base during the five months of fighting were horrendous, with shortages of food, water, and sleep but an abundance of rats. A massive aerial bombardment was launched in support of the marines isolated at the base, not only to inflict damage on NVA

forces but to provide the marines with badly needed supplies. The marines lost about 400 killed in action during the siege and the hill fights. Several hundred more Americans were wounded. Thirty-three South Vietnamese troops were killed and 187 wounded. An estimated 5,000 to 10,000 NVA troops were killed.

On July 3, 1983, Marine Corps veterans of Khe Sanh planted a ginkgo tree and placed this memorial tablet in memory of all those who were sacrificed in the fighting.

4-15: Benjamin O. Davis Sr., Section 2, Grave E-478-B

38° 52.808' N, 77° 4.223' W

Benjamin O. Davis Sr. entered military service at the beginning of the Spanish-American War in 1898 as a temporary first lieutenant in an all-black unit, the Eighth U.S. Volunteer Infantry. He mustered out nine months later and shortly thereafter enlisted in the

Ninth Cavalry Regiment, one of the original Buffalo Soldier units.

Tutored by Lieutenant Charles Young, the only African-American officer serving in the U.S. military at that time, Davis passed the test to become an officer and on February 2, 1901, was commissioned a second lieutenant of cavalry in the regular army. Only a few months later, he found himself in his second conflict, this time the Philippine-American War. He saw war for a third time in World War I when he was assigned to the Ninth Cavalry. After assignments in Wyoming, Ohio, Liberia, the border with Mexico, and a few other locations, Davis was promoted to brigadier general by President Franklin D. Roosevelt and General George C. Marshall, making him the first African-American general in the American military. He became commanding general of Fourth Brigade, Second Cavalry Division, at Fort Riley, Kansas, in January 1941, while the military was still segregated. He served as an advisor on race relations in the army during World War II in the European theater.

Davis retired from the army in 1948 after fifty years of service. His military decorations consisted of the Bronze Star Medal and the Distinguished Service Medal. The latter came with the following citation:

> For exceptionally meritorious service to the Government in a duty of great responsibility from June, 1941, to November, 1944, as an Inspector of troop units in the field, and as special War Department consultant on matters pertaining to Negro troops. The initiative, intelligence and sympathetic understanding displayed by him in conducting countless investigations concerning individual soldiers, troop units and other components of the War Department brought about a fair and equitable solution to many important problems which have since become the basis of far-reaching War Department policy. His wise advice and counsel have made a direct contribution to the maintenance of soldier morale and troop discipline and has been of material assistance to the War Department and to responsible commanders in the field of understanding personnel matters as they pertain to the individual soldier.

Davis was also awarded numerous foreign awards and honors, including the Croix de Guerre with palm from France and the Grade of Commander of the Order of the Star of Africa from Liberia. His son, Benjamin O. Davis Jr., was the first African-American general officer in the U.S. Air Force and was the commander of the World War II Tuskegee Airmen. He is buried nearby.

4-16: Benjamin O. Davis Jr., Section 2, Grave E-311-RH
38° 52.799' N, 77° 4.218' W

Benjamin O. Davis Jr. was the son of America's first African-American army general. The younger Davis attended West Point, where he became the fourth African-American to graduate, finishing 35th in a class of 276. While there, he was subjected to almost continuous

harassment and was shunned by other cadets. He had no roommates and ate his meals alone.

Upon his graduation, he took various assignments in the army, although he really wanted to fly. However, the segregated military had no black aviation units until President Franklin D. Roosevelt established an African-American squadron in the Army Air Corps, the Ninety-ninth Pursuit Squadron. Davis was named the squadron's leader. He earned his wings in 1942 and flew sixty missions. In September 1943, he was named commander of the 332nd Fighter Group, the famed Red Tails, who also had another nickname: the Tuskegee Airmen. Under Davis, the Tuskegee Airmen accumulated an enviable record against the German Luftwaffe, shooting down 111 enemy planes and destroying or damaging another 273 on the ground. A popular myth says they never lost a bomber to an enemy fighter, but that was not the case. Nevertheless, their record was an enviable one.

After the war, Davis served in various capacities as he continued to fight for civil rights. He is credited with playing a major role in the integration of the armed forces. He retired in 1970 as a lieutenant general. President William Clinton presented him with a fourth star in 1998.

Shortly after retirement, Davis was placed in charge of the federal sky-marshal program, designed to thwart the rash of plane hijackings of that era. In 1971, he became assistant secretary of transportation.

His military decorations include the Air Force Distinguished Service Medal, the Army Distinguished Service Medal, the Silver Star, the Legion of Merit with two oak leaf clusters, the Distinguished Flying Cross, the Air Medal with four oak leaf clusters, the Air Force Commendation Medal with two oak leaf clusters, and the Philippine Legion of Honor.

4-17: Chaplain's Hill Monuments, Section 2

38° 52.743' N, 77° 4.191' W

In a portion of Section 2 known as Chaplain's Hill lie chaplains from four wars. They include the first chief of chaplains, Colonel John T. Axton; Chief of Chaplains William A. Arnold, the first chaplain to become a general; and Major Charles Joseph Watters, who served in Vietnam and was posthumously awarded the Medal of Honor for his actions on November 19, 1967, when he was killed by a bomb while ministering to fallen soldiers.

The four monuments shown in the photo on page 62 were dedicated to the memory of chaplains who died while serving in the U.S. Armed Forces. The monument on the left was dedicated on May 21, 1989, to 83 Catholic chaplains who died in World War II, Korea, and Vietnam. Next to it, 23 chaplains who died in World War I are honored with a marker dedicated on May 5, 1926. Second from the right sits a monument to 134 Protestant chaplains who died in World Wars I and II. That marker was dedicated October 26, 1981. On the

extreme right sits a memorial to 14 Jewish chaplains who died in World War II, the Cold War era, and Vietnam; it was dedicated October 24, 2011.

4-18: Allen Buchanan, Section 9, Grave 5845
38° 52.737' N, 77° 4.289' W

Allen Buchanan was born in Indiana on December 22, 1876, and attended the U.S. Naval Academy, graduating in 1899. In 1914, he earned the Medal of Honor for actions at Veracruz, Mexico. While under continuous fire and in constant danger, he directed the First Seaman Regiment to ensure the city's capture. His citation reads,

The President of the United States of America, in the name of Congress, takes pleasure in presenting the Medal of Honor to Lieutenant Commander Allen Buchanan, United States Navy, for distinguished conduct in battle during the engagements of Vera Cruz, Mexico, 21 and 22 April 1914. In command of the 1st Seaman Regiment, Lieutenant Commander Buchanan was in both days' fighting and almost continually under fire from soon after landing, about noon of the 21st, until we were in possession of the city, about noon of the 22d. His duties required him to be

at points of great danger in directing his officers and men, and he exhibited conspicuous courage, coolness, and skill in his conduct of the fighting. Upon his courage and skill depended, in great measure, success or failure. His responsibilities were great, and he met them in a manner worthy of commendation.

He also earned the Navy Cross, the navy's second-highest award for valor, a few years later while serving as commander of the USS *Downes*. That citation reads,

The President of the United States of America takes pleasure in presenting the Navy Cross to Commander Allen Buchanan, United States Navy, for distinguished service in the line of his profession as Commanding Officer of the U.S.S. *Downes*, engaged in the important, exacting and hazardous duty of patrolling the waters infested with enemy submarines and mines, in escorting and protecting vitally important convoys of troops and supplies through these waters, and in offensive and defensive action, vigorously and unremittingly prosecuted against all forms of enemy naval activity during World War I.

Buchanan became the naval aide to the president of the United States in 1929 and a year later became chief of staff at the Naval War College. In February

1932, he retired and was placed on the retired list. He died January 12, 1940.

4-19: Berger H. Loman, Section 37, Grave 4909

38° 52.695' N, 77° 4.321' W

Berger Holton Loman was born in Bergen, Norway, on August 24, 1886. It is not recorded when he came to the United States, but he was here by the start of World War I. He entered the U.S. Army at Chicago and was placed in Company H, 132nd Infantry, Thirty-third Division.

On October 9, 1918, Loman and the rest of his company were under heavy fire near Consenvoye, France. Several of his companions had already been killed or wounded, and there was no sign the intense fire would lessen anytime soon. Still, Loman and the rest of his company crept forward. Finally, Company H was within a hundred yards of its objective when it became pinned down by heavy machine-gun fire. The order was given to take shelter wherever it could be found. It was apparent to Loman that it would be suicidal to try to advance any farther, and just as hazardous to retreat. He volunteered to move forward alone to eliminate the machine gun pinning the men down.

When permission was granted, he crawled forward with bullets passing just inches above his head. After several minutes, he reached a point on the flank of the machine-gun nest. Before the German gunners realized he was there, Loman opened fire, killing part of the crew and capturing the rest. Then, as the enemy took flight, he turned the machine gun on those in retreat. His actions saved numerous American lives and allowed Company H to continue its advance. For his valor, Private Berger Loman was awarded the Medal of Honor.

Before his time of service was up, Loman was promoted to private first class, then to corporal, the rank he held when he left the service. He died May 9, 1968, at the age of eighty-two.

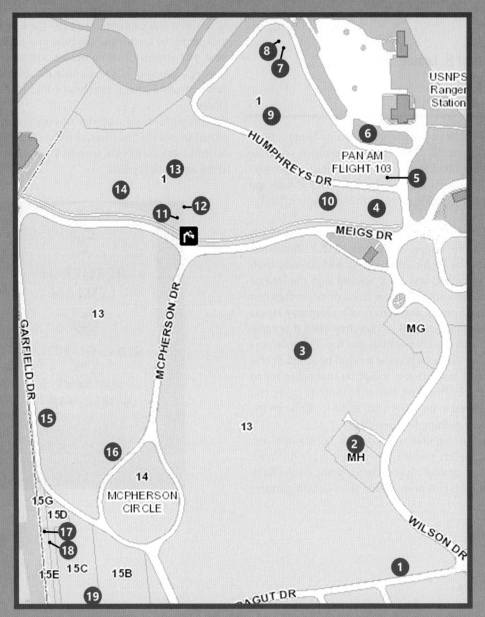

Courtesy of Arlington National Cemetery

CHAPTER 5

Sections 1, 13, 15, and Memorial Section MH

5-1: Exercise Tiger Memorial, Section 13
38° 52.632' N, 77° 4.471' W

On June 6, 1944, Operation Overlord, more commonly known as the D-Day invasion of Normandy, began. Its successful completion was at least partially the result of a dress rehearsal conducted by the Allies just two months earlier, an exercise known as Exercise Tiger that was kept secret from the world for decades.

The exercise took place at Slapton Sands, a beach in southwestern England that closely resembled the beaches at Normandy. General Dwight D. Eisenhower's plan was to expose the troops to conditions nearly identical to those they would experience in the coming invasion, including the use of live ammunition.

To ensure that the German army would not know of the invasion plans, the true nature of Exercise Tiger was not revealed to anyone, including the men involved. Unfortunately for the participants, a German patrol picked up the flotilla on its radar as it passed through the English Channel. Speedy German torpedo boats launched an attack on the Allied LSTs (an acronym for Landing Ship, Tanks but one the troops derisively said should mean "Long, Slow Targets"). Within a short time, 749 American troops were killed. The exercise ended so badly that consideration was given to postponing the D-Day invasion because ten officers who had knowledge of the invasion plans could not be accounted for. Fears arose that some or all of them had been captured, with the accompanying possibility that they might be forced to divulge what they knew. Any thoughts of postponement were dropped when the bodies of all ten were finally accounted for.

To prevent the leak of sensitive information and eliminate the possibility of decreased morale, news of the disaster was minimized. Doctors who treated the wounded were instructed to ask no questions, and the participants were warned of possible court-martial if they discussed it with anyone. Victims' families were simply told that their loved ones were missing in action.

Even after the war, little was said. In 1954, the army dedicated a granite monument at Slapton Sands recognizing the local residents who a decade earlier had left their homes for several months so the beach could be used as a makeshift battlefield. No mention was made of the men killed in the exercise.

Thirty years later, a submerged tank was found about a mile offshore and was brought to the beach. That tank now serves as a memorial to those who gave their lives.

Exercise Tiger revealed many areas in need of improvement and contributed immensely to the success of D-Day. In a cruel twist of fate, it turned out that more men were killed in Exercise Tiger than on Utah Beach—the very beach simulated in the exercise.

On January 18, 2013, the marker shown in the photo on page 65 was placed along Farragut Drive to memorialize those who lost their lives in the exercise. An Eastern white pine was planted at the same time in the names of those who made the ultimate sacrifice.

5-2: Joe R. Baldonado, Memorial Section MH, Grave 644

38° 52.695' N, 77° 4.498' W

Wishing to ensure that those deserving the Medal of Honor were not denied because of prejudice, Congress called for a review in 2002 of Jewish-American and Hispanic-American veteran records from World War II, the Korean War, and the Vietnam War. In the process of reviewing those records, it became apparent that several soldiers of either Jewish or Hispanic descent had met the criteria for the Medal of Honor. The 2002 Defense Authorization Act was amended to allow those soldiers to be so recognized. Each of the men had previously been awarded the Distinguished Service Cross, the nation's second-highest military award. Those awards were upgraded to the Medal of Honor in recognition of their heroism. On March 18, 2014, President Barack Obama awarded twenty-four army veterans the Medal of Honor for conspicuous gallantry.

One of those who received the belated award was Joe Baldonado, a twenty-year-old killed in Korea. Born in Colorado, Baldonado was the son of migrant workers from Mexico. His citation reads,

> Corporal Joe R. Baldonado distinguished himself by acts of gallantry and intrepidity above and beyond the call of duty while serving as an acting machinegunner in 3d Squad, 2d Platoon, Company B, 187th Airborne Infantry Regiment during combat operations against

an armed enemy in Kangdong, Korea on November 25, 1950. On that morning, the enemy launched a strong attack in an effort to seize the hill occupied by Corporal Baldonado and his company. The platoon had expended most of its ammunition in repelling the enemy attack and the platoon leader decided to commit his 3d Squad, with its supply of ammunition, in the defensive action. Since there was no time to dig in because of the proximity of the enemy, who had advanced to within twenty-five yards of the platoon position, Corporal Baldonado emplaced his weapon in an exposed position and delivered a withering stream of fire on the advancing enemy, causing them to fall back in disorder. The enemy then concentrated all their fire on Corporal Baldonado's gun and attempted to knock it out by rushing the position in small groups and hurling hand grenades. Several times, grenades exploded extremely close to Corporal Baldonado but failed to interrupt his continuous firing. The hostile troops made repeated attempts to storm his position and were driven back each time with appalling casualties. The enemy finally withdrew after making a final assault on Corporal Baldonado's position during which a grenade landed near his gun, killing him instantly. Corporal Baldonado's extraordinary heroism and selflessness at the cost of his own life, above and beyond the call of duty, are in keeping with the highest traditions of military service and reflect great credit upon himself, his unit and the United States Army.

Baldonado's body was never found.

5-3: George Washington Parke Custis, Section 13, Grave 6513
38° 52.747' N, 77° 4.538' W

George Washington Parke Custis was the grandson of Martha Washington by her first marriage. His parents died while he was a youngster, after which he went to Mount Vernon to live as the adopted son of George and Martha Washington.

Custis served in the U.S. Army in the Cor Light Dragoons from January 8, 1799, until his discharge on June 15, 1800, as a second lieutenant. He was also a volunteer in the defense of Washington during the War of 1812.

In 1802, he began construction of Arlington House in what is now the national cemetery. The house was both a home and a tribute to George Washington. Many of Washington's possessions were moved there when the house was completed in 1818.

In 1804, Custis married Mary Lee Fitzhugh. Tragedy visited the couple often; only one of its four children survived. Custis devoted most of his energies to the arts, rather than to running his varied business affairs. As a result, most of his ventures were unsuccessful. The exceptions were the acclaimed sheep and mules that he bred.

In 1831, his daughter, Mary Anna Randolph Custis, married a young army lieutenant in the home. That lieutenant, Robert E. Lee, would move into Arlington House and help Custis in the administration of his struggling business interests. When Custis died in 1857, the Lees inherited the estate. Custis was buried in a grave next to his wife. That grave was part of Section 13 when the estate became Arlington National Cemetery.

For more information on the history of Arlington, see Chapter 1.

5-4: Abner Doubleday, Section 1, Grave 61
38° 52.814' N, 77° 4.488' W

Abner Doubleday was born June 26, 1819, in Ballston Spa, New York. His grandfather fought in the American Revolution, and his father was a U.S. congressman.

Doubleday had already been a civil engineer for two years when he applied for admission to West Point, from which he graduated in 1842, ranked twenty-fifth in a class of fifty-six. Assigned to the artillery, he served in the Mexican and Seminole Wars but gained his fame

during the Civil War. Doubleday was at Fort Sumter when it came under attack in 1861 and is credited with firing the first defensive shot of the Civil War. He fought at the Second Battle of Bull Run, South Mountain, Antietam (where he was wounded), Fredericksburg, and Chancellorsville. When General John Reynolds was killed on the first day of fighting at Gettysburg, Doubleday took command of the First Corps, which held off superior Confederate numbers for several hours before falling back. After being relieved of command, he took part in the fighting over the next two days, receiving a neck wound at the end of Pickett's Charge. In November 1862, he was named a major general.

Doubleday retired from military service in 1873 and moved to San Francisco, where he established the city's first cable-car company. He is often incorrectly credited with inventing baseball. Visitors often leave baseballs and baseball-related memorabilia at his grave in tribute, as seen in the above photo. However, Doubleday never claimed credit for inventing the game, and

historians generally agree it originated as a version of rounders, a game played in Europe for many years prior to Doubleday's birth.

He died in New Jersey on January 26, 1893.

5-5: Wallace Fitz Randolph, Section 1, Grave 131-B
38° 52.831' N, 77° 4.484' W

Born in Pennsylvania on June 11, 1841, Wallace Randolph was just twenty years old when he enlisted as a private in the Seventeenth Pennsylvania Infantry in April 1861. Within a few months, he was discharged so he could accept a second lieutenant's commission from President Abraham Lincoln in the Fifth U.S. Field Artillery. He received a brevet promotion to captain for his service in the battles around Winchester, Virginia, in 1863, and a second brevet to major in 1865, at the close of the war.

In 1863, Randolph was seriously wounded when his battery was captured by Confederates. He was placed in Libby Prison and was part of the famous tunnel escape from that facility a year later, making his way

ing the Spanish-American War. In March 1901, President William McKinley appointed Randolph as chief of the Artillery Corps when the artillery arm of the service was reorganized. Randolph retired in January 1904 with the rank of major general.

In his later years, he suffered from depression, a condition believed to have contributed to his death by suicide in 1910 at age sixty-nine. This twelve-pounder Napoleon cannon marks his final resting place. Randolph is said to have commented shortly before his death that he had spent his entire life behind an artillery piece, so he wouldn't mind spending eternity under one. His "headstone"—the only such marker in the entire cemetery—made that possible. Unusual markers such as Randolph's are no longer permitted in Arlington.

5-6: Pan Am Flight 103 Memorial, Section 1
38° 52.853' N, 77° 4.495' W

On December 21, 1988, Pan Am Flight 103 was en route from Frankfurt to Detroit, via London and New York. Less than an hour after a change of aircraft in London, a bomb exploded on board, destroying the plane and killing all 243 passengers and 16 crew members. Debris from the aircraft fell onto the town of Lockerbie, Scotland, killing an additional 11 people on the ground. Of the victims, 189 were American citizens, including 35 students from Syracuse University on their way home for the holidays after a semester of study in London. Another 43 were British citizens, with the remainder coming from nineteen other nations. The bomb had been placed by a Libyan terrorist. In 2003, Libyan leader Muammar Gaddafi accepted responsibility for the Lockerbie bombing and paid compensation to the families of the victims. Gaddafi denied giving the order for the attack, despite information to the contrary.

On December 21, 2014, the twenty-sixth anniversary

through hostile country to the Union lines at Williamsburg, Virginia.

After the war, he continued his military service during labor strikes in 1877 in Pennsylvania. In the great Chicago strike of 1894, he commanded the battalion of federal artillery that was sent to maintain peace. He became colonel of the First Artillery in 1889 and served as a brigadier general of volunteers in Cuba dur-

of the bombing, this Scottish cairn pictured above was dedicated in Arlington to memorialize those killed in the attack. The cairn is constructed of 270 sandstone blocks, one for each victim. The blocks were quarried in Lockerbie and sent to American by the Scottish town. The names of the victims are engraved on the base of the cairn.

5-7: Robert F. Sink, Section 1, Grave 320-A
38° 52.896' N, 77° 4.547' W

Robert Sink was introduced to the American public in the popular television series *Band of Brothers*, the World War II story of Easy Company, 506th Regiment, 101st Airborne Division. Sink, however, made his mark long before that, having had a long and distinguished military career following his 1927 graduation from West Point. During the subsequent seven years, he served in the Eighth Infantry, the Sixty-fifth infantry,

and the Thirty-fourth Infantry. After graduating from Infantry School, Sink served in the Fifty-seventh Infantry in the Philippines and with the Twenty-fifth Infantry at Fort Huachuca, Arizona, followed by a stint with the 501st Parachute Infantry Battalion at Fort Benning, Georgia.

Advancing in both rank and responsibility, Sink was called on in 1942 to organize, train, and command the 506th Parachute Infantry Regiment of the 101st Airborne. It was here that he eventually became known as the commander of the Band of Brothers. He was so closely associated with the 506th PIR that it became known as "the Five-Oh-Sink."

Following the war, Sink served in numerous capacities, including commander of the Strategic Army Corps and commander of U.S. forces in Panama. He retired from active service as a lieutenant general in 1961 and died four years later. Among his many awards are the Silver Star with two oak leaf clusters, the Legion of Merit with oak leaf cluster, and the Air Medal with oak leaf cluster. He also received citations from several

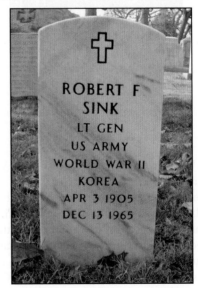

foreign governments, including Belgium, Korea, the Netherlands, and Great Britain.

Sink, who made two combat parachute jumps, was qualified as a master parachutist, a designation bestowed on only the most elite. He went on to celebrate each birthday by making a parachute jump. He died December 13, 1965.

5-8: Jonathan Mayhew Wainwright, Section 1, Grave 358-A-B

38° 52.898' N, 77° 4.554' W

Jonathan Wainwright graduated from West Point in 1906 and entered the cavalry upon his commissioning. He served as assistant chief of staff for the Eighty-second Infantry Division during World War I. He rose to the rank of major general and commanded the Philippine Division under Douglas MacArthur at the beginning of World War II, assuming the responsibility of resisting the Japanese invasion that began just a few weeks after the attack on Pearl Harbor.

When MacArthur left in 1942, Wainwright was named temporary lieutenant general in command of American forces in the Philippines. His own replace-

ment, General Edward King, was forced to surrender Bataan on April 9, 1942, after a three-month-long defense with little food or ammunition.

On Corregidor, Wainwright saw his outmanned and poorly supplied forces slowly driven back by relentless Japanese assaults, and he and his men were eventually forced to follow King's surrender, effectively ending the U.S. command in the Philippines. Wainwright's capture made him the highest-ranking American POW in World War II. He was held in prison camps in Luzon, Formosa, and Manchuria and was finally rescued by Russian troops in 1945. He gained a small measure of revenge a few weeks after his rescue when he witnessed the Japanese surrender on the deck of the USS *Missouri*.

For his courage and leadership, Wainwright was awarded the Medal of Honor, over MacArthur's protests. MacArthur was furious that Wainwright had surrendered, viewing his action as a failure of leadership.

Wainwright died September 2, 1953. His funeral was conducted in the lower level of the Memorial Amphitheater, making him only the seventh person accorded that honor.

5-9: Louis Cukela, Section 1, Grave 427-A-B

38° 52.863' N, 77° 4.560' W

Born in Austria in 1888, Louis Cukela came to the United States in 1913. A short time later, he enlisted in the U.S. Army, serving as a corporal in Company H, Thirteenth Infantry, and mustering out in June 1916.

His life as a civilian was interrupted just seven months later when he enlisted in the marines, serving as a gunnery sergeant in the Sixty-sixth Company, Fifth Marine Regiment. When the United States entered World War I, Cukela was sent to France, where, on July 18, 1918, he found himself fighting near Villers-Cotterêts. As his company advanced, it was stopped by

5-10: Meigs Family Grave: Montgomery Meigs, Section 1, Grave 1-EH; and John Rodgers Meigs, Section 1, Grave 1-SH
38° 52.820' N, 77° 4.520' W

fierce enemy resistance. Ignoring the warnings of his mates, Cukela crawled forward under heavy fire to an enemy gun emplacement, where he bayoneted several of the crew and drove off the rest, capturing the gun. Using enemy hand grenades, he then neutralized a second gun, capturing it as well, along with four members of the second gun crew.

For his actions, Cukela was awarded the Medal of Honor by both the army and the navy, making him one of only nineteen double recipients of America's highest military honor. In addition, he received the Silver Star, as well as numerous awards from several foreign governments.

Cukela was wounded twice in World War I, although there is no record that he received a Purple Heart. He left the marines in June 1940 as a major. Called back to duty just four weeks later, he served in Norfolk and Philadelphia throughout World War II. He retired for good in May 1946, having served nearly thirty-two years of active duty.

As quartermaster general for the Union army during the Civil War, Montgomery Meigs was highly skilled at obtaining men and war materiel while weeding out dishonest suppliers. Long known as an excellent engineer, one of his many projects having been the construction of the Capitol dome, the West Point graduate was also recognized as an outstanding general and became one of President Lincoln's most trusted military advisors.

In mid-summer 1864, his abilities were challenged when he was tasked with finding a solution to the rapidly filling military cemeteries in the Washington area. The Civil War would not end for nearly another year, and existing cemeteries were nearly filled, while the casualty list grew daily.

Meigs held a long-festering bitterness toward the Confederacy and quickly saw an opportunity to solve the cemetery crisis while garnering a measure of revenge against those he saw as traitors to the flag. He found what he believed to be the perfect place for a cemetery: the estate of fellow West Point graduate and former colleague Robert E. Lee in Arlington, Virginia, a property already confiscated by the Federal government. Meigs ordered that twenty-six dead Union soldiers be buried in the garden immediately adjacent to Lee's mansion. By the end of the war, that number grew to seventeen thousand on the property. (For further details, see Chapter 1.)

After the war, Meigs did the preliminary design for the National Museum in Washington, now known as the Arts and Industries Building. He served on the board of regents for the Smithsonian Institution and in the 1880s designed what is perhaps his greatest work, the Pension Building in Washington, now a National Historic Site.

Meigs died in 1892 and was buried with high military honors. His wife, grandfather, uncle, and son are buried in the same grave. His son, First Lieutenant John Rodgers Meigs, was killed in a brief gunfight with Confederate scouts in the Shenandoah Valley in 1864 and is depicted in the smaller of the two monuments on the Meigs grave. The figure on the top represents the younger Meigs as he was found lying along a road, pistol by his side.

5-11: James M. Lingan, Section 1, Grave 89-A
38° 52.810' N, 77° 4.620' W

Born around 1752, James M. Lingan was working in a store in Georgetown when the Revolutionary War broke out. He volunteered in the Continental Army just nine days after the signing of the Declaration of Independence, serving in the Rawlings Additional Regiment. He was wounded and captured by the British at Fort Washington and placed on a prison ship, where he languished for more than three years.

Following Lingan's release at the end of the war, George Washington appointed him collector of the port of Georgetown. At about the same time, Lingan became a brigadier general in the Maryland State Militia. He was also a founding member of the Society of the Cincinnati, the oldest military hereditary society in the United States.

Lingan, a vocal advocate for freedom of the press, supported the publisher of an antiwar newspaper who wrote an article that criticized the United States for participating in the War of 1812. An angry mob stormed the publisher's office, forcing the local militia to accompany Lingan and others to the Baltimore jail, where they took refuge. After destroying the newspaper's offices and presses, the mob turned its attention to the jail, killing Lingan on July 28, 1812. He was buried in a private cemetery in Washington, his funeral attended by more than fifteen hundred mourners. Lingan was reinterred in Arlington in 1908, some ninety-six years after his death.

5-12: Isaiah Mays, Section 1, Grave 630- B
38° 52.818' N, 77° 4.614' W

Born into slavery, Isaiah Mays enlisted in Company B of the Twenty-fourth U.S. Infantry, a Buffalo Soldier regiment. On May 11, 1889, Mays was part of a contingent of Buffalo Soldiers who were escorting U.S. Army paymaster Joseph W. Wham as he delivered a military payroll of more than twenty-eight thousand dollars. Between Fort Grant and Fort Thomas in Arizona, the men were ambushed by a group of robbers. Within thirty minutes, the Buffalo Soldiers were surrounded. Wounded badly in both legs, Corporal Mays crawled nearly two miles to a ranch to seek assistance.

The payroll was never recovered, although several were arrested in connection with the robbery. At the trial, the all-white jury chose to believe the denials of the white suspects over the testimony of the Buffalo Soldiers, and all were acquitted. A government investigation concluded that the soldiers had done all they could in defending the payroll, and on February 15, 1890, Mays and Sergeant Benjamin Brown were awarded the Medal of Honor for their actions. The citation that accompanied his medal noted his "gallantry in the fight between Paymaster Wham's escort and robbers. Mays walked and crawled 2 miles to a ranch for help."

Despite receiving the nation's highest military award, however, Mays was denied a pension when he applied in 1923. Now indigent, Mays was committed to the Arizona State Hospital, a facility that also housed the mentally ill and those afflicted with tuberculosis. Mays died there in 1925 and was buried in a pauper's grave. A small bricklike marker identified his grave.

In 2001, the cemetery, by then a run-down vacant lot in downtown Phoenix, was cleaned up, and Mays was given a Medal of Honor headstone by the government. In 2009, through the efforts of several military organizations, a court order was issued to have his remains exhumed and cremated. His ashes were placed in a specially designed urn, and Mays was interred in Arlington in a ceremony befitting a Medal of Honor recipient.

5-13: Edward P. Doherty, Section 1, Grave 690
38° 52.834' N, 77° 4.634' W

Edward Doherty was born in Canada in 1840. From 1861 until 1870, he served in the Seventy-first New York State Militia, the Sixteenth New York Cavalry, the Third Provisional New York Cavalry, the Fifth U.S. Cavalry, and the First Cavalry.

The assassination of President Abraham Lincoln in 1865 triggered one of the most intense manhunts in American history. The search for John Wilkes Booth was ten days old when Doherty, a first lieutenant, was ordered to form a detachment from the Sixteenth New York Cavalry and report to Colonel Lafayette C. Baker. Two days later, Doherty's detachment caught up with Booth and his accomplice, David Herold, on the farm of Richard Garrett just outside Port Royal, Virginia. Booth and Herold had taken refuge in Garrett's barn. Doherty's men surrounded the barn, and Doherty ordered the two fugitives to surrender. Herold did so, but

Booth refused. The barn was set afire, and Booth, who had fractured his leg when he leaped from the presidential box at Ford's Theatre after shooting Lincoln, could be seen hobbling on a crutch inside the burning structure. Despite orders from Secretary of War Edwin Stanton that Booth was to be taken alive, Sergeant Boston Corbett shot him through a crack in the wall of the barn, saying he thought Booth was about to fire at the troops outside. Corbett's shot proved mortal to Booth, who died about two hours later on Garrett's front porch.

Stanton had authorized a total of $75,000 in reward money. Doherty, as the leader of the detachment, was awarded the largest portion, $7,500, by a special War Department commission. A congressional committee of claims, however, decreased Doherty's share to $2,500 and presented Lafayette Baker and Everton Conger, a detective who had participated in the chase, $17,500 each. After several protests, a third and final award was presented. This time, Doherty's share was increased to $5,250, while Conger's was reduced slightly to $15,000 and Baker's was dropped to $3,750. Baker's cousin Luther Baker, another detective who had worked on the case, was given $3,000. Four other investigators split $5,000, while the remainder of the reward money was divided evenly among the twenty-six cavalrymen who captured Booth, each man receiving $1,653.85.

In addition to receiving a share of the reward, Doherty was promoted to captain. He remained in military service until 1870 and died of heart disease in 1897.

5-14: Albert Barnitz, Section 1, Grave 759
38° 52.824' N, 77° 4.658' W

Albert Barnitz was born in 1835 in Bloody Run (now Everett), Pennsylvania, and attended Kenyon College and

Cleveland Law College, during which time he wrote a popular book of poetry titled *The Mystic Delvings*.

When the Civil War began, he enlisted in the Thirteenth Ohio Infantry, a three-month unit. At the end of his enlistment, he joined the Second Ohio Cavalry, advancing to the rank of senior captain. While on a raid in Tennessee in 1863, he was severely injured when his horse fell on him. After Barnitz recovered, he rejoined his regiment, only to be wounded at Ashland Station, Virginia, while leading a charge on foot after his horse was shot from under him. He was awarded a brevet to major for gallantry and meritorious service in this action. After another recovery period, he rejoined the Second Ohio Cavalry under his new commander,

George Armstrong Custer, and served until the end of the war.

When the conflict ended, Barnitz and his men were ordered to serve as provost guard in Springfield, Missouri. There, in 1865, Barnitz gained fame by arresting Wild Bill Hickok for killing a man in a duel. Barnitz mustered out shortly afterward.

Not finding civilian life to his liking, he sought and received a commission as a captain in the Seventh U.S. Cavalry, again serving under Custer. At the Battle of the Washita, he received a wound that may have saved his life by forcing him to retire before the Seventh was massacred at the Battle of Little Big Horn. Prior to his retirement, he was breveted to colonel for what was described as his "distinguished gallantry."

Following his retirement, Barnitz returned to Cleveland to continue his law studies and was in demand as a speaker at political rallies and military reunions. His writings on his career in the Seventh are recognized today as among the best representations of frontier life. He died at the age of seventy-seven, at which time his autopsy revealed that a piece of his uniform had been forced into his body by his Washita wound, the fragment having been undetected for forty-four years.

5-15: Daniel M. Keys, Section 13, Grave 13615
38° 52.714' N, 77° 4.715' W

When Quartermaster General Montgomery C. Meigs formally proposed Arlington as the location for what would become the national cemetery, the earliest headstones were made of wood and painted white. As would be expected, those wooden headstones quickly fell victim to the elements, rotting and reaching a point where they were no longer legible.

After the Civil War, Meigs designed a new headstone made of melted-down ordnance. His design solved two problems. It made more permanent grave markers available, and it answered the question of what to do with weaponry that was no longer needed. These became known as Meigs Markers.

Only one such marker remains in Arlington, all the others having been replaced by the standard granite markers issued by the government or by individualized markers constructed of granite, marble, or similar, more permanent materials.

The remaining marker sits at the grave of Daniel Keys, a captain in the Independent West Virginia Volunteers who died in 1883. The headstone placed on his grave after his burial has stood the test of time.

5-16: McCullough Brothers, Section 13, Grave 13724

38° 52.682' N, 77° 4.672' W

This grave is unusual in that it contains the remains of four brothers, all of whom fought in the same regiment in the Civil War, the 100th Pennsylvania Volunteer Infantry. The regiment was recruited from southwestern Pennsylvania, an area settled by the Roundheads of the English Revolution. Keeping with tradition, the 100th Pennsylvania adopted the nickname "Roundheads."

Brothers Jacob, John, Nathaniel, and Joseph McCullough all enlisted in the regiment. None got through the war unscathed. Jacob was killed at Cold Harbor on June 2, 1864, and Joseph died on July 19, 1864, of wounds suffered the previous month at the siege of Petersburg. John was wounded July 30, 1864, also at Petersburg, but survived the war, being discharged on May 21, 1865. He died in 1869. Nathaniel also was wounded, at Cold Harbor on June 2, 1864. He survived the war and lived until 1908.

The names of all four brothers are listed on the rear of the monument.

5-17: James Parks, Section 15E, Grave 2

38° 52.653' N, 77° 4.711' W

James "Uncle Jim" Parks was born a slave at the Arlington estate about 1843 and is the only person buried at the national cemetery who was born on the property. One of sixty-three slaves at the estate, Parks was a field

plantation to Lieutenant Colonel Charles G. Mortimer, quartermaster for the Marine Corps, locating wells, springs, slave quarters, the slave cemetery, the dance pavilion, old roads, the icehouse, the blacksmith shop, and kitchens for the restoration. Parks stated that all of his grandparents and parents were buried in the slave cemetery.

Although Parks never had the opportunity to serve in the military, his faithful service at Arlington was recognized when the secretary of war granted special permission for him to be buried in Arlington. On August 23, 1929, Parks was laid to rest with full military honors.

5-18: Luzerne A. Blue, Section 15D, Grave 272

38° 52.646' N, 77° 4.708' W

Luzerne Atwell "Lu" Blue was born March 5, 1897, in Washington, D.C. In 1916, he signed a professional baseball contract with the Martinsburg Blue Sox of the Blue Ridge League. In his first season, he gave an indication of what was to come when he hit two grand slam home runs in one game, one batting left-handed and one right-handed. The Detroit Tigers purchased his contract the next season.

His professional baseball career was interrupted by World War I, when he served in the infantry. When he returned home, he resumed playing baseball, reaching the major leagues with the Tigers in 1921. A first baseman, he played seven seasons with the Tigers, three for the St. Louis Browns, and two for the Chicago White Sox. He played in one game with the Brooklyn Dodgers before retiring in 1933.

A first baseman, Blue was known for his outstanding defense but was also a feared batter. And he was one of the best of his time at drawing bases on balls,

slave, so he rarely saw the inside of the mansion. However, he did remember what happened outside and often spoke of dances held in the pavilion near the river.

Before the cemetery was established, Parks helped construct Forts McPherson and Whipple, which became Fort Myer, now part of Joint Base Myer–Henderson Hall. At the beginning of the Civil War, Parks was eighteen years old. In 1864, when the cemetery was established, he began digging graves and helped with some of the earliest burials. He eventually prepared the grave of Quartermaster General Montgomery Meigs, the man responsible for establishing Arlington as a cemetery.

Parks married twice and fathered twenty-two children. He continued to work at Arlington until 1925. When the exterior of the mansion was restored in 1928, he provided valuable information on the layout of the

finishing in the top ten in walks in ten of his twelve full seasons. He had 100 or more walks in four seasons and led the American League in that category in 1929. Blue finished his career with 1,092 walks and an on-base percentage of .402. He is one of forty-eight players in history with twice as many walks as strikeouts in at least five thousand career plate appearances. He batted .300 or higher in five seasons and finished with a lifetime batting average of .287.

Lu Blue died July 28, 1958.

5-19: Children's Graves, POWs, Foreign Nationals, Section 15
38° 52.622' N, 77° 4.662' W

Visitors to Section 15 often leave confused by the many children buried here. And some are more than a bit disturbed to see three enemy soldiers among the rows of American burials. Both can be explained.

Most of the children were infants. Until the 1960s, this area was the de facto cemetery for nearby Fort Myer, now Joint Base Myer–Henderson Hall. Anyone affiliated with the post could be interred in this section, including the children of those assigned there. While the causes of death are not shown on the markers, the U.S. Public Health Service has noted that pneumonia and influenza caused high numbers of infant deaths in 1947. A flu epidemic was also reported that year. In 1951, another deadly strain of flu hit during the winter and spring. In addition, Centers for Disease Control and Prevention records indicate that the United States suffered its most deadly polio season in 1951, with 57,879 reported cases. An examination of the children's headstones reveals an abundance of deaths in those two years.

The three Axis soldiers from World War II buried in this section were prisoners of war, all believed to have been captured in the African campaign. One is German soldier Anton Hilberath (Section 15B, Grave 347-1, 38° 52.621' N, 77° 4.665' W), and the other two are Italians Mario Batista (Section 15B, Grave 347-4, 38° 52.618' N, 77° 4.665' W) and Arcangelo Prudenza

(Section 15B, Grave 347-5, 38° 52.617' N, 77° 4.665' W). All three were held in POW camps on Maryland's Eastern Shore and died in 1946. The Geneva Convention required that any POW or foreign national who died in a foreign country during World War II was to be buried in the closest national cemetery of that country. Arlington was the closest to eastern Maryland. Cemetery records indicate that seventeen other foreign nationals are also buried in this section, including six British service members, two Danish sailors, and a pair of Danish marines.

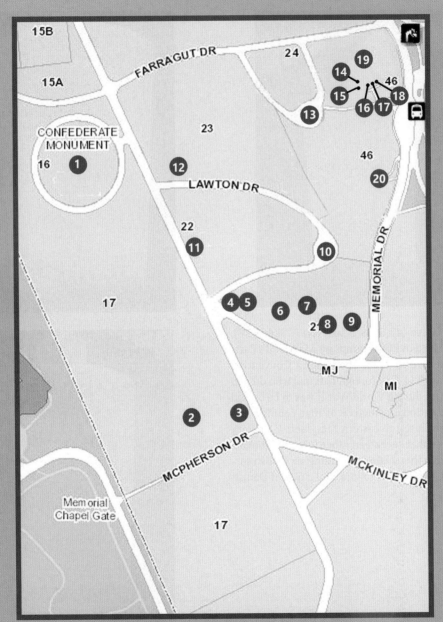

6-1: Confederate Memorial, Section 16

38° 52.567' N, 77° 4.637' W

For many years following the Civil War, bitter feelings between North and South remained, and although hundreds of Confederate soldiers were buried at Arlington, it was considered a Union cemetery. Family members of Confederates were not permitted to decorate the graves of their loved ones and in extreme cases were even denied entrance to the cemetery.

Slowly, the bitterness began to fade. When the Spanish-American War began, geographical differences were set aside as young men from all parts of the country answered the call to arms. Seeing this easing of feelings, Congress authorized in June 1900 that a section of Arlington be set aside for the burial of Confederate dead.

On June 4, 1914, the birthday of Confederate president Jefferson Davis, the Confederate Monument was unveiled. President Woodrow Wilson delivered an address. Veterans of both the Union and the Confederacy placed wreaths on the graves of their former foes to symbolize the long-overdue reconciliation.

The monument was designed by world-renowned sculptor Moses Ezekiel, a graduate of Virginia Military Institute and a Confederate veteran who fought at New Market. He died in Rome, Italy, and his remains were later returned to Arlington. He is now buried at the monument's base. Three other Confederate soldiers are also buried at the base. They are Lieutenant Harry C. Marmaduke, who served in the Confederate navy; Captain John M. Hickey of the Second Missouri Infantry; and Brigadier General Marcus Joseph Wright, who com-

manded brigades at Shiloh and Chickamauga.

Among the 482 persons interred in this section are 46 officers, 351 enlisted men, 58 wives, 15 Southern civilians, and 12 unknowns. They are buried in concentric circles around the main monument, their graves marked with headstones with the pointed tops common to Confederate markers in all national cemeteries. Legend states the reason for the pointed tops is to keep Yankees from sitting on them.

The monument is highly symbolic. A figure of a woman is at the top, her left hand extending a laurel wreath toward the South. Her right hand holds a pruning hook resting on a plow stock, symbolizing the biblical passage inscribed at her feet: "And they shall beat their swords into plowshares and their spears into pruning hooks." The plinth on which she stands is embossed with four cinerary urns symbolizing the four years of the Civil War. Supporting the plinth is a frieze of thirteen inclined shields, each depicting the coat of arms of one of the thirteen Confederate states. A fourteenth shield represents Maryland, which did not join the Confederacy but supported the South in the war. At the base of the plinth, Minerva, goddess of war and wisdom, lifts a fallen woman who represents the Confederacy. On either side of the fallen woman are figures—soldiers, sailors, sappers, and miners—representing branches of the Confederate service. Completing the frieze are six vignettes illustrating the effect of the war on Southerners of all races. The base features several inscriptions, including the seal of the Confederacy with the Latin phrase, "*Victrix Causa Diis Placuit Sed Victa Caton*," meaning, "The victorious cause was pleasing to the gods, but the Lost Cause to Cato." The inscription on the rear of the monument reads,

> Not for fame or reward
> Not for place or for rank
> Not lured by ambition
> Or goaded by necessity
> But in simple
> Obedience to duty
> As they understood it
> These men suffered all
> Sacrificed all
> Dared all—and died

6-2: Isaac Gause, Section 17, Grave 19595
38° 52.437' N, 77° 4.563' W

Isaac Gause was born in Trumbull County, Ohio, on December 9, 1843. On October 10, 1861, he mustered into the Second Ohio Volunteer Cavalry at Camp Wade near Cleveland, serving as a corporal in Company E.

On September 13, 1864, the regiment found itself in battle near Berryville, Virginia, as part of General Philip Sheridan's Shenandoah Valley campaign. During a reconnaissance patrol along the Berryville and Winchester Pike, Gause's company engaged the Eighth South Carolina Infantry. In the struggle, Gause captured the South Carolina regiment's flag, earning him the Medal of Honor. He received his medal just six days later.

Gause was one of six Second Ohio Cavalry soldiers—and one of only seven Jewish soldiers in the entire Union army—to be awarded the Medal of Honor for bravery. He died April 23, 1920.

6-3: John Cook, Section 17, Grave 18613
38° 52.441' N, 77° 4.525' W

John Cook was born in Hamilton County, Ohio, on August 16, 1847, and volunteered into the Union army at the age of thirteen, becoming the bugler for the Fourth U.S. Artillery.

On September 17, 1862, young Johnny Cook and the rest of the Fourth's Battery B came under heavy fire along the Hagerstown Pike just outside Sharpsburg, Maryland. The Battle of Antietam was under way, and the carnage that early morning was already beyond belief.

As the battery's cannons were being unlimbered, the unit's captain was badly wounded. Being a bugler, Cook was more expendable than the rest of the cannon crew, so he assisted the captain to the rear. There, the captain ordered Cook to return to the battery and let the lieutenant know that he would have to take command.

On arriving back at the battery, Cook saw that all the cannoneers were either dead or wounded and that the battery was in danger of being overrun. He quickly grabbed a pouch of ammunition from a dead cannoneer and began loading and firing one of the cannons. To his surprise, General John Gibbon, who was passing by, dismounted and helped fire the gun beside him.

Confederate troops made three charges against the Fourth Artillery, killing or wounding forty-four men and nearly as many horses, but they were pushed back each time. When the fighting ended, dead Confederates lay within ten feet of the guns.

After the war, Cook moved back home, married, and raised a family. In 1880, he and his family moved to Washington, where he took a job at the Government Printing Office. Then, in 1894, he was surprised to learn he had been awarded the Medal of Honor for his actions at Antietam thirty-two years earlier. At the time, he had been only fifteen, making him one of the youngest soldiers ever to receive the award.

Cook died August 3, 1915, at the age of sixty-eight.

6-4: Battle of the Bulge Memorial, Section 21
38° 52.497' N, 77° 4.534' W

On December 16, 1944, a desperate Adolf Hitler launched a counterattack through the densely forested Ardennes region of Wallonia in Belgium, France, and Luxembourg that pushed through the Allied lines, creating a large bulge in the line as seen on maps. The Allies rallied however, and launched their own counterattack to seal the breach in the line. In some of the coldest weather on record for that area, the Allies defeated the Germans in savage fighting, with heavy casualties on both sides. U.S. forces incurred their highest casualties for any operation during the war. Germany never fully recovered from its defeat. The Battle of the Bulge signaled the beginning of the end for the Third Reich.

The Veterans Benefits Act of 2002 (Public Law 107-330) was passed on December 6 of that year. A section of the law authorized the erection of a memorial to honor those who fought in the Battle of the Bulge. The memorial was to be placed in Arlington National Cemetery.

The Battle of the Bulge Memorial, commemorating the action that lasted from December 16, 1944, to January 25, 1945, was dedicated May 8, 2006. Some three hundred veterans of the battle attended the unveiling.

The inscription on the front of the memorial reads,

TO WORLD WAR II AMERICAN SOLDIERS
WHO FOUGHT IN THE BATTLE OF THE
BULGE—THE GREATEST LAND BATTLE IN
THE HISTORY OF THE UNITED STATES ARMY

6-5: Spanish-American War Nurses Memorial, Section 21

38° 52.497' N, 77° 4.526' W

The Spanish-American War was the first American conflict in which nurses were assigned as a special quasi-military unit. Often working under hostile fire, many of them lost their lives. Some are now buried not far from this monument.

Colonel Anita Newcomb McGee, founder of the Army Nurse Corps and president of the Society of Spanish-American War Nurses, directed the efforts to erect the memorial. Dr. McGee was the only woman

with the rank of assistant surgeon in the U.S. Army. She is buried in the cemetery's Section 1.

The marker is a large granite stone that features the Maltese cross, the insignia of the Society of Spanish-American War Nurses. The front is engraved simply, "To Our Comrades." On the rear, a small bronze plaque states,

IN MEMORY OF
THE WOMEN WHO GAVE THEIR LIVES
AS ARMY NURSES IN 1898

ERECTED BY
THE SOCIETY OF
SPANISH AMERICAN WAR NURSES

6-6: Jane A. Delano, Section 21, Grave 6

38° 52.491' N, 77° 4.513' W

Born at Townsend, New York, on March 12, 1862, Jane Delano graduated from the Bellevue Hospital of Nursing in New York City in 1886. During the Spanish-American War, she served as a volunteer nurse with the American Red Cross.

In 1909, she became the second superintendent of the Army Nurse Corps. The same year, she was named chairman of the National Committee on Red Cross Nursing Service, while working simultaneously as president of the American Nurses Association and as chairman of the board of directors of the *American Journal of Nursing.*

From 1909 until the beginning of World War I, Delano created several major programs for the Red Cross and cowrote with Isabel McIssac the first Red Cross textbook on elementary hygiene and home care of the sick. In 1912, she resigned from the Army Nurse Corps to devote herself full-time to being a Red Cross volunteer.

She remained active with the Red Cross throughout World War I and was the founder of the American Red Cross Nursing Service, the reserve nursing service of the Army Nurse Corps. At the close of the war, she went on an inspection tour of hospitals in Europe where American nurses were serving but contracted an ear infection over the winter and had to curtail her visits. When conservative treatment failed to cure her infection, she had several mastoid operations. Unfortunately, those also proved unsuccessful, and her condition continued to deteriorate until she died April 15, 1919. Her last words were, "I must get back to my work."

Delano was buried in the American military cemetery at Savenay, France. Before her death, she had expressed hope that she could be buried in Arlington. Her wish was fulfilled on September 18, 1920, when she was reinterred here.

6-7: Nurses Memorial, Section 21
38° 52.492' N, 77° 4.490' W

The Nurses Memorial, featuring a ten-foot-tall depiction of a military nurse, sits on a hill in Section 21, known as "the Nurses' Section." The graves surrounding it are the final resting places of army, navy, and air force nurses. Dr. Anita Newcomb McGee, one of the founders of the Army Nurse Corps and one of those responsible for the Spanish-American War Nurses Memorial, was also instrumental in getting the Nurses Memorial erected.

Sometimes called "the Spirit of Nursing Monument," this memorial was carved by Frances Rich to honor nurses who served in the U.S. armed forces in World War I. The original inscription on the monument's base simply read, "Army and Navy Nurses."

In 1970, navy captain Delores Cornelius, deputy director of the Navy Nurse Corps, requested to expand the original intent to include all military nurses. Later that same year, she received permission, and a plaque was installed over the original inscription a few months later. That plaque reads,

THIS MONUMENT WAS ERECTED IN 1938
AND REDEDICATED IN 1971
TO COMMEMORATE DEVOTED SERVICE
TO COUNTRY AND HUMANITY BY
ARMY, NAVY, AND AIR FORCE NURSES

The statue is now considered a memorial to nurses in all branches of the service and is no longer limited to those who served in World War I.

6-8: Ruby Grace Bradley, Section 21, Grave 318
38° 52.488' N, 77° 4.479' W

One of the most decorated women in American military history, Colonel Ruby Bradley was awarded thirty-four medals and citations of bravery, including two Legion of Merit medals, two Bronze Stars, two Presidential Emblems, the World War II Victory Medal, and the United Nations Service Medal. She was also the recipient of the Florence Nightingale Medal, the Red Cross's highest international honor.

Bradley joined the Army Nurse Corps in 1934 as a surgical nurse. When the Japanese attacked Pearl Harbor in 1941, she was serving at Camp John Hay in the Philippines. Three weeks later, she was captured. In 1943, she was moved to the Santo Tomas Internment Camp

in Manila, where she and several other imprisoned nurses were referred to by fellow captives as "Angels in Fatigues." For the next several months, she provided medical treatment to the prisoners and hid food in her pockets for starving children in the camp, ignoring her own hunger. On the brink of starvation, she lost enough weight that her prison uniform became much too large for her. Rather than seeing her starvation as an inconvenience, she considered it an opportunity to use the extra material to smuggle surgical equipment into the camp, which she used to assist in 230 operations and the delivery of thirteen children.

On February 3, 1945, Bradley was freed after three years as a prisoner of war when American troops stormed the Japanese camp. She weighed eighty pounds. She returned home to West Virginia to live a life of peace, only to return to the battlefield five years later. During the war in Korea, she served as a front-line army nurse in evacuation hospitals. When her facility was in danger of being overrun by a hundred thousand Chinese soldiers, she refused orders to leave until she had loaded the sick and wounded onto a plane. She escaped just in time, as her ambulance exploded behind her.

In 1963, after three decades of military service, Bradley retired from the army.

Over the years, many of her awards were lost or misplaced. In 1999, when she was ninety-one, the army replaced those awards, which included the Meritorious Unit Emblem, the American Defense Service Medal, the American Campaign Medal, the Asiatic-Pacific Campaign Medal, the Army Occupational Medal with Japan clasp, three Korea Service medals, the Philippine Liberation Medal, and the Philippine Independence Ribbon.

Colonel Ruby Bradley suffered a heart attack and died May 28, 2002, at the age of ninety-four in Hazard, Kentucky.

6-9: Juanita R. Hipps, Section 21, Grave 769-1

38° 52.489' N, 77° 4.453' W

Juanita Redmond was born July 1, 1912, and entered the army as a nurse during World War II. She served in Bataan and Corregidor and was one of "the Angels of Bataan," those nurses who risked their lives to assist the wounded in that area.

When Bataan and Corregidor fell, seventy-eight nurses were captured and imprisoned. Lieutenant Redmond was one of only eight who were able to escape. In 1943, she wrote *I Served on Bataan*, which became a bestseller and the basis for the movie *So Proudly We Hail*, a story about military nurses sent to the Philippines during World War II.

Throughout the war, she traveled to recruit nurses and assist in war-bond drives. She was one of the first nurses to earn Golden Flight Wings. She also assisted in establishing the Army Air Corps Flight Nurse Program. In 1946, she married General William Grover Hipps and accompanied him on trips for the military around the United States, as well as to Iran and the Far East.

Colonel Juanita Redmond Hipps died February 25, 1979, and was buried in Arlington with full military honors. Among her awards were the Purple Heart, the Bronze Star, three Presidential Unit Citations, and United States and Philippine Campaign Ribbons. The Air Force Association has named its highest award in the field of nursing the Juanita Redmond Award.

6-10: Spanish-American War Memorial, Section 22

38° 52.522' N, 77° 4.472' W

In 1898, the United States and Spain fought a ten-week-long conflict over Cuban independence. The United States had about three hundred men killed, not including the loss of life on the USS *Maine*.

On May 21, 1902, this impressive monument was unveiled and dedicated, with the principal address given by Theodore Roosevelt. Sponsored by the National Society, Colonial Dames of America, it was intended to serve as a memorial to those who died in that war.

The monument is approximately fifty feet high and takes the form of a Corinthian column of Barre granite. On top of the column is a sphere of Quincy granite on which is mounted a bronze eagle. On each corner of the base is a highly polished black granite sphere eighteen inches in diameter. Along the top edge of the upper base (above the bronze tablets) are eleven bronze stars on each of the four sides, for a total of forty-four. In the rear of the monument are four guns mounted on concrete stands. The two outer guns are captured Spanish cannons and are made of bronze. The two inner guns are U.S. naval guns.

A bronze plaque on the front of the base reads,

TO THE SOLDIERS AND SAILORS
OF THE UNITED STATES
WHO GAVE THEIR LIVES FOR THEIR COUNTRY
IN THE WAR OF 1898–99 WITH SPAIN

THIS MONUMENT IS DEDICATED
IN SORROW, GRATITUDE AND PRIDE
BY
THE NATIONAL SOCIETY
OF THE COLONIAL DAMES
OF AMERICA
IN THE NAME OF ALL
THE WOMEN OF THE NATION
1902

On October 11, 1964, a second bronze tablet, also dedicated by the Colonial Dames, was placed on the rear of the monument. That tablet reads,

TO THE GLORY OF GOD AND
IN GRATEFUL REMEMBRANCE
OF THE MEN AND WOMEN OF
THE ARMED FORCES WHO IN
THIS CENTURY GAVE THEIR
LIVES FOR OUR COUNTRY
THAT FREEDOM MIGHT LIVE

6-11: Rough Riders Monument, Section 22
38° 52.525' N, 77° 4.560' W

This large granite stone on page 91 is dedicated to the memory of the men of the First U.S. Volunteer Cavalry, better known as the Rough Riders. The Rough Riders served with distinction during the Spanish-American War and are best known for their charge up San Juan Hill, led by Leonard Wood and Teddy Roosevelt.

The monument was erected in 1906 but not officially dedicated until April 12, 1907. The insignia of the First U.S. Volunteer Cavalry is displayed on its west face. Also listed are the battles in which the Rough Rid-

ers took part: Las Guasimas, San Juan, and Santiago. The names of all the officers and enlisted men of the First Cavalry who lost their lives during the Spanish-American War are engraved on the side.

The inscription on the bronze tablet affixed to the front of the monument reads,

IN MEMORY OF
THE DECEASED MEMBERS
OF THE 1ST U.S.
VOLUNTEER CAVALRY
SPANISH-AMERICAN WAR
ERECTED BY THE MEMBERS AND
FRIENDS OF THE REGIMENT
1906

6-12: George Arrington, Section 23, Grave 16728-1-A

38° 52.568' N, 77° 4.560' W

On May 11, 1889, a band of robbers bore down on a small detachment of men from the Twelfth U.S. Infantry. Among those in the detachment was Private George Arrington of Charleston, South Carolina. The detachment was serving as an escort for Major Joseph W. Wham, paymaster for the army, who was delivering the payroll. In the ensuing fight, the robbers were driven off. Private Arrington distinguished himself with honor. For his efforts, he was awarded the Distinguished Service Cross. (For another account of this incident, see Chapter 5, site 5-12.)

His accompanying citation reads in part, "The Distinguished Service Cross is presented to George Arrington, Private, U.S. Army, for gallant and meritorious conduct while serving with a detachment escorting Major Joseph W. Wham, paymaster, U.S. Army, in an encounter with a band of robbers by whom the party was attacked between Forts Grant and Thomas, Arizona, May 11, 1889."

Arrington died August 4, 1943, and was interred in Arlington three days later.

6-13: USS *Maine* Mast, Section 24
38° 52.590' N, 77° 4.483' W

On the night of January 25, 1898, the battleship *Maine*, under the command of Admiral Charles D. Sigsbee, sailed into Havana Harbor to provide a deterrent to guerilla activities and to evacuate American citizens, if necessary.

Three weeks later, the *Maine* exploded, killing 260 officers and men. Many of the dead were buried in a Havana cemetery. As tensions between the United States and Spain escalated, many Americans grew certain the Spanish were responsible. Fanned by the American press, accusations of sabotage by Spain gave rise to the slogan, "Remember the *Maine!*"

A subsequent U.S. Naval Court of Inquiry determined that the *Maine* was destroyed by a submerged mine, although it stopped short of assigning blame. A second inquiry in 1911 also could not say with certainty what had occurred. In 1976, however, Admiral Hyman Rickover conducted a new investigation, which reached the conclusion that the explosion was caused by spontaneous combustion in the ship's coal bins, a problem that afflicted other ships of the period.

In 1899, the remains of those buried in Havana were disinterred and brought to Arlington, where they were reinterred with full military honors.

In 1911, the *Maine* was raised and the masts removed. The main mast was brought to Arlington, where it was placed on a base and dedicated May 30, 1915. The foremast, meanwhile, was placed as a monument at the U.S. Naval Academy in Annapolis, Maryland, giving rise to the tongue-in-cheek claim that the *Maine* is now the longest ship in the navy. When the ship was raised, the remains of sixty-six sailors were recovered. Of those, only one could be identified, and his remains were returned to his family for burial. The sixty-five unknown remains were brought to Arlington and interred on March 23, 1912, with their shipmates, most of whom are buried in the area on the north side of the memorial. What remained of the *Maine* was towed out to sea and scuttled with full honors in water six hundred fathoms deep.

The base of the monument was built to represent the turret of a battleship. Around its sides are inscribed the names of those who lost their lives when the ship exploded. Above the door is the inscription,

ERECTED IN MEMORY OF THE OFFICERS AND MEN
WHO LOST THEIR LIVES IN THE DESTRUCTION
OF THE USS *MAINE* AT HAVANA, CUBA,
FEBRUARY FIFTEENTH MDCCCXCVIII

On the south side of the memorial sit two bronze cannons captured from the Spanish. The anchor was brought to Arlington from the Boston Navy Yard. A bronze plaque on it reads,

USS *MAINE*
BLOWN UP
FEBRUARY FIFTEENTH 1898
HERE LIE THE REMAINS OF ONE HUNDRED
AND SIXTY THREE
MEN OF THE *MAINE*'S CREW
BROUGHT FROM HAVANA, CUBA
REINTERRED AT ARLINGTON
DECEMBER TWENTY EIGHT 1899

While historians will never know exactly what happened the night the *Maine* went down, the incident plunged the United States and Spain into war.

6-14: USS *Monitor* Unknowns, Section 46
38° 52.606' N, 77° 4.446' W

On March 8, 1862, the Confederate ironclad *Virginia* slipped into Hampton Roads, Virginia. It had been constructed from the wreckage of the former USS *Merrimack*, which was intentionally scuttled and burned when the Union's Gosport Navy Yard was evacuated in response to Virginia's secession from the Union.

Once in Hampton Roads, the CSS *Virginia* rammed the USS *Cumberland*, sinking the Union vessel. The USS *Congress*, having run aground in an effort to avoid the same fate, became an easy target for the *Virginia*, whose guns pounded it into submission. The *Virginia* then retired for the evening.

During the night, the Union ironclad *Monitor* arrived. The next morning, the *Monitor* and the *Virginia* met in the first battle of ironclads in naval history. Neither was able to inflict appreciable damage on the other, and both eventually withdrew. The historical contest would become known as the Battle of Hampton Roads, or as "the *Monitor* versus the *Merrimack*," despite the latter ship's name change.

Ten months later, on December 31, 1862, the *Monitor* sank near Cape Hatteras, North Carolina, during a storm. Of the sixty-two crew members on board, sixteen were lost.

In 1974, the wreckage of the *Monitor* was found. An expedition was launched in 2002 to recover some of its artifacts. That expedition discovered the remains of two crew members from the gun turret.

On March 8, 2013, a burial service was held at Arlington for the two unknown sailors. Their names appear on this memorial among those of the lost crewmen. For now, it remains unknown which two of the sixteen lie beneath the marker.

6-15: F. R. "Dick" Scobee, Section 46
Grave 1129-4, 38° 52.604' N, 77° 4.446' W

Francis Richard "Dick" Scobee, commander of the space shuttle *Challenger*, was born May 19, 1939, in Cle Elum, Washington. He enlisted in the air force upon graduating from high school in 1957 and was subsequently stationed at Kelly Air Force Base, Texas. There, he attended night school, acquiring two years of college credit, which led to his selection for the Airman's Education and Commissioning Program. He graduated from the University of Arizona with a bachelor of science degree in aerospace engineering in 1965 and received his commission that same year. He earned his wings in 1966 and, after a combat tour in Vietnam, returned home and attended the U.S. Air Force Aerospace Research Pilot School at Edwards Air Force Base, California. After graduating in 1972, he participated in various flight-test programs, logging flight time in forty-five different types of aircraft.

Scobee was selected as an astronaut candidate in January 1978. After completing a one-year training and evaluation period, he was declared eligible for assignment as a pilot on future space shuttle flight crews. In addition to his astronaut duties, he served as an instructor pilot on the NASA/Boeing 747 shuttle carrier airplane.

His first space flight launched from Kennedy Space Center on April 6, 1984. His crew participated in two extravehicular activities and made the first repair of a satellite in orbit. The mission lasted seven days before landing at Edwards Air Force Base on April 13, 1984. Upon the completion of this flight, he had logged a total of 168 hours in space.

Lieutenant Colonel Scobee was commander on STS 51-L, better known as the *Challenger*, when it launched from Kennedy Space Center on January 28, 1986. Only seventy-three seconds into the mission, the

spacecraft exploded and broke up. All seven astronauts on board were killed.

Scobee's awards included the Air Force Distinguished Flying Cross, the Air Medal, and two NASA Exceptional Service Medals. He also was posthumously awarded the Congressional Space Medal of Honor. On his birthday in 1986, he was interred at Arlington near the *Challenger* Memorial.

6-16: *Challenger* Memorial, Section 46
38° 52.605' N, 77° 4.443' W

After three delays due to weather conditions, the space shuttle *Challenger* finally lifted off on January 28, 1986, at 11:38 A.M. Little more than a minute later, the world was horrified when the shuttle exploded in flight, killing all seven crew members. This marked the first time American astronauts had died during a flight.

The explosion occurred more than nine miles above the earth's surface. Flaming debris fell into the ocean for more than an hour. It was two months before the remains were recovered from the ocean floor about eighteen miles off Cape Canaveral. While some could be identified, others could not. Early on the morning of May 20, 1986, the unidentified remains were buried here. On March 21, 1987, the memorial below was dedicated.

The names and likenesses of the crew members are shown on the plaque on the front of the marker. Those crew members were Captain Michael Smith, the pilot (buried in Section 7A, Grave 208); Commander Francis "Dick" Scobee (whose cremated remains were interred in Section 46, Grave 1129); Ronald E. McNair, mission specialist; Ellison Onizuka, mission specialist; Christa McAuliffe, payload specialist (a teacher and the first civilian on a space flight); Gregory B. Jarvis, payload specialist; and Judith A. Resnik, mission specialist. The poem "High Flight," written by John Gillespie Magee Jr., is inscribed on the reverse side.

An investigation into the tragedy revealed that two rubber O-rings failed due to unusually cold temperatures just prior to the launch. The failure allowed flames to break out from the booster, damaging the external fuel tank and causing the spacecraft to fall apart.

The crew members of the *Challenger* were honored when the Mars rover Opportunity's landing site was named *Challenger* Memorial Station.

6-17: Iran Rescue Monument, Section 46

38° 52.606' N, 77° 4.441' W

Following his overthrow by extremists under the Ayatollah Khomeini in 1979, the shah of Iran came to the United States for cancer treatment. Furious that the shah was now out of reach of the new rulers, a mob of Iranians stormed the U.S. embassy in Tehran, destroying property and seizing sixty-six American hostages. The hostages were held for several days without the release of any information on their condition or whereabouts. Finally, the extremists released all the female and African-American hostages, followed later by a man suffering from a medical condition, leaving fifty-three. The Iranians demanded the shah's return for trial and execution for crimes against Iranian citizens. The United States refused to turn him over, countering that the taking of the hostages was a violation of international law granting diplomats immunity from arrest.

In December 1980, the shah left the United States to live in Egypt, angering the Iranians further. Meanwhile, the hostages were blindfolded and paraded in front of television cameras in an effort to humiliate and intimidate them. Over the next several months, neither side showed a willingness to comply with the other's demands, and negotiations reached an impasse.

Finally, on April 25, 1980, President Jimmy Carter authorized a secret rescue mission, Operation Eagle Claw, to rescue the hostages. Delta Force commandos were to be flown by helicopter to a location outside Tehran that was to serve as the launching point for the mission. The helicopters, which departed from an aircraft carrier in the Persian Gulf, required a refueling stop. C-130 transport planes were dispatched to the rendezvous point, Desert One, where the refueling was to be done. Two helicopters were forced to drop out when a sandstorm caused mechanical problems. A third chopper developed a hydraulic leak and was cut from the

mission. The commander, army colonel Charles Beckwith, believed the loss of these three helicopters made the chance for success unlikely, and the mission was scrubbed.

Shortly after the decision to abort the mission, a fourth helicopter collided with a C-130 loaded with fuel, killing eight men. The mission's failure meant the hostages would remain in the hands of their captors until January 20, 1981, some 444 days after their capture.

This monument is dedicated to the memory of the eight servicemen who died in Operation Eagle Claw. The white stone marker bears a bronze plaque listing the names and ranks of the three marines and five airmen. Three of the airmen—Major Richard Bakke, Major Harold Lewis Jr., and Sergeant Joel Mayo—are buried together in Section 46, Grave 1129-3, not far from the group memorial.

6-18: *Columbia* Memorial, Section 46

38° 52.606' N, 77° 4.439' W

Sitting just feet from a similar memorial to the space shuttle *Challenger*, this memorial honors the astronauts killed in the explosion of the *Columbia* seventeen years later. The *Columbia* launched for the first time on April 12, 1981, and had completed twenty-seven missions before it disintegrated during reentry on February 1, 2003, resulting in the death of all seven crew members. The debris trail extended across a large portion of Louisiana and Texas.

The seven crew members were Commander Richard D. Husband; William C. McCool, the pilot; Michael P. Anderson, payload commander; David M. Brown, mission specialist 1; Kalpana Chawla, mission specialist 2; Laurel Blair Salton Clark, mission specialist 4; and Ilan Ramon, payload specialist 1. The remains of three members of the crew were interred in Section 46 not far from the memorial; they are air force lieutenant colonel Michael P. Anderson, in Grave 1180-1; navy captain and medical doctor Laurel Blair Salton Clark, in Grave 1180-2; and navy captain David M. Brown, in Grave 1180-3.

Touchdown for the *Columbia* had been set for 9:16 A.M. that fateful day. The craft had been in orbit for sixteen days and had completed 255 circuits of the earth. The shuttle was on its way toward a successful reentry when, over north-central Texas, something went terribly wrong. Investigators determined that a piece of insulating foam had struck the underside of the shuttle's wing when it lifted off on January 16. The impact dislodged sections

of the shield designed to protect the shuttle from heat generated during reentry. When the shuttle reentered the earth's atmosphere, super-hot gases created by friction contacted the exposed surface of the wing where the insulating tiles had been. The heat penetrated the wing and caused significant internal damage, leading to the structural failure.

The front side of the memorial features a bronze replica of a mission patch designed by crew members. The names of the *Columbia* astronauts are etched into the bronze plaque on the rear of the marker, which is set on Vermont marble.

The Mars rover Spirit's landing site was named *Columbia* Memorial Station.

6-19: Canadian Cross of Sacrifice, Section 46
38° 52.619' N, 77° 4.445' W

When Great Britain declared war on Germany in August 1914, Canada was also brought into World War I. The United States would not enter the conflict

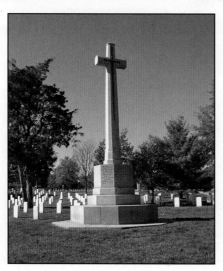

until April 1917. During that three-year interim, many Americans crossed the border to fight in the Canadian armed forces. More than three thousand of those Americans lost their lives.

In 1925, seven years after the close of the war, Canadian prime minister Mackenzie King proposed that a memorial to those Americans be constructed. The proposal met with nearly unanimous approval in the United States, President Calvin Coolidge quickly endorsing King's suggestion.

On Armistice Day 1927, this monument was dedicated. Donated by the Canadian government and designed by Canadian architect Reginald Bloomfield, it consists of a twenty-four-foot-tall cross emblazoned with a large bronze sword. The inscription on the base of the cross comes from Prime Minister King's comments and reads,

ERECTED BY THE
GOVERNMENT OF
CANADA
IN HONOUR OF THE
CITIZENS OF THE
UNITED STATES
WHO SERVED IN
THE CANADIAN
ARMY AND GAVE
THEIR LIVES IN
THE GREAT WAR
1914–1918

Similar inscriptions on other faces of the monument were added following World War II and Korea.

6-20: Audie L. Murphy, Section 46, Grave 366-11
38° 52.558' N, 77° 4.434' W

Orphaned at age sixteen, young Audie Murphy enlisted to fight in World War II a year later. At five foot

any time. From that position, he contested the enemy's advance, using the only machine gun available. He was wounded in the leg but remained at his position for nearly an hour, directing artillery fire and firing his weapon. Exposed to fire on three sides, Murphy was credited with single-handedly killing or wounding 50 enemy soldiers, many of them within ten yards of his position. With the German advance halted, he gathered his men and led them in a counterattack that ultimately drove the enemy from Holtzwihr. Only then did he accept medical treatment for his wound. For this, Murphy was awarded the Medal of Honor.

By the end of the war, Murphy had been wounded three times and earned twenty-eight medals, all before his twenty-first birthday. He returned to a hero's welcome in the United States, where James Cagney convinced him to become an actor. Murphy went on to make more than forty films, including the movie version of his wartime memoirs, *To Hell and Back.*

After nearly two decades of acting, he retired and started a career in private business. Within a few years, his business failed, plunging him into bankruptcy in 1968. Murphy is said to have suffered what we know today as post-traumatic stress disorder for the remainder of his life. In 1971, at the age of forty-six, he died when a private plane in which he was a passenger crashed into a mountain during a heavy rainstorm. He was buried in Arlington with full military honors on June 7, 1971.

In addition to his Medal of Honor, Murphy received the Distinguished Service Cross, the Silver Star with oak leaf cluster, the Legion of Merit, the Bronze Star with "V" device and oak leaf cluster, the Purple Heart with two oak leaf clusters, and numerous other medals. He also received awards from France and Belgium, and the Texas legislature awarded him the Texas Legislative Medal of Honor.

five and 110 pounds, he was turned down by both the Marine Corps and the paratroopers. Anxious to serve, he turned to the army, in which he became America's most-decorated World War II soldier.

Assigned to the Fifteenth Infantry Regiment, Third Infantry Division, Murphy fought in North Africa, Sicily, Italy, France, and Germany. He quickly advanced in rank, in part because of his skills but also because so many officers above him became casualties. He eventually earned a battlefield commission.

On January 26, 1945, near the village of Holtzwihr in eastern France, Murphy's forward position came under attack by the Germans. As six Panzer tanks and 250 infantrymen advanced, Murphy ordered his men to fall back to better defensive positions. With no support, he climbed onto an abandoned, burning tank destroyer, ignoring the likelihood that it could explode at

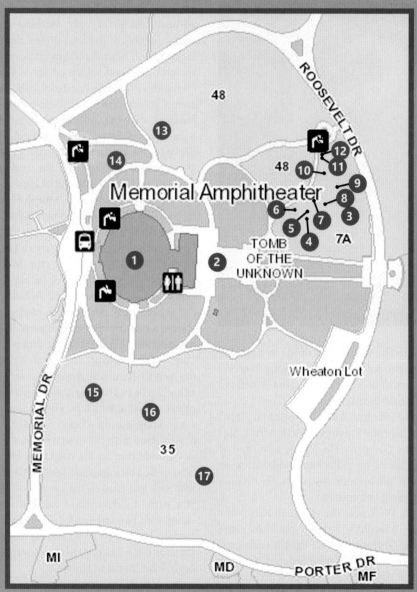

48

ROOSEVELT DR

13

14

12
11
48
10
9
8
3
7
6
5
4
7A

Memorial Amphitheater

TOMB
OF THE
UNKNOWN

1

2

MEMORIAL DR

Wheaton Lot

15

16

35

17

MI

MD

PORTER DR
MF

Courtesy of Arlington National Cemetery

CHAPTER 7

Sections 7A, 35, 48, Memorial Amphitheater, and Tomb of the Unknowns

7-1: Memorial Amphitheater

38° 52.585' N, 77° 4.379' W

When the Old Amphitheater in Section 26, now known as the James Tanner Amphitheater (see Chapter 3, site 3-15, and Chapter 4, site 4-3), was deemed too small for the crowds coming to the events held there, a new facility was needed. Judge Ivory Kimball, a former officer in the Union army, petitioned Congress during several sessions to build such a structure. On March 4, 1913, Congress authorized its construction. Judge Kimball participated in the ground-breaking ceremony on March 1, 1915, but did not live to see his dream completed. He died May 15, 1916, and is buried in Section 3, Grave 1538.

On October 13, 1915, President Woodrow Wilson laid the cornerstone, which held fifteen items: a Bible, copies of the Declaration of Independence and the Constitution, a 1915 American flag, designs and plans for the amphitheater, Pierre Charles L'Enfant's map design of the city of Washington, autographs of the amphitheater commission, one of each American coin in use in 1915, one of each American postage stamp in use in 1915, a 1914 map of Washington, the *Congressional Directory*, *Boyd's City Directory for the District of Columbia*, an autographed photo of President Wilson, the cornerstone dedication program, and a copy of the *Washington Evening Star*'s account of the ceremonies and the campaign to build the amphitheater.

Dedication of the Memorial Amphitheater took place on May 15, 1920. Now the home of the Tomb of the Unknowns, it is also the site of the cemetery's

in Arlington, a quote from Horace is etched above the west entrance: *"Dulce et decorum est pro patria mori"* ("It is sweet and fitting to die for one's country").

7-2: Tomb of the Unknowns
38° 52.583' N, 77° 4.330' W

On November 11, 1918, an armistice ended World War I. More than 116,000 Americans had died in the fighting. Many would never be identified.

European nations announced plans to honor their unknown dead. France and England were the first, on November 11, 1920. Hearing of the French plans, Brigadier General William Connor, commander of American forces in France, proposed a similar project for the United States. The proposal was not approved by army chief of staff Peyton C. March, who felt that America's dead would all eventually be identified. He also noted that the United States had no suitable place for such a memorial, as the French had with their Arc de Triomphe or the British with Westminster Abbey. He argued that it was a matter for Congress, rather than the army.

On December 21, 1920, Congress did just that. Congressman Hamilton Fish Jr. of New York introduced a resolution proposing that an unknown American soldier killed in France be returned to the United States and buried in a tomb to be constructed in Arlington. Congress approved that resolution on March 4, 1921.

On October 22, 1921, the body of an unidentified American was exhumed from each of the four American cemeteries in France: Aisne-Marne, Meuse-Argonne, Somme, and St. Mihiel. Four others were selected as alternates, should the exhumation of any of the first four reveal evidence of identity. One body from each cemetery was carefully examined to determine that he was really an American, that he had died of combat wounds, and that there was no clue as to

ceremonies on Memorial Day, Veterans Day, and Easter. The amphitheater has hosted the state funerals of many famous Americans, such as General of the Armies John J. "Black Jack" Pershing.

The amphitheater has a capacity of about five thousand people. The Memorial Display Room, between the amphitheater and the Tomb of the Unknowns, houses plaques and other tributes presented in honor of the service members interred at the Tomb of the Unknowns. A small chapel sits beneath the amphitheater stage.

The names of forty-four American battles from the Revolutionary War through the Spanish-American War are inscribed around the frieze above the colonnade. The names of fourteen army generals and fourteen admirals prior to World War I are inscribed on each side of the amphitheater stage. Above the stage is inscribed a quote from President Abraham Lincoln's Gettysburg Address: "We here highly resolve that these dead shall not have died in vain." Inside the apse is a quote from General George Washington's June 26, 1775, letter to the Provincial Congress: "When we assumed the soldier we did not lay aside the citizen." In a statement of gratitude and respect to those who rest

his identity. Then the bodies were placed in identical caskets and shipping cases. The next day, the four were transported to Chalons-sur-Marne for the selection ceremony. The men's burial records were destroyed to further guarantee anonymity.

When the caskets arrived at city hall in Chalons-sur-Marne, they were met by a large delegation of French and American officials. City hall had already been decorated with French and American flags; inside, palms, potted trees, and flags lined the corridors. French troops carried the shipping cases into the reception room, where they were adorned with American flags. A French honor guard stood watch until late that night, when six American pallbearers arrived. From that point, a combined American-French guard maintained constant vigil.

The next morning, the caskets were rearranged so that each rested on a shipping case other than the one in which it had arrived, eliminating the likelihood that anyone could determine even the cemetery from which a body came. The man chosen to select the unknown soldier was Sergeant Edward F. Younger of the

Ninth Infantry of the Army of Occupation in Germany. (Younger is now buried at Arlington in Section 18, Grave 1918-B. See Chapter 9, Site 9-2.)

After music by a French military band, officials paid their respects and made speeches. Then Sergeant Younger led the way from the main hall, carrying a spray of white roses presented by a Frenchman who had lost two sons in the war. With the French band softly playing a hymn, Younger walked around the caskets several times before placing the roses on one to indicate his selection. He then saluted the one he had chosen. The roses remained on the casket, to be buried with the unknown American in Arlington.

The body was then transferred to a special casket brought from the United States. This casket was sealed, and the empty casket was returned to the reception room, where one of the three remaining bodies was placed in it so the casket could not be identified. The caskets of the three remaining unknown Americans were then transported to Meuse-Argonne Cemetery, 152 miles east of Paris, for immediate burial.

The casket of the unknown soldier of World War I

was draped with an American flag and carried to the catafalque in the main hall. After a public viewing, the unknown soldier was carried in procession through Chalons-sur-Marne to the railroad station, where he was placed aboard a special funeral train provided by the French government and taken to Le Havre, where a formal departure ceremony was held October 24.

Following the ceremony, the body of the unknown soldier was placed aboard the cruiser USS *Olympia*, Admiral George Dewey's old flagship, to be transported to the United States. The *Olympia* was escorted by the destroyer USS *Reuben James*, destined to become the first American warship sunk in World War II. A seventeen-gun salute was offered when the ships cleared harbor and again when the French escorts dropped astern just outside French territory.

On November 9, the *Olympia* docked at Washington Navy Yard, where it was greeted by the Third U.S. Cavalry and its mounted band, along with several dignitaries, including General of the Armies John J. Pershing. Following a reception ceremony, the casket was taken to the Capitol rotunda, where it was placed on the Lincoln catafalque. Public viewing began the next morning and continued until midnight, by which time ninety thousand persons had passed the bier.

On November 11, a long procession escorted the casket from the Capitol to Arlington. Among those in the march were President Warren G. Harding and former president Woodrow Wilson, military officers and enlisted men from all branches, Medal of Honor recipients, Supreme Court justices, state governors, and members of the Senate and the House.

At a ceremony held in the Memorial Amphitheater, the president placed the Medal of Honor and the Distinguished Service Cross on the casket. Representatives of several of America's allies also presented medals; those decorations can now be seen in the amphitheater's Memorial Display Room. The casket was then carried the short distance to the burial site, where a

committal service was held. That service featured honors and prayers from Native Americans; the headdress of Crow chief Plenty Coups, who offered the prayers, is also displayed in the Memorial Display Room. At the end of the ceremony, the unknown soldier was laid to rest on a two-inch bed of soil taken from the battlefields of France.

It took ten more years for the monument to be completed and the sarcophagus to be placed into position. The fifty-ton white marble monument contains three figures on the side facing Washington; they represent peace, victory, and valor. The side facing the amphitheater bears the inscription,

HERE RESTS IN
HONORED GLORY
AN AMERICAN
SOLDIER
KNOWN BUT TO GOD

For years following the burial, letters arrived from mothers across the country hoping to learn if the unknown soldier may have been their son.

More than a quarter-century after the unknown soldier of World War I was laid to rest, the process of

selecting an unknown soldier was to be repeated. On July 23, 1948, the Department of the Army issued orders for the selection of an unknown serviceman from World War II. Detailed plans were developed, but the project was canceled when hostilities broke out in Korea in June 1950. In August 1955, Secretary of Defense Charles E. Wilson asked the Department of the Army to renew and implement plans to select an unknown serviceman of World War II. A year later, on August 3, 1956, Congress also authorized the burial of an unknown serviceman from the Korean War. New plans were drafted for selecting the unknown servicemen of World War II and the Korean War. All services would participate. By May 12, 1958, after several reviews and revisions, the final version was published. A provision of the plan was that two crypts, rather than separate new tombs, would be utilized.

The selection process for both unknowns began overseas while plan review was still in progress. The bodies of thirteen unknown American servicemen who had fought in the transatlantic phase of World War II were exhumed at cemeteries in Europe and Africa and shipped in identical caskets to the American cemetery at Epinal, France. On May 12, Major General Edward J. O'Neill selected one of them. That casket was flown to Naples, Italy, and placed on the USS *Blandy*. Escorted by the USS *Canberra*, the *Blandy* sailed to a point off the coast of Virginia, where the final choice of a World War II unknown was made. The twelve bodies not selected were reburied.

Meanwhile, a World War II serviceman from the Pacific theater was also selected. Remains of two unknown Americans were taken from the National Cemetery of the Pacific in Hawaii, while four more were taken from Fort McKinley American Cemetery and Memorial in the Philippines. All six caskets were then moved to Hickam Air Force Base in Hawaii. On May 16, 1958, air force colonel Glenn T. Eagleston chose one. The remaining five were reinterred in the National Cemetery of the Pacific.

The day before Colonel Eagleston made his selection, the bodies of four unknown Americans killed in the Korean War had been disinterred from the National Cemetery of the Pacific. Army master sergeant Ned Lyle chose one of those to be honored as the unknown soldier of the Korean War. Those not selected were buried in Hawaii.

That casket and the one selected to represent the Pacific theater of World War II were flown to Guantanamo Bay, Cuba. There, they were placed aboard the USS *Boston*, which sailed for a rendezvous with the *Canberra* for the final selection of the unknown soldier of World War II.

The *Blandy*, the *Canberra*, and the *Boston* met on May 26 at the rendezvous point off the coast of Virginia. The first casket, representing the European theater of World War II, was transferred from the *Blandy* to the *Boston*. All three unknowns were transferred from the *Boston* to the *Canberra* and taken to the *Canberra*'s missile-handling room, where three morticians from Washington, D.C., removed the steel caskets from their shipping cases, took turns changing the positions of the caskets bearing the two World War II dead, and transferred the bodies of all three soldiers to bronze caskets in preparation for the selection ceremony.

The ceremony began with the *Canberra*'s band playing a funeral march as white-clad sailors wearing black armbands brought the three caskets on deck. The casket bearing the Korean War serviceman was placed in the middle of the three, with the World War II representatives on either side. Hospital Corpsman First Class William R. Charette, a Korean War Medal of Honor recipient, had been selected to choose the unknown soldier of World War II. Charette marched around the row of caskets, saluted, then lifted a floral wreath from a nearby stand. Marching behind the caskets, he stopped, glanced to his left, then placed the wreath at the casket on the right and saluted again.

Following the selection ceremony, the caskets of the Korean War and World War II servicemen were transferred back to the *Blandy*. Accompanied by the USCG *Ingham*, the two sailed for the Naval Gun Factory in Washington, D.C. The World War II soldier not chosen was then buried at sea in a ceremony eight miles offshore.

In Washington, the caskets of the selected unknown servicemen, accompanied by a guard of honor, were placed on the fantail ceremonial area of the *Blandy* in preparation for the reception ceremony the next day. At that ceremony, the navy band played hymns while dignitaries took their positions. The colors were presented and the body bearers, divided into two groups, each led by two chaplains, boarded the ship to remove the caskets. The navy band sounded four ruffles and flourishes, then played hymns as the caskets were borne from the *Blandy*; the World War II unknown was removed first, followed by the unknown from Korea. Both caskets were then taken in a procession to the Capitol, where they were placed on catafalques in the center of the rotunda. An honor guard was positioned around the two, the World War II soldier keeping the senior position on the right. Vice President Richard Nixon placed a wreath at the head of the biers, an act repeated by Speaker of the House Sam Rayburn and the dean of the diplomatic corps, Dr. Guillermo Sevilla Sacasa of Nicaragua. With the wreath-laying ceremony completed, the rotunda was opened to the public, which was admitted from midmorning until early evening on May 28 and again from eight in the morning on May 29 until noon on May 30.

At one in the afternoon on May 30, 1958, the body bearers removed the caskets from the rotunda, those carrying the unknown soldier of World War II leading. A color guard, two clergymen, and military officials walked ahead of the caskets. The procession halted at the top of the Capitol steps while the U.S. Navy Band sounded four ruffles and flourishes and then began a hymn. As the hymn played, the caskets were carried down the steps and secured to the caissons for transport to Arlington. As the procession solemnly made its way to the cemetery, a saluting battery on the Washington Monument grounds began firing minute guns. The firing would continue until the close of ceremonies at the cemetery except for a pause during two minutes of silence observed at the amphitheater. When the minute guns finished firing, a twenty-one-gun salute was fired at the cemetery.

As the caissons entered the cemetery through the Memorial Gate, twenty jet fighters and bombers passed overhead, each formation showing the missing man. At the amphitheater, the U.S. Army Band played four ruffles and flourishes, followed by a hymn, while the bearers removed the caskets from the caissons and, led as before by clergy and colors, carried them inside. The unknown soldier of World War II was borne through the south entrance and the Korean War unknown soldier through the entrance on the north. Each casket was set on a movable bier and wheeled around the colonnade to the apse, where the World War II soldier was placed in front of President Dwight Eisenhower and the Korean War soldier in front of Vice President Nixon. While the caskets were being brought to the apse, the U.S. Marine Band played hymns. After the caskets were situated, that band played the national anthem. After prayers and two minutes of silence, the army chorus led the audience in singing "America," after which President Eisenhower placed a Medal of Honor on each casket. When all the tributes and prayers concluded, the unknown soldiers were taken to the amphitheater's Trophy Room, accompanied by the presidential party. The audience made its way to the plaza at the Tomb of the Unknown Soldier for the burial service. A priest, a minister, and a rabbi each conducted the burial service of his faith. Following the Third Infantry's twenty-one-gun salute, an eight-man squad fired the traditional three volleys. Immediately afterward, the bugler sounded taps. The body bearers then folded the flags, which were presented to the president and vice president, who in turn gave them to cemetery officials for safekeeping, completing the ceremony.

On June 2, 1958, each crypt was covered with a concrete slab and topped with white marble. The marble tops bore only years: 1941–1945 for the World War II soldier and 1950–1953 for the Korean soldier. At the same time, the years 1917–1918 were carved in the pavement in front of the tomb of the World War I unknown soldier.

The Tomb of the Unknowns remained unchanged for a quarter-century, until America's involvement in Vietnam stirred demands and political pressure to have an unknown soldier from that war interred at Arlington.

The National League of POW-MIA Families, among others, opposed the idea on the premise that modern technology would likely be able to identify every recovered body. Its argument was difficult to dispute. When the World War I unknown soldier had been selected, more than sixteen hundred remains were un-

identified. There were more than eighty-five hundred unidentified World War II dead, largely because so many more had participated in that conflict. When the unknown soldier from Korea was selected, the number of unknown remains had dropped to eight hundred. However, because of prompt evacuation of the dead and wounded by helicopter, improved military record-keeping, and scientific advances in identification, there had never been more than four Vietnam unknowns at the Central Identification Laboratory (CIL), headquartered in Hawaii, at any one time.

Those in favor of having an unknown Vietnam veteran interred at the Tomb of the Unknowns continued to apply political pressure, however. Groups including the Veterans of Foreign Wars and the American Legion were prominent in the effort. Political expediency began to take over, as Americans were eager to put the unpopular war behind them. Finally, in 1973, Congress directed the secretary of defense to include an unknown soldier from Vietnam in the Tomb of the Unknowns.

Of the four sets of unidentified remains at the laboratory in Hawaii, one was a Southeast Asian, leaving only three to select from. Two of those were close to being identified, leaving only one possible choice. Those remains, consisting of six bones, were given the identification number X-26. Other items recovered with the body included the remnants of a flight suit, a pistol holster, a parachute, and a one-man inflatable raft, indicating the man had likely been a fighter pilot. With the information available, CIL officials remained reluctant to say X-26 could never be identified, but they were overruled by officials eager to end the controversy. To preserve the selection's anonymity, all records pertaining to the case were ordered destroyed and lab personnel were told not to discuss any aspect of the investigation.

On May 17, 1984, an official ceremony to designate the remains as the Vietnam unknown was held at Pearl Harbor Naval Base. Marine sergeant major

Allan J. Kellogg, a Medal of Honor recipient in Vietnam, placed a wreath at the foot of the casket, after which pallbearers placed it aboard the USS *Brewton* for transport to Washington via Alameda Naval Base, Travis Air Force Base, and Andrews Air Force Base. Once in Washington, the remains were moved to the Capitol rotunda. Again, the public was admitted to pay respects.

On a sultry Memorial Day, May 28, 1984, a military funeral procession carried the casket on an army caisson from the Capitol to Arlington, accompanied by a series of twenty-one-gun salutes. A quarter-million people lined the route. As the procession made its way to Arlington, more than a hundred Medal of Honor recipients, military and political officials, and invited guests gathered at the Memorial Amphitheater for the ceremony.

President Ronald Reagan, one of those who had pressed for the unknown soldier from Vietnam to be included at the Tomb of the Unknowns despite the likelihood of eventual identification, presided over the ceremony. He praised the soldier and challenged the government of North Vietnam to account for all missing soldiers. His speech concluded, the president awarded the Medal of Honor to the unknown soldier. On behalf of the soldier's family, he accepted the folded flag from the honor guard. The ceremony concluded with a bugler blowing taps. Later that day, the casket was lowered into the crypt.

One might think the story ended there, but it didn't. Against orders, an official in Hawaii had not destroyed the items found with the body. Unknown to army headquarters, Major Johnie Webb, a decorated Vietnam veteran himself, had placed those items in the casket, where they remained.

In 1994, air force captain Patricia Blassie received a phone call from a man who identified himself as Ted Sampley, a former Green Beret. He said he had re-searched the story of the unknown soldier from Vietnam to determine his identity and had eliminated every possibility except one. Sampley was convinced the soldier was Patricia's brother Michael, who had been shot down near An Loc, South Vietnam, on May 11, 1972. Blassie's family had never been informed by the military that the wreckage of his plane had been located or that remains were recovered, so Patricia was skeptical. That was supported when the family contacted the Air Force Casualty Office, which could not confirm Sampley's theory.

Three years later, CBS News correspondent-in-training Vince Gonzales read an article Sampley had written about his theory. His curiosity piqued, Gonzales began gathering additional information, using the Freedom of Information Act. CBS assigned newsman Eric Engberg to work with Gonzales on a possible story as the Blassie family wrestled with the decision about going public with the information. The family finally agreed to let the story be aired, and on January 19, 1998, Engberg reported it on the evening news. In that report, a courageous Patricia Blassie, not knowing how her actions would be perceived by the air force, requested that DNA testing be performed on the body in the Tomb of the Unknowns.

Defense Secretary William Cohen directed Rudy de Leon, undersecretary for personnel and readiness, to look into the allegations and make a recommendation on Patricia Blassie's request. De Leon's investigation concluded that the evidence supported the CBS report. On May 14, 1998, the Vietnam unknown was disinterred during a formal ceremony. In attendance were the Blassie family, Ted Sampley, and the families of eight other pilots who had been shot down in the An Loc area at about the time Michael Blassie was lost.

When the casket was opened at the Armed Forces Institute of Pathology, Johnie Webb's claim that the crash-site items were in the casket was confirmed. Fur-

thermore, testing showed that the mitochondrial DNA of the remains in the casket perfectly matched that of Blassie's family members.

Lieutenant Michael Blassie's remains were taken home to St. Louis, where they were reinterred in Jefferson Barracks National Cemetery. The Medal of Honor that had been placed on his casket is now on display in the amphitheater's Memorial Display Room. The crypt for the Vietnam unknown will remain empty. The original inscription of "Vietnam" and the dates of the conflict have been changed to "Honoring and Keeping Faith with America's Missing Servicemen, 1958–1975." With the technology now available, it is unlikely there will ever be another unknown soldier.

Since 1948, the tombs have been guarded around the clock. All the guards are volunteers from the Third U.S. Infantry (the Old Guard). They are accepted only after completing extremely rigorous training and testing, conducted in several phases. After serving on tomb guard duty for more than nine months, candidates receive their permanent Tomb Guard Identification Badge. As of this writing, only 646 candidates have been awarded the badge. Only the Astronaut Badge is

more exclusive. The Tomb Guard Identification Badge is a lifelong honor and can be rescinded if the holder ever does anything deemed unbecoming a tomb guard or that dishonors the tomb in any way. The badge can be revoked even if the behavior occurs after the individual leaves military service. The guard walking the mat wears no indication of rank, so as not to outrank the unknowns, whatever their ranks may have been.

The guard is changed in an impressive ceremony every half-hour from April 1 through September 30. From October 1 until March 31, it is changed every hour on the hour. This procedure continues around the clock, even if no visitors are present to see it. Each guard takes his responsibility seriously, as seen in the Sentinels Creed, posted in the tomb guard quarters.

The changing of the guard begins with an announcement by the relief commander, followed closely by the new guard's arriving and unlocking the bolt of his rifle to indicate to the relief commander that he can

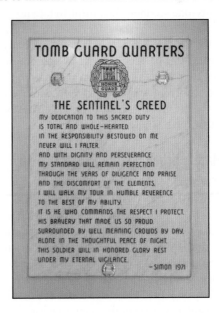

begin the ceremony. At that point, the relief commander approaches the tomb and salutes. He then turns to the crowd members and requests that they stand and remain silent and respectful throughout the ceremony.

Following the ceremonial white-glove inspection of the sentinel's weapon, the relief commander and the relieving sentinel meet the sentinel who is going off duty. That meeting takes place at the center of the mat on which the guards walk. The three salute the tomb, after which the relief commander orders the relieved sentinel, "Pass on your orders!"

The sentinel responds, "Post and orders, remain as directed."

The sentinel who is coming on duty replies, "Orders acknowledged."

He then steps onto the mat. When the relief commander passes by, the new sentinel begins walking at a cadence of ninety steps per minute. He marches twenty-one steps down the black mat and turns toward the east for twenty-one seconds, then turns to face north, placing the weapon on the shoulder closer to the visitors to signify that he stands between the tomb and any possible threat. After pausing another twenty-one seconds, he takes twenty-one steps down the mat and repeats the process. Twenty-one was chosen because it symbolizes the twenty-one-gun salute, the highest military honor that can be bestowed.

7-3: Matt L. Urban, Section 7A, Grave 40
38° 52.605' N, 77° 4.260' W

The back of Lieutenant Colonel Matt Urban's headstone tells his story. The recipient of twenty-nine medals, he is one of the most decorated soldiers in American history.

Born Matthew Louis Urbanowicz, Urban entered active duty on July 2, 1941. He served as a first lieutenant and captain in the Ninth Infantry Division's Sixtieth

Regiment during World War II, when he was wounded seven times in Tunisia, Sicily, France, and Belgium. One of those wounds was so severe that he was not expected to live, yet he kept returning to combat. Seemingly invincible, he gained a reputation among German soldiers as "the Ghost." He was promoted to major and lieutenant colonel on October 2, 1944, and October 2, 1945, respectively. Still suffering the effects of his wounds, he was medically retired from the army on February 26, 1946.

Urban's exploits became legendary in the Ninth Division, culminating in his receiving the Medal of Honor from President Jimmy Carter in 1980. His citation covered a series of heroic acts over a fifty-one-day period in 1944 and reads as follows:

On 14 June, Captain Urban's company, attacking at Renouf, France, encountered heavy enemy small arms and tank fire. The enemy tanks were unmercifully raking his unit's positions and inflicting heavy casualties. Captain Urban, realizing that his company was in imminent danger of being decimated, armed himself with a bazooka. He worked his way with an ammo carrier through hedgerows, under a continuing barrage of fire, to a point near the tanks. He brazenly exposed himself to the enemy fire and, firing the bazooka, destroyed both tanks. Responding to Captain Urban's action, his company moved forward and routed the enemy.

Later that same day, still in the attack near Orglandes, Captain Urban was wounded in the leg by direct fire from a 37mm tank-gun. He refused evacuation and continued to lead his company until they moved into defensive positions for the night. At 0500 hours the next day, still in the attack near Orglandes, Captain Urban, though badly wounded, directed his company in another attack. One hour later he was again wounded. Suffering from two wounds, one serious, he was evacuated to England.

In mid-July, while recovering from his wounds, he learned of his unit's severe losses in the hedgerows of Normandy. Realizing his unit's need for battle-tested leaders, he voluntarily left the hospital and hitchhiked his way back to his unit near Saint-Lô, France. Arriving at the 2d Battalion Command Post at 1130 hours, 25 July, he found that his unit had jumped-off at 1100 hours in the first attack of Operation Cobra. Still limping from his leg wound, Captain Urban made his way forward to retake command of his company. He found his company held up by strong enemy opposition. Two supporting tanks had been destroyed and another, intact but with no tank commander or gunner, was not moving. He located a lieutenant in charge of the support tanks and directed a plan of attack to eliminate the enemy strong-point. The lieutenant and a sergeant were immediately killed by the heavy enemy fire when they tried to mount the tank. Captain Urban, though physically hampered by his leg wound and knowing quick action had to be taken, dashed through the scathing fire and mounted the tank. With enemy bullets ricocheting from the tank, Captain Urban ordered the tank forward and, completely exposed to the enemy fire, manned the machine gun and placed devastating fire on the enemy. His action, in the face of enemy fire, galvanized the battalion into action and they attacked and destroyed the enemy position.

On 2 August, Captain Urban was wounded in the chest by shell fragments and, disregarding the recommendation of the Battalion Surgeon, again refused evacuation. On 6 August, Captain Urban became the commander of the 2d Battalion. On 15 August, he was again wounded but remained with his unit.

On 3 September, the 2d Battalion was given the mission of establishing a crossing-point on the Meuse River near Heer, Belgium. The enemy planned to stop the advance of the allied Army by concentrating heavy forces at the Meuse. The 2d Battalion, attacking toward the crossing-point, encountered fierce enemy artillery, small arms and mortar fire which stopped the attack. Captain Urban quickly moved from his command post to the lead position of the battalion. Reorganizing the attacking elements, he personally led a charge toward the enemy's strong-point. As the charge moved across the open terrain, Captain Urban was seriously wounded in the neck. Although unable to talk above a whisper from the paralyzing neck wound, and in danger of losing his life, he refused to be evacuated until the enemy was routed and his battalion had secured the crossing-point on the Meuse River. Captain Urban's personal leadership, limitless bravery, and repeated extraordinary exposure to enemy fire served as an inspiration to his entire battalion. His valorous and intrepid actions reflect the utmost credit on him and uphold the noble traditions of the United States.

His many citations included the Bronze Star with two oak leaf clusters, the Silver Star with oak leaf cluster, the Purple Heart with six oak leaf clusters, the Legion of Merit, and awards from the governments of France and Belgium.

Urban died March 4, 1995, of complications from one of his war wounds.

7-4: Michael J. Novosel, Section 7A, Grave 178-C
38° 52.604' N, 77° 4.275' W

At 5'3¾", Michael Novosel was a quarter-inch short of the standard to become a pilot in World War II, but he somehow was able to talk his way into the Flight Cadet Training program in Lake Charles, Louisiana. He graduated, earned his wings, and became a bomber pilot, flying a B-29 Superfortress. During the war, he dropped bombs over Tokyo and was part of the flyover during the Japanese surrender ceremony on the USS *Missouri*.

He left active duty in 1949, joining the U.S. Air Force Reserve and becoming a pilot for Southern Airways. When hostilities broke out in Vietnam, Lieuten-

ant Colonel Novosel attempted to return to active duty, but the air force refused him. Novosel then joined the army as a warrant officer and began flying medical evacuation helicopters, known as "Dust Offs."

On October 2, 1969, during his second tour of Vietnam, he received word that wounded South Vietnamese soldiers were pinned down near an enemy training area. He immediately headed for the location, where he was met by intense ground fire that forced him away six times. He was finally able to complete fifteen separate flights into the training area to remove the wounded. On the last extraction, he hovered backward into a barrage of enemy fire to keep as much of the airframe as possible between his crew and the enemy. Just as a wounded soldier was being pulled aboard, Novosel was hit by shrapnel in the right hand and leg. Despite his wounds, Novosel regained control of his aircraft and flew the wounded to safety.

In all, Novosel and his crew saved twenty-nine soldiers during this mission, for which he was awarded the Medal of Honor. At the age of forty-eight, he was the army's oldest Medal of Honor recipient in Vietnam. During two Southeast Asia tours, he flew 2,534 missions and evacuated more than fifty-five hundred wounded, gaining him the nickname "Dean of the Dust Offers."

Upon his retirement in February 1985, he was the last active-duty military aviator on flying status who had seen combat duty in World War II. He died of cancer on April 3, 2006, at the age of eighty-three.

7-5: Frank Reynolds, Section 7A, Grave 180
38° 52.609' N, 77° 4.275' W

World War II veteran and television news anchor Frank Reynolds was born November 29, 1923. Following graduation from Wabash College, he enlisted in the army, serving as a combat infantryman. He was

awarded the Purple Heart for wounds he received in hand-to-hand combat with soldiers of the elite German SS. He mustered out of the army with the rank of staff sergeant.

He began his broadcasting career in Chicago, working his way up to anchor ABC's *World News Tonight*. Normally calm and unflappable, Reynolds is remembered for losing his composure while broadcasting the events surrounding the shooting of President Ronald Reagan. After all the major networks announced that White House press secretary James Brady had died from a head wound, word came in that Brady in fact had not died. Anxious for confirmation, Reynolds grew noticeably perturbed on camera, shouting out to nobody in particular that someone better find out what was going on, so it could be reported with accuracy.

Reynolds won the George Foster Peabody Award for excellence in broadcast journalism in 1979 and served as the original anchor of *America Held Hostage*, a series of special reports that eventually became the newsmagazine *Nightline* in 1980. He was fifty-nine years old when he died of viral hepatitis and multiple myeloma on July 20, 1983. His old friend President Reagan was among more than a thousand dignitaries, journalists, and friends in attendance at his funeral.

7-6: Michael John Smith, Section 7A, Grave 208-1
38° 52.608' N, 77° 4.285' W

Michael John Smith was born April 30, 1945, and graduated from the U.S. Naval Academy in 1967. He received his aviator wings in May 1969 and served a tour in Vietnam, as well as two assignments as a flight instructor for naval test pilots.

In 1980, he was selected for the Astronaut Corps. His first space mission came as pilot on STS 51-L, known better to the public as the space shuttle *Challenger*. On January 28, 1986, the shuttle lifted off after a number of delays. The weather was unusually cold, the temperature in the twenties. A little more than a minute after liftoff, the shuttle exploded, killing all aboard. Debris fell from the sky for more than an hour. (For details on the explosion, see Chapter 6, site 6-16.)

Had he lived, Smith would also have been the pilot for space shuttle mission 61-N (*Discovery*), scheduled for launch in the fall of 1986. He was posthumously awarded the Congressional Space Medal of Honor, as were the other six astronauts on the shuttle. He also received the Defense Distinguished Service Medal (posthumous), the Navy Distinguished Flying Cross, three

Air Medals, thirteen Strike/Flight Air Medals, the Navy Commendation Medal with "V" device, the Navy Unit Citation, and the Vietnam Cross of Gallantry with silver star.

Michael J. Smith Field, an airfield in his hometown of Beaufort, North Carolina, is named in his honor.

7-7: Joseph Jacob Foss, Section 7A, Grave 162
38° 52.614' N, 77° 4.272' W

General William L. Nyland, assistant commandant of the Marine Corps, summed up the life of South Dakota native Joseph Foss in one succinct sentence at Foss's funeral when he said, "The history of Joe Foss was written in the skies over Guadalcanal."

Foss graduated from the University of South Dakota and joined the marines, earning his wings in March 1941, nine months before the United States was drawn into World War II. On October 9, 1942, he landed on Guadalcanal, where he would gain lasting fame as the leader of a group of fliers known as Foss's Flying Circus for its acrobatic maneuvers. Foss went on to shoot down twenty-six Japanese planes, becoming an ace and breaking the 1918 aerial record of Eddie Rickenbacker, who shot down twenty-five German planes in World War I. Foss also was credited with severely damaging, and probably destroying, another fourteen enemy planes. He accomplished this in just forty-four days, earning a Medal of Honor for the feat and getting his picture on the cover of *Life* magazine. On January 15, 1943, he shot down three more enemy planes, setting a record of achievement unmatched by any other World War II pilot. Ten days later, he led an attack on a much larger Japanese force in which four fighters were shot down and the enemy bombers were forced to turn back without releasing a single bomb.

After leaving the military, Foss in 1955 became the youngest governor in the history of South Dakota. He

was thirty-nine years old. He also served as commissioner of the American Football League, headed the National Rifle Association, organized the South Dakota Air National Guard, and hosted the popular ABC television series *The American Sportsman*.

Foss suffered an apparent aneurysm in October 2002 and died January 1, 2003, at the age of eighty-seven without regaining consciousness. In addition to the Medal of Honor, he was awarded the Distinguished Flying Cross, the Silver Star, the Bronze Star, and the Purple Heart.

7-8: James H. Doolittle, Section 7A, Grave 110
38° 52.611' N, 77° 4.267' W

James "Jimmy" Doolittle left the University of California in his junior year to enlist in the Army Signal Corps when the United States entered World War I. He spent the war as a flying instructor. When the war was over, he remained in the army, earning his BA

in 1922. In September of that year, he made the first cross-country flight, flying from Florida to San Diego in twenty-one hours and nineteen minutes, with only one refueling stop. He received the Distinguished Flying Cross for this accomplishment. He followed this by getting both a master's degree and a doctorate from the Massachusetts Institute of Technology. He also took a leave of absence from the army.

Over the next few years, Doolittle regularly set new speed records, winning the Schneider Cup Race, considered the World Series of seaplane racing, in 1925. His average speed of 232 miles per hour was the fastest a seaplane had ever flown. In 1928, he assisted in the development of artificial horizontal and directional gyroscopes, testing them by making the first flight completely by instruments. In March 1930, he became a major in the Specialist Reserve Corps and continued his assault on the world's speed records, setting the 1932 world's high speed record for land planes. He won the Bendix Trophy Race from Burbank, California, to Cleveland in a Laird biplane and followed that up by winning the prestigious Thompson Trophy Race at Cleveland with an average speed of 252 miles per hour.

Doolittle returned to active duty when World War II began. It was after being promoted to lieutenant colonel that his career reached its zenith. In January 1942, Doolittle planned the first aerial raid on the Japanese homeland. He volunteered to lead a force of sixteen B-25 medium-range bombers off the aircraft carrier *Hornet* in a daring one-way mission to targets in Tokyo, Kobe, Osaka, and Nagoya. The April 18, 1942, mission saw Doolittle bail out. All other participants in the attack did the same. Several lost their lives, although Doolittle landed safely in a rice paddy. For planning and leading this mission, Doolittle was awarded the Medal of Honor.

Promoted to brigadier general the day after the Tokyo attack, Doolittle became commanding general of the Twelfth Air Force in North Africa in September 1942. His next promotion was to major general in November. Five months later, he took command of the North African Strategic Air Forces. He became commander of the Fifteenth Air Force in the Mediterranean theater in November 1943 and from January 1944 to September 1945 commanded the Eighth Air Force in Europe and the Pacific as a lieutenant general. He held this position until the end of the war.

Doolittle went on inactive reserve status in May 1946 and joined Shell Oil as a vice president. He later became a director at Shell. In March 1951, he was appointed special assistant to the air force chief of staff, in which role he worked on projects that led to the air force's ballistic missile and space programs.

He retired from air force duty on February 28, 1959, and died September 27, 1993, his place as an aviation pioneer and war hero solidified in history. In addition to his Medal of Honor, Doolittle received two Distinguished Service Medals, the Silver Star, three Distinguished Flying Crosses, the Bronze Star, four Air Medals, and decorations from Great Britain, France, Belgium, Poland, China, and Ecuador.

7-9: Stuart Allen Roosa, Section 7A, Grave 73
38° 52.620' N, 77° 4.262' W

Stuart Roosa attended Oklahoma State University and the University of Arizona, graduated with honors and a BS in aeronautical engineering from the University of Colorado, was presented an honorary doctorate of letters from the University of St. Thomas (in Houston, Texas) in 1971, and completed the advanced management course at Harvard Business School in 1973. He earned his air force wings while at the University of Colorado.

Roosa graduated from the aerospace test-pilot school and became a test pilot and fighter pilot, flying the F-84F and F-100 aircraft and logging fifty-five hundred hours of flying time, five thousand of those in jet aircraft. In 1966, he was selected by NASA to become an astronaut.

He was a member of the astronaut support crew for the Apollo IX flight and completed his first space flight on Apollo XIV from January 31 to February 9, 1971, piloting the command module *Kitty Hawk* around the moon. After Alan Shepard and Edgar Mitchell descended to the surface in the lunar module *Antares*, Roosa conducted a variety of assigned photographic and visual observations. In completing his first space flight, Roosa logged a total of 216 hours and 42 minutes in space.

He served as backup command pilot for the Apollo XVI and XVII missions and was assigned to the space shuttle program until his retirement in 1976. Roosa died December 12, 1994, due to complications of pancreatitis.

7-10: Gregory "Pappy" Boyington, Section 7A, Grave 150
38° 52.627' N, 77° 4.269' W

Gregory "Pappy" Boyington was born in Idaho on December 4, 1912, and attended the University of Washington, where he was a champion wrestler. He served in the Marines Corps prior to World War II but resigned to become part of the famed Flying Tigers under Claire Chennault. He returned to the marines shortly after the bombing of Pearl Harbor, serving in the South Pacific, where, in September 1943, he became commanding officer of Fighter Squadron 214, better known by its nickname, "the Black Sheep Squadron."

On January 3, 1944, Boyington destroyed his twenty-sixth enemy plane while on a mission over Rabaul in Papua New Guinea. A short time afterward, he was shot down and captured by the Japanese. He remained a prisoner until he was liberated at the end of the war.

Shortly after his return to the United States, Boyington was awarded the nation's highest honor, the Medal of Honor. On October 4, 1945, he also received the Navy Cross. His Medal of Honor citation reads,

For extraordinary heroism and valiant devotion to duty as commanding officer of Marine Fighting Squadron 214 in action against enemy Japanese forces in the Central Solomons area from 12 September 1943 to 3 January 1944. Consistently outnumbered throughout successive hazardous flights over heavily defended hostile territory, Maj. Boyington struck at the enemy with daring and courageous persistence, leading his squadron into combat with devastating results to Japanese shipping, shore installations, and aerial forces. Resolute in his efforts to inflict crippling damage on the enemy, Major Boyington led a formation of 24 fighters over Kahili on 17 October and, persistently circling the airdrome where 60 hostile aircraft were grounded, boldly challenged the Japanese to send up planes. Under his brilliant command, our fighters shot down 20 enemy craft in the ensuing action without the loss of a single ship. A superb airman and determined fighter against overwhelming odds, Major Boyington personally destroyed 26 of the many Japanese planes shot down by his squadron and, by his forceful leadership, developed the combat

readiness in his command which was a distinctive factor in the Allied aerial achievements in this vitally strategic area.

Boyington retired from the Marine Corps on August 1, 1947, the same day he was promoted to colonel. He wrote his autobiography, *Baa Baa Black Sheep*, in 1958. The book was adapted into a television series in the 1970s. He died January 11, 1988.

7-11: Lee Marvin, Section 7A, Grave 176
38° 52.629' N, 77° 4.271' W

Nine months after the United States entered World War II, Lee Marvin enlisted in the Marine Corps at the age of eighteen. While attending Quartermaster School, he was promoted to corporal, although he soon found himself a private again following a series of incidents.

After undergoing training in Hawaii, he shipped out to Saipan in June 1944. This strategically located island was needed by the United States for the purpose of establishing an air base that could be used by long-range bombers. In a brutal three-week battle, the island was taken for the United States.

Marvin made twenty-one landings on Pacific islands as a scout sniper. On Saipan, he received a wound in the assault on Mount Tapochau that severed his sciatic nerve and earned him a Purple Heart. Hospitalized for thirteen months, Marvin was unable to return to active duty in time to see any further combat and received a medical discharge in 1945.

After returning home, he worked at part-time jobs and acted in bit parts in small Off-Broadway plays. In 1950, he moved to Hollywood, acting mostly in war movies. His tough-guy personality eventually earned him a starring role as Frank Ballinger in the television series *M Squad*, and his career began to take off. In 1965, he was awarded an Academy Award and a Golden Globe, both for best actor in the movie *Cat Ballou*.

Marvin died of a heart attack on August 29, 1987.

7-12: Joe Louis, Section 7A, Grave 177
38° 52.631' N, 77° 4.271' W

Joseph Louis Barrow was born in 1914 and dropped his last name when he signed up for his first amateur fight. He lost that bout but went on to win the national Amateur Athletic Union light-heavyweight title. His amateur record was fifty wins and four losses, forty-three of his victories coming through knockouts.

After winning his AAU title, Louis turned professional, losing only three times in sixty-eight fights. Of his sixty-five wins, fifty-four were knockouts. On June 22, 1937, he knocked out James J. Braddock in eight rounds to become world heavyweight champion. He retired twelve years later, having defended his title twenty-five

times, only three of those bouts going the full fifteen rounds.

Nicknamed "the Brown Bomber," Louis is best remembered for one fight. That was his bout on June 22, 1938, in Yankee Stadium against Max Schmeling, a German fighter held up to the world by Adolf Hitler as the epitome of the Aryan race. Schmeling had already knocked Louis out two years earlier, but the Brown Bomber was not to be denied in the second fight, knocking Schmeling out at two minutes, four seconds of the first round. Newspapers declared Louis's win a victory for the free world.

Louis is remembered to a lesser degree for defending his title once a month for an entire year, always against lesser opponents. Skeptics referred to those opponents as Louis's "Bum of the Month Club."

Few are aware that Louis also served in the army, enlisting in the same unit as Jackie Robinson. Since he was part of the Special Services Division, most of his duties involved fighting exhibition matches for the troops; he fought ninety-six bouts before an estimated two million troops. He also assisted in recruiting.

By the time Louis mustered out, he had attained the rank of technical sergeant. On September 23, 1945, he was awarded the Legion of Merit for his contribution to the general morale of the troops. He also donated more than a hundred thousand dollars for army and navy relief.

In Louis's later years, he encountered problems with the Internal Revenue Service, finally settling in 1965. He died in Las Vegas on April 12, 1981, of cardiac arrest.

7-13: James N. "Nick" Rowe, Section 48, Grave 2165-A

38° 52.645' N, 77° 4.368' W

Colonel James "Nick" Rowe graduated from West Point in 1960. He served in Vietnam as a Special Forces officer until he was captured by enemy forces on October 29, 1963. Kept in a bamboo cage in the Mekong Delta, he was subjected to torture and daily death threats. He resisted every attempt by his captors to extract information and made several unsuccessful attempts to escape, gaining him the sobriquet "'Mr. Trouble'" from his jailers.

Finally tiring of his resistance, his captors scheduled him for execution in late December 1968. Before they could carry out their plan, however, Rowe took advantage of a sudden flight of American helicopters that appeared while he was outside the prison camp. Overpowering his guards, he ran into a clearing, where the helicopters rescued him, still clad in black prisoner pajamas. Once rescued, he learned he had been promoted to major during his five years of captivity. He was one of only thirty-four Americans who escaped captivity during Vietnam.

Rowe left the army in 1976 but returned in 1981,

when he was appointed chief of a Green Beret training program at Fort Bragg, North Carolina. Four years later, he was placed in command of the First Special Warfare Training Battalion at Fort Bragg. He held that post until May 1987, when he was assigned to the Philippines. There, he served as chief of the army division of the Joint U.S. Military Advisory Group, providing counterinsurgency training for the Philippine military. He worked closely with the CIA and was involved in the program to penetrate the New People's Army and its parent Communist Party.

On April 21, 1989, members of the New People's Army attacked Rowe in his car in the Manila suburb of Quezon City, killing him instantly. Although wounded, his driver survived. Rowe's body was returned to the United States, where a memorial service at Fort Bragg was attended by several hundred mourners. He was laid to rest in Arlington on May 1, 1989.

On May 2, 2014, the Defense Intelligence Agency named one of its buildings in Charlottesville, Virginia, in Rowe's honor. The mission of those who work in the building is locating soldiers who remain missing in action or who were last known to be prisoners of war.

7-14: Korean War Memorial Bench, Section 48
38° 52.624' N, 77° 4.393' W

Located adjacent to the Memorial Amphitheater, the Korean War Memorial Bench was placed in Arlington in 1987 next to a Korean white pine tree donated by the Republic of Korea in 1965. The pine tree was replaced with a Korean mountain ash by President Roh Tae-woo in 1989. The bench was dedicated in memory of Americans lost in the Korean War, as shown in the inscription:

"THE BEGINNING OF THE END OF WAR LIES IN REMEMBRANCE"
—HERMAN WOUK
IN SACRED MEMORY OF THOSE AMERICANS WHO
GAVE THEIR LIVES DURING THE KOREAN WAR,
1950–1953
54,246 DIED, 8,177 MISSING IN ACTION,
389 UNACCOUNTED FOR POWS
FIRST INTERNATIONAL TRIBUTE, JULY 27, 1987

The war was initially between North and South Korea. China and the Soviet Union joined in with the North Koreans, while a United Nations force led by the United States fought on the side of South Korea. The signing of an armistice on July 27, 1953, created the Korean Demilitarized Zone.

The bench was dedicated July 27, 1987, as the result of a joint effort of the Korean War Veterans Association and No Greater Love, Inc.

7-15: Richard Nott Antrim, Section 35, Grave 2613
38° 52.533' N, 77° 4.414' W

Born on December 17, 1907, in Peru, Indiana, Richard Nott Antrim graduated from the U.S. Naval Academy in 1931. He was serving as executive officer of the USS *Pope* on March 1, 1942, when it was sunk by the Japanese. As the senior officer among the 150 survivors, he organized the men and distributed rations. Under his direction, all of his command survived until a Japanese destroyer pulled them from the sea a week

later. He would be awarded the Navy Cross for his actions.

Taken to a prisoner-of-war camp on Celebes (now the island of Sulawesi in Indonesia), Antrim and his crew suffered regular beatings and torture for the slightest infraction of the rules. Shortly after their arrival, a naval officer failed to bow low enough to a guard, sending the guard into a frenzy. He began administering a savage beating. Antrim yelled at the guard to stop, immediately drawing the attention of other guards. With the beating temporarily halted, Antrim explained to the guards that the man was new to the camp and not yet familiar with Japanese customs. Despite Antrim's pleas, the camp commandant was unmoved. He ordered that the officer be punished with fifty lashes as the other prisoners watched. Fifteen blows into the punishment, the unfortunate victim lapsed into unconsciousness. Three of the guards began kicking him. Again, Antrim stepped forward, this time announcing that he would take the remaining thirty-five lashes, bringing a roar of approval from the prisoners. The stunned Japanese, not expecting Antrim's offer, gathered to determine their next course of action. The commandant ordered the unconscious officer to be taken to the dispensary. He then gave Antrim a slight bow in a show of respect, again bringing a shout of approval from the prisoners. Antrim's actions brought a temporary halt to the senseless beatings, as well as a new respect from the guards.

When the POWs were liberated in September 1945, word of Antrim's bravery became known to naval officials, and on January 30, 1947, he was awarded the Medal of Honor.

Antrim remained on active duty until ill health caused by his years as a POW forced his retirement in April 1954 as a rear admiral. He died March 8, 1969, at Mountain Home, Arkansas.

7-16: Leonard A. Funk Jr., Section 35, Grave 2373-4

38° 52.524' N, 77° 4.371' W

First Sergeant Leonard Funk was born in Braddock Hills, Pennsylvania, on August 27, 1916. He enlisted in the army in June 1941 and was assigned to Company C, 508th Parachute Infantry, which went to England as part of the Eighty-second Airborne Division. He made two combat jumps, the first into Normandy on D-Day, June 6, 1944, and the second into Holland during Operation Market Garden, September 17, 1944, when he earned the Distinguished Service Cross for leading his men in an attack on an enemy stronghold.

On January 29, 1945, in Holzheim, Belgium, Funk led a makeshift platoon of clerks in an assault against fifteen German-occupied houses. In the midst of a snowstorm, the clerk platoon captured thirty Germans without suffering a casualty, while the rest of the unit captured fifty more. The eighty prisoners were herded into the yard of a nearby house. Four soldiers were left behind to guard the prisoners until another company arrived, while Funk and the rest of the platoon returned to the fight.

A short time later, Funk and another soldier returned to the house to retrieve the four soldiers left as guards. While they were gone, however, German troops had overtaken the guards, released the prisoners, and prepared them for an attack. When Funk walked into the yard, he was immediately confronted by a Nazi officer, who ordered his surrender. Surrounded by a hundred Germans with weapons pointed at the captured Americans, Funk pretended to surrender, then swung his Thompson submachine gun into positon and shot the officer. The surprised German troops returned fire, killing Funk's companion. Funk continued to fire as the disarmed American soldiers seized weapons the Germans had dropped and joined the fight. In less than a minute, his force killed twenty-one Germans, wounded twenty-four more, and took the remainder prisoner.

In a White House ceremony in August 1945, Funk received the Medal of Honor for his actions. He also earned several other awards including the Silver Star, the Bronze Star, the Purple Heart with two oak leaf clusters, and honors from France, Belgium, and the Netherlands.

When discharged in June 1945, he returned home and labored as a clerk for two years, then went to work for the Veterans Administration. He retired as a division chief in the Pittsburgh regional office in 1972. Funk died of cancer on November 20, 1992.

7-17: William E. Daniel, Section 35, Grave 218
38° 52.496' N, 77° 4.351' W

William E. Daniel has the distinct honor of being the first recipient of the Tomb of the Unknown Soldier Guard Identification Badge. A replica of the badge appears on his headstone and is shown in enlarged form on page 123.

Daniel became a tomb sentinel in February 1957 and served until June 1960. He received his badge on February 7, 1958—prior to that date, no special insignia was worn—and was present May 30, 1958, when the unknowns from World War II and the Korean War were interred.

Including his time as tomb sentinel, Daniel served in the army for twenty-two years. He fought in World War II and was captured July 4, 1944, in Saint-Lô,

France, following the D-Day offensive. He was a prisoner of war until June 1945, when he escaped with several other Allied soldiers.

He retired in 1965 and for the next ten years served as an instructor in the Reserve Officer Training Corps in Birmingham, Alabama. In 1996, he returned his tomb badge, which is now on display in the tomb quarters. He made his gesture as a gift to all soldiers who guard the tomb.

Daniel died January 30, 2009, and is buried just a short distance from where he served as a faithful sentinel for the Tomb of the Unknowns.

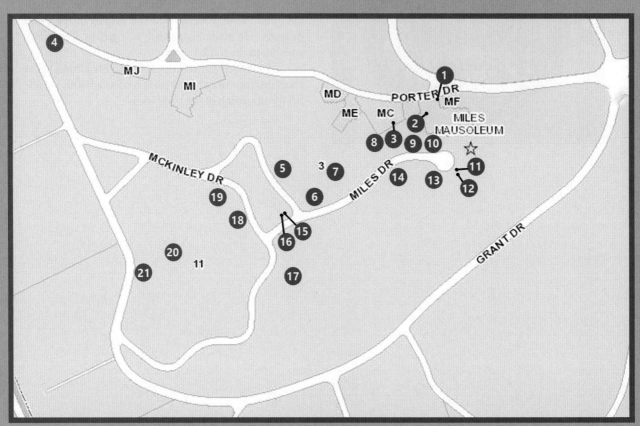

MJ

MI

MD

ME   MC

PORTER DR

MF

MILES MAUSOLEUM

1

2

8   3

9   10

11

12

MCKINLEY DR

5

3   7

MILES DR

6

14

13

19

18

15

16

GRANT DR

20

11

17

21

8-1: Robert Lee Krag, Memorial Section MF, Grave 1

38° 52.447' N, 77° 4.265' W

Robert Lee Krag was born January 5, 1928, in Hannaford, North Dakota. His first assignment following graduation from the U.S. Naval Academy was the aircraft carrier USS *Franklin D. Roosevelt* (CVA 42), on which he served for three years. At the end of his tour on the *Franklin D. Roosevelt*, he attended the Massachusetts Institute of Technology, where he received his master's degree in naval engineering, placing highest in his class. He then entered submarine training at New London, Connecticut, and was assigned to the USS *Albacore* (AGSS 569) when he graduated.

In July 1961, Krag was reassigned to the staff of the Submarine Force, U.S. Atlantic Fleet, where he represented the commander on all sea trials. Two years later, he was on the USS *Thresher* (SSN-593), a nuclear-powered attack submarine, when the ship was lost. The *Thresher* carried a crew of 112, plus 17 technical observers, when it went to sea on April 9, 1963. Krag was one of those technical observers. The mission was a post-overhaul deep-diving exercise about two hundred miles off Cape Cod. The *Thresher* was accompanied by the USS *Skylark*, a submarine rescue ship assigned to provide surface support and communications for the deep-diving sea trials.

Shortly before 8:00 A.M. on April 10, the *Thresher* started toward its designated test depth. Five minutes later, it contacted the *Skylark* that it had reached four hundred feet and that no leaks had developed. Approximately thirty minutes after beginning its descent,

the *Thresher* reached its test depth. Shortly after that, its transmissions began to degrade. At 9:17 A.M. the *Skylark* lost contact with the *Thresher* except for one garbled message that sounded like the submarine was exceeding its test depth. No reason for that could be determined. One minute later, the *Skylark*'s equipment detected a high-energy, low-frequency noise characteristic of an implosion. The *Thresher* was not heard from again.

Several ships began a search of the area using

underwater cameras, sonar, and other detection devices. Although some small pieces of debris were spotted, it was not until late June 1963 that the bathyscaphe *Trieste* located the main debris field.

Several other men from the *Thresher* are memorialized at various locations in the cemetery, among them Chief Engineman Tilman J. Arsenault, Lieutenant Robert Biederman, Lieutenant Commander John Billings, Lieutenant Michael Collier, Lieutenant Commander Michael DiNola, Chief Sonarman Ellwood Forni, Lieutenant Commander John Lyman Jr., Petty Officer Second Class Anthony Rushetski, Seaman Burnett M. Shotwell, Seaman David Wasel, Fire Control Technician First Class Charles L. Wiggins, and Lieutenant (j.g.) John Wiley.

The sinking of the *Thresher* remains the world's worst submarine disaster. Legislation has been introduced to place a memorial to the submarine and its crew in Arlington but has not received final approval.

8-2: Alexander David Goode, Memorial Section MF, Grave 40-2

38° 52.440' N, 77° 4.260 W

One of the most selfless acts of heroism during World War II took place in February 1943 in the icy waters off the coast of Greenland. A U.S. Army transport ship, the USAT *Dorchester*, was carrying 774 troops and 130 crew members from New York to an American military base in Greenland. Among those on board were four chaplains: Methodist minister George L. Fox; Alexander D. Goode, a rabbi; Clark V. Poling, a minister in the Dutch Reformed Church; and John P. Washington, a Roman Catholic priest. The four spent their time on board trying to maintain morale among the young soldiers, talking with them, offering prayer, and even holding nightly amateur floor shows.

On the evening of February 2, a German U-boat was detected following the three-ship convoy. An urgent request for antisubmarine patrol planes was sent, but all planes were patrolling elsewhere and were unavailable. Although all the men on board received orders to sleep in their regular clothing and wear life jackets, many in the ship's hold failed to comply, due to the heat of the nearby engines and the bulkiness of the life jackets.

Shortly after one the next morning, the U-223 fired its torpedoes, striking the *Dorchester* on its starboard side near the engine room below the water line. Power and radio contact were knocked out, and a hundred men were killed in the blast. The order came to abandon ship. Panic-stricken men, many with no clothing or life vests, struggled to get topside. Those who made it onto the listing deck overcrowded the lifeboats to the point of capsizing. Rafts were tossed into the sea but drifted away before anyone could get into them.

As chaos mounted, the four chaplains quietly spread out among the soldiers, trying to calm the frightened and offering prayers to the wounded. They also opened a storage locker and began handing out life jackets but soon ran out. When a young soldier yelled that he had no life jacket, one of the chaplains offered his own. The other three quickly did the same. The four chaplains locked arms and braced themselves as the ship listed even further. As they prayed, the *Dorchester* slipped beneath the waves. Of the 902 men aboard, 675 died, many from hypothermia in the freezing waters.

News of the tragedy and the heroic conduct of the four chaplains caused a sensation in America. On December 19, 1944, the four posthumously received the Distinguished Service Cross for extraordinary heroism. In 1961, Congress authorized a Special Medal for Heroism, which had never been given before and is never to be given again.

A native of Brooklyn, Goode had moved with his family to Washington. After World War I, when the body of the unknown soldier was brought to Arlington, he attended the ceremonies, walking the entire distance from his home, thirty miles round-trip. Following in his father's footsteps, he became a rabbi. After the attack on Pearl Harbor, he enlisted in the army. When he was assigned to an Army Air Corps base in North Carolina, he wrote to congressmen and senators and pulled strings to get assigned to Europe, where he thought he could do the most good. His memorial headstone illustrates that he never got there.

8-3: Sullivan Brothers, Memorial Section MC, Graves 30-M through 34-M

38° 52.434' N, 77° 4.290' W

Albert Leo (age nineteen), Madison Abel (twenty-two), Joseph Eugene (twenty-three), Francis Henry (twenty-five), and George Thomas (twenty-seven) represented the entire male population of the seven-sibling Sullivan family of Waterloo, Iowa. When the five Sullivan brothers heard that a close friend had been killed in the Japanese attack on Pearl Harbor, they resolved to enlist in the U.S. Navy. To get their names on the enlistment papers, however, the navy had to accommodate one non-negotiable provision set down by the brothers: that they be permitted to serve together. The navy ultimately placed them all on the USS *Juneau*.

On November 12, 1942, the Sullivans and their ship were part of a convoy en route from New Caledonia to Guadalcanal to provide reinforcements and supplies to marines who had been fighting on the latter island since August. On the other side of Guadalcanal,

a Japanese convoy was undertaking a similar mission to aid its troops. At 1:45 A.M., the two task forces met in a thirty-minute battle in which the Japanese lost a battleship and two destroyers and the Americans saw five of their thirteen ships sunk or badly damaged. The *Juneau* suffered heavy damage from a torpedo that nearly severed its keel.

At dawn, the surviving American ships limped back to base. Later that same morning, a Japanese submarine fired a torpedo that struck the damaged *Juneau* in the ammunition storage area. The resulting explosion destroyed the ship. Four of the five Sullivan brothers were killed. George was among the eighty survivors.

The survivors drifted for more than a week in intense heat, with no food, surrounded by sharks. On the tenth day, witnesses reported that George, probably delirious from his wounds and the conditions, said he was going to take a bath. Slipping out of the safety of the raft, he attracted a shark, which pulled him under the water. He was not seen again. Only ten of the original survivors were rescued.

When naval officials went to the home of Tom and Aletta Sullivan to inform them of their loss, one reportedly said he had news about their boys. Mr. Sullivan is said to have inquired, "Which one?" The official sadly answered, "All of them."

The deaths of the five Sullivan brothers became a major story. War-bond rallies were held in the name of the family. Mr. and Mrs. Sullivan and their daughter Genevieve put their grief aside and visited more than two hundred shipyards and defense plants, urging the workers to labor even harder so the war could be brought to a quick end.

A movie was made about the five brothers, and the navy named a destroyer after them. That ship served from 1943 to 1965, earning nine battle stars during World War II and two more in Korea. In 1977, a second destroyer was named in their honor. That ship, the *Sullivans* (DDG-68), remains on duty.

The memorial headstones to the five brothers were placed side by side, each bearing the inscription, "Brothers in Arms."

8-4: John Leonard Lavan, Section 3, Grave 1352-E

38° 52.460' N, 77° 4.505' W

Born on October 28, 1890, in Grand Rapids, Michigan, John Leonard Lavan attended the University of Michigan Medical School. While at Michigan, he played baseball for Branch Rickey, attracting the attention of major-league scouts and signing with the St. Louis Browns before receiving his medical degree. He played for the Browns for two months and was then purchased by the Philadelphia Athletics. It proved a fortuitous move for the young shortstop, as he earned a World Series title with the Athletics, although he didn't get into any of the Series games. He used his World Series share to pay off his medical-school tuition and to complete his medical degree in 1914. After his release

by the Athletics, he returned to the Browns, playing with the St. Louis team until 1917.

In 1917, with World War I threatening, Lavan applied for a commission in the Navy Medical Corps, after which he served two years as a physician at the Great Lakes Training Center. He was also able to continue his baseball career, playing for the Washington Senators in 1918 and the St. Louis Cardinals from 1919 to 1924. In his twelve-year major-league career, Lavan accumulated 954 hits. His lifetime batting average was .245, with his best year coming in 1920, when he batted .289.

He retired from military service after World War II as a commander in the Naval Reserve. A practicing medical doctor, Lavan served as a health officer in several different cities. He also served as director of research for the National Foundation of Infantile Paralysis, known today as the March of Dimes.

8-5: James Thomas Cruse, Section 3, Grave 1758

38° 52.401' N, 77° 4.359' W

Midshipman James Cruse was one of two sons of Brigadier General Thomas Cruse, a Medal of Honor recipient in the Indian Wars. General Cruse is buried not far from his son, in Section 3, Grave 1763.

Until July 15, 1907, James Cruse's career in the navy was largely uneventful. On that date, he was serving on the battleship *Georgia* off the coast of Massachusetts. Along with other vessels of the Atlantic fleet, the *Georgia* was engaged in target practice. Suddenly, during the loading of an eight-inch gun, a violent explosion ripped through the gun's turret, instantly killing eight of the crew and injuring thirteen others. Among the injured was Cruse, who suffered severe burns of his hands and face. Nearby ships immediately sent launch-

es carrying doctors and medical supplies. When one of the surgeons leaned over the nineteen-year-old to offer medical aid, Cruse uttered the words that would become his famous epitaph: "Never mind me. I am all right. Look after those other fellows." But Cruse was not all right, and he died a painful death four days later.

Similar previous explosions on the *Missouri, Massachusetts, Iowa*, and *Kearsarge* had resulted in modifications to the loading systems of battleships, including the *Georgia*. Those changes had led officials to believe that loading powder into the guns was safe, so the cause of the *Georgia*'s explosion was a mystery. Investigation eventually revealed that a "flare back," caused by the shutting off of the air blast too soon while a light wind was blowing into the muzzle of the gun, had ignited the powder in the loader's arms.

namese at the time of his death at age forty-three. He had also served in Korea.

Nolde was a professor of military science at Central Michigan University prior to joining the army. In his honor, the university established the William B. Nolde Scholarship. In addition, the William B. Nolde Lecture Series takes place every two years, with military leaders and others being invited to lecture on leadership.

Nolde was laid to rest February 5, 1973, with full military honors, including the riderless horse, Black Jack. His funeral attracted national attention and was attended by many dignitaries. Thousands more viewed it on television.

8-7: Thomas Ellwood Rose, Section 3, Grave 1818
38° 52.406' N, 77° 4.315' W

Born in Bucks County, Pennsylvania, on March 12, 1830, Thomas Rose enlisted as a private in the Twelfth Pennsylvania Volunteers in April 1861. He was named a captain in the Seventy-seventh Pennsylvania in October of that year and rose to become the regiment's colonel in January 1863.

Captured at the Battle of Chickamauga in Tennessee on September 20, 1863, Rose escaped at Weldon, North Carolina, and was recaptured the next day. Sent to Libby Prison in Richmond, he immediately began plotting his escape, joining with Captain Andrew Hamilton of the Twelfth Kentucky Cavalry. The men engineered eight unsuccessful attempts at breaking out before Rose, Hamilton, and 13 additional Union officers dug a fifty-three-foot tunnel in seventeen days. The exodus through that tunnel on February 9, 1864, became the largest prisoner-of-war escape in American military history, 109 Union officers making their way out of the tunnel. Of those, 59 made their way back to Union lines, 2 drowned, and 48 were recaptured. Rose was one of those recaptured. As the leader of the

8-6: William B. Nolde, Section 3, Grave 1775-B
38° 52.394' N, 77° 4.350' W

Vietnam, the longest war in U.S. history to that point, was finally drawing to a close. A truce had been negotiated at the Paris Peace Accords, and American soldiers looked forward to going back to "the world." With only eleven hours to go before the cease fire was to take effect, Colonel William B. Nolde was killed by an artillery shell near An Loc. Although others would die later, Nolde's was the last American death recorded before the cease fire, giving him the distinction of officially being the last American to die in the war. Those who perished later were not listed as casualties of the war. Nolde was serving as an advisor to the South Viet-

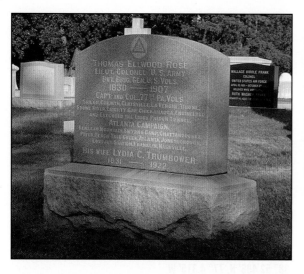

8-8: Floyd Bennett, Section 3, Grave 1852-B
38° 52.428' N, 77° 4.293' W

escape, he was placed in a damp cell in the basement of the prison for thirty-eight days, subsisting on only bread and water. When he was removed from the cell, his uniform, hair, and beard were covered with mold.

On April 21, 1864, Rose was exchanged for a Confederate colonel, only to be wounded two months later at Kennesaw Mountain, Georgia. He was breveted a brigadier general on July 22, 1865, and mustered out on December 6, 1865.

After the Civil War, he enlisted in the army as a captain in the Eleventh U.S. Infantry. He was breveted a major on March 2, 1867, for gallantry at Liberty Gap and to lieutenant colonel that same date for gallantry and meritorious service at Chickamauga. He transferred to the Sixteenth U.S. Infantry in 1870 and retired from military service on March 12, 1894.

Rose died of a cerebral hemorrhage on November 6, 1907.

Floyd Bennett left school at age seventeen to become a mechanic and part-owner of a garage. His background followed him when he enlisted in the U.S. Navy and signed up for aviation training. Although Bennett earned his wings, the navy assigned him to serve as an aviation mechanic, against his wishes.

In 1925, he was assigned to an aviation group headed by Lieutenant Commander Richard E. Byrd (see Chapter 4, site 4-12) that was slated to explore Greenland later that year. The transfer to Byrd's group changed Bennett's life. The following year, Bennett and Byrd made a second expedition, Bennett serving as Byrd's personal pilot. Their goal was to become the first team to fly over the North Pole. When they returned the same day they left, their claim of flying over the pole was met with skepticism. Later evidence proved that the skepticism was justified. But in the meantime, Bennett and Byrd were presented with the Medal of Honor for being the first to fly over the pole.

In 1927, Byrd and Bennett planned the first nonstop flight from the United States to France. That dream was dashed when Bennett was seriously injured after crashing on takeoff during a practice flight. Not long afterward, Charles Lindbergh flew from Long Island to Paris, accomplishing what Bennett and Byrd had hoped to do.

In 1928, while on a mission to salvage an aircraft that had gone down off Labrador, Bennett became ill. He died of pneumonia in Quebec on April 25, 1928. Three years later, New York City's first municipal airport was named Floyd Bennett Airport in his honor.

8-9: Walter Reed, Section 3, Grave 1864
38° 52.422' N, 77° 4.264' W

Walter Reed was born in Belroi, Virginia, on September 13, 1851. He attended the University of Virginia, earning his medical degree at age nineteen; he remains the youngest person to receive a medical degree from that institution. He took additional training at Bellevue Medical College in New York City.

When Reed entered the army, he was commissioned as an assistant surgeon with the rank of lieutenant. In 1890, he became the attending surgeon and examiner of recruits in Baltimore. Three years later,

he was named curator of the Army Medical Museum. The new position brought with it a promotion to major. Five years later, he was appointed chairman of a commission that was being organized to study yellow fever among U.S. soldiers in Cuba. His research proved that the disease was transmitted by mosquitoes, rather than from contaminated drinking water, as had been believed.

Reed died November 22, 1902, at age fifty-one from appendicitis. Walter Reed National Military Medical Center is named for him.

8-10: Jonathan Letterman, Section 3, Grave 1869
38° 52.422' N, 77° 4.248' W

Born on December 10, 1824, Jonathan Letterman graduated from Jefferson Medical College in Philadelphia and joined the army in 1849. The son of a surgeon, he served as a captain and assistant surgeon in Florida, Minnesota, and New Mexico until April 16, 1862, when he was promoted to major and full surgeon and assigned to the Army of the Potomac as medical director.

In that position, he observed that it often took more than a week to remove wounded soldiers from a battlefield. Letterman immediately took action to rectify the problem, developing a three-stage system that included front-line aid stations for triage and preliminary treatment, field hospitals for more advanced treatment, and larger semi-permanent hospitals for long-term treatment. He also started the first Ambulance Corps, training stretcher bearers and ambulance drivers to pick up the wounded and transport them to field dressing stations. His system gained widespread recognition at Antietam, where more than twenty-three thousand casualties were removed from the field in just twenty-four hours. Letterman's changes also provided for an

8-11: Edmund Rice, Section 3, Grave 1875
38° 52.412' N, 77° 4.243' W

This unusual headstone marks the final resting place of Brigadier General Edmund Rice, whose justifiable pride in his Medal of Honor is reflected in the marker's design.

Rice served as a captain in the Fourteenth Massachusetts Infantry during the Civil War until the regiment was disbanded in 1861, at which time he transferred to the Nineteenth Massachusetts Infantry. He fought in numerous battles including Gettysburg, where he was badly wounded and was awarded his Medal of Honor. The citation recognized him for "conspicuous bravery on the third day of the battle on the countercharge against Pickett's division where he fell severely wounded within the enemy's lines."

Rice had previously been wounded in the leg at Antietam and was badly wounded a third time and captured in 1864 at Spotsylvania Court House. While being transported to a prison camp, he cut through the door of the freight car in which he was riding and jumped to safety while the train was moving. He

overhaul of the military medical personnel system, calling for the hiring of civilian doctors to serve as contractors, recruiting women as nurses, and drilling and testing military doctors on their medical knowledge. One of his best-known accomplishments was the establishment of Camp Letterman at Gettysburg, where more than fourteen thousand Union and sixty-eight hundred Confederate wounded received treatment.

Recognized as "the Father of Modern Battlefield Medicine," Letterman was credited with saving thousands of soldiers. In March 1864, the Letterman System was officially adopted for the U.S. Army by an act of Congress. Letterman resigned from the army in December 1864 and moved to San Francisco, where he died March 15, 1872. On November 13, 1911, the army hospital at the Presidio was named Letterman General Hospital in his honor.

reached Union lines twenty-three days later, after walking nearly four hundred miles. During the war, he was breveted for gallant service at Antietam, Gettysburg, and the Wilderness.

After his discharge from the army in 1865, he became an inventor, primarily of military implements. He received patents for such inventions as an improved bayonet, an improved trowel bayonet, an improved bayonet scabbard, and an improved individual shelter tent. Rice also served in the Indian Wars, the Spanish-American War, and the war in the Philippines. He retired from the army in 1903 as a brigadier general.

8-12: Vinnie Ream Hoxie, Section 3, Grave 1876
38° 52.409' N, 77° 4.242' W

Members of the Winnebago Indian tribe taught Lavinia Ream Hoxie to paint and draw when she was a child in her native Wisconsin. She later had formal training in literature, art, and music.

When the family moved to Washington, Vinnie, as she was known, worked as a postal clerk, one of the earliest women to do so. She also labored part-time in a sculptor's studio, making relief medallions and portrait busts of congressmen and other public figures. Impressed with her work, one of these influential men introduced her to President Abraham Lincoln, suggesting she do a bust of the president. Reluctant at first, the president finally acquiesced, a decision that would catapult Vinnie to international fame. She thus became the first female artist commissioned to sculpt a statue for the government and the last artist for whom Lincoln sat before his death.

When Lincoln was assassinated, Congress wished to memorialize him with a full-sized statue. Remembering that Vinnie had done the president's bust and developed a close relationship with him, Congress voted to commission her to sculpt his full-sized work.

Still only eighteen, Vinnie began the project immediately, going so far as to borrow the clothes the president was wearing when he was killed. The end result was the marble figure that stands in the rotunda of the Capitol. Dedication took place on January 25, 1871, with President Ulysses Grant in attendance.

The statue above Vinnie's grave, representing the poetess Sappho, is one of her many works.

8-13: Albert B. Sabin, Section 3, Grave 1885-RH

38° 52.408' N, 77° 4.257' W

Albert Bruce Sabin was born in Poland in 1906 and came to the United States with no understanding of English. He eventually graduated from New York University with a medical degree and began his polio research at Rockefeller Institute for Medical Research. He joined the army at the outbreak of World War II and served with the Board of Investigation of Epidemic Diseases as a lieutenant colonel, in which role he developed vaccines for a number of diseases, including one against Japanese encephalitis. He also explored the possibility that some viruses could be linked to some types of cancer.

After the war, he resumed his research into the prevention and treatment of polio, one of the most contagious diseases of his time. Although Dr. Jonas Salk had already developed an injectable vaccine, Sabin believed an oral vaccine would be more effective and easier to administer. In the mid-1950s, he perfected his oral polio vaccine, which was tested on prisoners who volunteered to be part of the research. Prior to that testing, Sabin had tested the vaccine on himself and members of his own family.

Sabin's vaccine helped reduce the number of reported cases of polio from more than twenty-one thousand in 1952 to virtually none just a few years later. Over the next forty years, an estimated half-million lives were saved and five million cases of paralytic polio were prevented. The last ten years of that period found Sabin working in extreme pain, partially paralyzed by spinal calcification.

Sabin received more than forty honorary degrees, as well as the National Medal of Science, the Presidential Medal of Freedom, the Medal of Liberty, and the Order of Friendship of Peoples, awarded by the USSR. He died in Washington in 1993 from heart failure.

8-14: Frank D. Baldwin, Section 3, Grave 1894

38° 52.412' N, 77° 4.282' W

Frank Baldwin entered the Michigan Horse Guards with the rank of second lieutenant at the outbreak of the Civil War, serving with distinction dur-

8-15: Roger Bruce Chaffee, Section 3, Grave 2502-F

38° 52.389' N, 77° 4.365' W

Born in 1935 in Grand Rapids, Michigan, Roger Chaffee had many interests as a youth, including target shooting, music, and airplanes. He joined the Boy Scouts and advanced rapidly, becoming an Eagle Scout within a few years.

Like his fellow astronaut Virgil "Gus" Grissom, Chaffee was a graduate of Purdue University; Chaffee's degree was in aeronautical engineering. He earned extra money teaching freshman math classes while still a student himself. He entered the navy in 1957, serving as safety officer and quality control officer for Heavy Photographic Squadron 62 at Naval Air Station Jacksonville in Florida.

ing that conflict. He was awarded the Medal of Honor when, according to his citation, he "led his company in a countercharge at Peach Tree Creek, Ga., 12 July 1864, under a galling fire ahead of his own men, and singly entered the enemy's line, capturing and bringing back 2 commissioned officers, fully armed, besides a guidon of a Georgia regiment."

After the war, Baldwin immediately enlisted in the regular army. On November 8, 1874, he received a second Medal of Honor for his heroics at McClellan's Creek, Texas. The citation for this award describes how he "rescued, with 2 companies, 2 white girls by a voluntary attack upon Indians whose superior numbers and strong position would have warranted delay for reinforcements, but which delay would have permitted the Indians to escape and kill their captives."

In 1890, he was breveted a captain for gallantly leading a successful attack on Sitting Bull's encampment in Montana. He retired from active service in 1906 and served from 1917 to 1919 as adjutant general of Colorado. Major General Frank D. Baldwin died April 23, 1923.

In 1963, he was selected by NASA in the third group of astronauts. On March 21, 1966, he became part of the crew for the AS-204 mission, the first three-man Apollo flight. The other two crew members were Gus Grissom and Ed White.

On January 27, 1967, the crew entered the command module for what all three expected to be a grueling but routine preflight test. However, as the test progressed, fire broke out. Before the astronauts could exit the module, it was completely engulfed. All three men perished.

White's body was taken to West Point for burial. Chaffee and Grissom were placed adjacent to one another in Arlington. All three astronauts were posthumously awarded the Congressional Space Medal of Honor. Chaffee was also awarded the U.S. Navy Air Medal.

Chaffee, Grissom, and White have been honored by having their names affixed to the three hills on Mars that are visible from the rover Spirit's landing site.

8-16: Virgil I. Grissom, Section 3, Grave 2503-E
38° 52.389' N, 77° 4.365' W

Virgil Grissom, better known to the American public as Gus, was born in 1926 and earned a bachelor of science degree in mechanical engineering from Purdue University. He received his wings in March 1951 and flew a hundred combat missions in Korea in F-86s with the 334th Fighter Interceptor Squadron. He was awarded the Distinguished Flying Cross and the Air Medal with cluster for his service.

After his return from Korea, he became a test pilot and was one of the seven original Mercury astronauts selected by NASA in April 1959. On July 21, 1961, he achieved his dream when he piloted *Liberty Bell 7*, the second and final suborbital Mercury test. This flight lasted fifteen minutes and thirty-seven seconds, at-

tained an altitude of 118 statute miles, and traveled 302 miles down range from the launch pad at Cape Kennedy. Grissom narrowly escaped with his life when the capsule sank after splashdown. The capsule was not recovered until 1999.

On March 23, 1965, he served as command pilot on the first manned Gemini flight. When given the customary opportunity to name the spacecraft, Grissom showed his sense of humor (and his unhappy memory of his first space flight) when he christened it the *Molly Brown*, a reference to the famous *Titanic* survivor and socialite. When unamused NASA officials asked him to rename it, Grissom suggested, "How about the *Titanic*?" Officials relented, but it was the last mission for which astronauts were allowed to name their spacecraft.

Grissom was named to serve as command pilot for

the AS-204 mission, the first three-man Apollo flight. Ed White and Roger Chaffee were the other two astronauts. On January 27, 1967, tragedy struck during a preflight training session when fire swept through the command module. All three men were killed.

Grissom is buried immediately beside Chaffee. In addition to his Congressional Space Medal of Honor, Grissom was awarded two NASA Distinguished Service Medals, the NASA Exceptional Service Medal, and the Air Force Command Astronaut Wings.

8-17: Thomas Selfridge, Section 3, Grave 2158
38° 52.353' N, 77° 4.357' W

U.S. Army first lieutenant Thomas Etholen Selfridge, one of America's first aviators, is perhaps better known for his dubious distinction of being the country's first military air casualty.

Selfridge proved himself a successful aviator. He was a test pilot of sorts, making his first flight while lying prone in the center of a large tetrahedral kite called *Cygnet I*, designed by Alexander Graham Bell. The kite was towed by a tugboat; the flight lasted seven minutes.

In 1908, as a member of the Aerial Experiment Association, he designed the association's first airplane, called the *Red Wing*, for its red silk–covered wings. When he piloted the association's second plane a short time later, he became the first army officer ever to make a flight. Later that year, he was assigned to a board responsible for testing the Army Signal Corps' first dirigible. Selfridge made numerous test flights in this dirigible before it was officially accepted.

His next assignment saw him as part of a group conducting the first tests to see if an airplane could fly forty miles an hour, carry two persons, and be portable enough to be transported by a mule-drawn wagon. After Orville Wright made the first successful flight at

Fort Myer, the airplane continued to impress observers for the next two weeks.

The unfortunate incident that led to Selfridge's death took place September 17, 1908, when Selfridge was the passenger on a plane piloted by Orville Wright. The plane had made four successful circles around the Fort Myer parade grounds when a propeller broke off. The plane plummeted to the ground from a height of about 150 feet, just outside the cemetery and not far from where Selfridge is buried. Selfridge suffered a fatal skull fracture, while Wright suffered nonfatal rib and thigh fractures.

A plaque on Joint Base Myer–Henderson Hall near

its boundary with Arlington marks the location of the crash.

8-18: Nathan Bedford Forrest III, Section 11, Grave 824-A

38° 52.388' N, 77° 4.393' W

The great-grandson of famed Confederate general Nathan Bedford Forrest, Nathan Bedford Forrest III was born in Memphis, Tennessee, on April 7, 1905. After studying for two years at Georgia Tech, he received an appointment to West Point, graduating in 1928. He was commissioned a second lieutenant and advanced through the ranks to brigadier general in November 1942. He was serving as chief of staff of the Second Air Force and as an observer in a B-17 heavy bomber of the Eighth Air Force when he went missing during a raid over the submarine yards of Kiel, Germany, on June 13, 1943. Other pilots reported seeing several parachutes opening as his plane went down, giving hope that he may have survived and been taken prisoner. That hope was dashed when his body washed ashore three months later at the seaplane base at Rügen Island,

Germany. Forrest was buried September 28, 1943, in a small cemetery near Wiek, Germany. Six years later, he was reinterred in Arlington.

Forrest was the first American general to become a casualty in the attack on Germany. In addition to a Purple Heart, he was posthumously awarded the Distinguished Flying Cross.

8-19: Francis Gary Powers, Section 11, Grave 685-2

38° 52.392' N, 77° 4.410' W

Francis Gary Powers was commissioned a second lieutenant in the U.S. Air Force in 1950. Upon completion of advanced training, he became an F-84 Thunderjet pilot and was discharged in 1956 with the rank of captain.

Now out of the service, he joined the Central Intel-

ligence Agency's U-2 project, a program in which pilots flew at altitudes above seventy thousand feet, their mission being to take high-resolution photos of military installations and other important sites in countries hostile to the United States. On May 1, 1960, after Powers had already flown twenty-seven successful missions, his plane was hit by a surface-to-air missile over the Soviet Union. Unable to activate the plane's self-destruct mechanism, Powers parachuted to the ground and was captured by the KGB, the main security agency for the Soviet Union. The plane landed nearly intact, and the Soviets were able to retrieve the state-of-the-art camera.

On August 17, 1960, armed with the photographic evidence from Powers's plane, the Soviet Union convicted him of espionage and sentenced him to a total of ten years in prison—three years of imprisonment, followed by seven years of hard labor. On February 10, 1962, after twenty-one months of captivity, Powers was exchanged in a spy swap for KGB colonel Vilyam Fisher (a.k.a. Rudolf Ivanovich Abel).

Although he underwent intense interrogation while a prisoner, Powers did not divulge any vital information, despite what the Associated Press called "cajolery, trickery, insults and threats of death." The American public, however, took a different view, many calling Powers a coward for not committing suicide using a poisoned needle he had been given before the flight. Others criticized him for failing to destroy his plane, camera, and photos. He was even investigated by a Senate Armed Services Select Committee, which eventually concluded he had done nothing wrong and had conducted himself honorably.

Needing a job, Powers accepted a position as a test pilot for Lockheed, where he worked for seven years until the CIA requested he be terminated for writing a book titled *Operation Overflight*, which the agency feared might reveal sensitive information. He then became a helicopter pilot and traffic reporter in Los Angeles.

On August 1, 1977, while Powers was returning from covering brush fires in Santa Barbara County, his helicopter crashed a few miles from Burbank Airport, where he was based. Both Powers and cameraman George Spears were killed.

Although Powers had received few accolades on his return to the United States following his captivity, he was awarded numerous medals, some posthumously, as the Cold War died down. Among them were the Intelligence Star, the Silver Star, the Distinguished Flying Cross, the National Defense Service Medal, and the Prisoner of War Medal.

8-20: Charles "Pete" Conrad Jr., Section 11, Grave 113-3
38° 52.365' N, 77° 4.452' W

Charles Conrad, known to his friends as Pete, was born June 2, 1930, in Philadelphia. He joined the navy following his graduation in 1953 from Princeton University, becoming a naval aviator and serving at various times as a test pilot, flight instructor, and performance engineer. In 1962, he was selected as an astronaut by NASA. He went on to fly four missions in space. Those missions are engraved on the rear of his grave marker.

His first flight was the eight-day Gemini V mission in 1965, which established the space endurance record and pushed the United States ahead of the Soviet Union in the lead for man-hours in space. In 1966, he served as commander of Gemini XI, docking with another orbiting craft and setting a space altitude record of 850 miles. He then served as commander of Apollo XII in 1969, becoming only the third person to walk on the moon. On his final mission, he served as commander of Skylab II, the first U.S. space station. One

of his tasks was to repair damage suffered by Skylab on liftoff. By the end of this mission, Pete Conrad had spent 1,179 hours and 38 minutes in space, a personal endurance record. He retired from the navy in December 1973 after serving twenty years, eleven of them as an astronaut.

Among Conrad's many awards were the Congressional Space Medal of Honor, two NASA Distinguished Service Medals, two NASA Exceptional Service Medals, the Navy Astronaut Wings, two Navy Distinguished Service Medals, and two Distinguished Flying Crosses. He was enshrined in the Aviation Hall of Fame in 1980.

Conrad died July 8, 1999, from injuries sustained in a motorcycle accident, becoming the third of the twelve moon walkers to die, James Irwin of Apollo XI having passed away in 1991 and Alan Shepard of Apollo XIV in 1998.

8-21: Ellis Spear Middleton II, Section 11, Grave 38

38° 52.359' N, 77° 4.461' W

Perhaps no story from Arlington National Cemetery better illustrates the love of a parent than that of Captain Ellis Spear Middleton. Middleton was reported missing in action in September 1944, one of many young men unaccounted for during that time. The twenty-four-year-old had enlisted in the Army Air Corps before Pearl Harbor and had flown several successful missions.

As time passed with no information, Middleton's frustrated parents launched a search of their own in an effort to find his body, or at least to learn what had happened to him. They arranged for thirty thousand circulars and advertisements to be placed throughout Europe, hoping their son's fate could be determined.

After three years with no news, a letter arrived

informing them that their son's body had been buried by Nazi paratroopers in the Kleve Forest and erroneously marked with the inscription, "Unknown German Soldier." The family subsequently learned that Captain Middleton had been shot down September 23, 1944, over Arnhem, Netherlands, after he had downed three Nazi planes. Some thirty-five people worked to locate his remains and reinter them in the U.S. cemetery at Neuville-en-Condroz in Belgium.

In 1948, the Middletons traveled to Europe to visit their son's grave and see where he had been shot down. They also made a point to meet with those who had helped unravel the mystery. Middleton's remains were disinterred and flown to Arlington for his final burial on May 2, 1949.

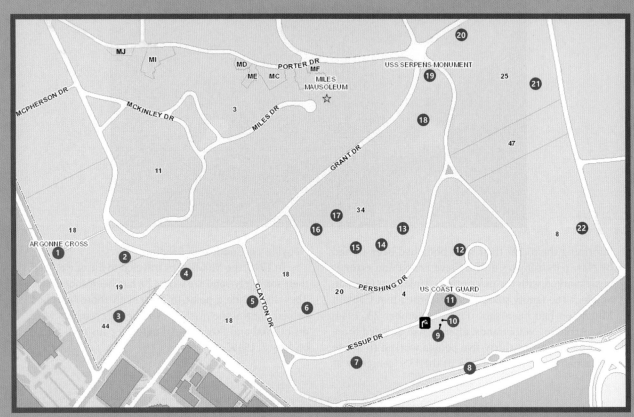

9-1: Argonne Cross, Section 18
38° 52.293' N, 77° 4.535' W

As the death toll escalated in World War I, it was necessary to bury the dead quickly in cemeteries throughout Europe. After the war, efforts to provide more proper burials for fallen servicemen were initiated. From April 1920 through July 1921, many of those remains were disinterred and either reinterred in other cemeteries in Europe or returned to the United States.

By the time the project was completed, the remains of approximately twenty-one hundred men had been brought to Arlington. The Argonne Cross was erected to their memory. It sits in a grove of nineteen pine trees, symbolizing the Argonne Forest, where many of the men fought. An eagle and wreath are carved at the juncture of the arm and stem of the cross. An inscription on one side of the base reads,

IN MEMORY OF YOUR MEN IN FRANCE
1917–1918

A second inscription, on the opposite side, reads,

ERECTED - THROUGH - THE - EFFORTS - OF - THE
ARGONNE - UNIT - AMERICAN - WOMENS - LEGION

9-2: Edward F. Younger, Section 18, Grave 1918-B
38° 52.286' N, 77° 4.466' W

With World War I already raging and the United States two months from becoming directly involved, Edward Younger enlisted in the army in February 1917. Within a short time, he became a seasoned combat veteran, fighting at Château-Thierry, St. Mihiel, the Somme offensive, and the Meuse-Argonne offensive. Wounded twice, he reenlisted in 1919 and was stationed with the Fifteenth Infantry of the army of occupation in Mayen, Germany, when he was chosen as one of six soldiers to go to France to select the unknown soldier.

Younger later reported that the six who were selected assumed they were to serve as pallbearers. However, when they arrived at Chalons-sur-Marne, they were informed otherwise by Major Robert Harbold, the officer in charge of grave registrations. Four coffins had been placed in the chapel, one from each of the major cemeteries where American war dead were

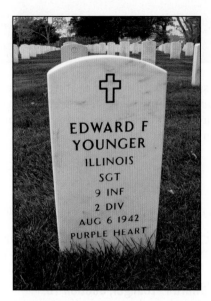

buried. When Younger and the other five men lined up in formation, Harbold told them of their real mission. Carrying a bouquet of roses, he passed in front of the six, finally handing the roses to Younger, indicating it would be his honor to make the selection.

On November 24, 1921, the apprehensive Younger proceeded into the chapel, where he was left alone to make his selection. He instinctively knelt in prayer, then walked around the coffins three times, unable to make his decision. Suddenly, he stopped behind one of them. He had no idea what drew him to the one he chose, saying it was almost as if something had pulled him to that particular coffin. He gently placed the roses on the coffin, paid his respects, and quietly left the chapel.

After leaving the army, Younger worked for the post office in Chicago. He died August 6, 1942, believing to the end that he probably knew the soldier he had selected to represent the unknown dead of World War I. (See the entry for the Tomb of the Unknowns, Chapter 7, for more details.)

9-3: Beauford Theodore Anderson, Section 44, Grave 292

38° 52.239' N, 77° 4.472' W

Beauford Anderson was born in Eagle River, Wisconsin, on July 6, 1922. He joined the army in 1942 and was assigned to the newly activated Ninety-sixth Infantry Division. In October 1944, Anderson saw his first combat, landing on the beach at Leyte as part of the effort to retake the Philippines. In that fighting, Anderson received a Bronze Star after he crossed open terrain under heavy enemy fire to bring two wounded men to safety, then gave them first aid until they could be evacuated.

Anderson was not done fighting. In April 1945, his unit was struck in the early-morning hours by a Japanese attack. Anderson ordered his men to take cover, then single-handedly faced the charging Japanese, armed with only his carbine. After he emptied

his magazine, he threw an unexploded enemy mortar round into the oncoming force. The round exploded in the midst of the Japanese, killing and wounding several. As the Japanese continued advancing, Anderson grabbed a box of mortar shells, pulled the safety pins, and banged the bases on a rock to arm them. He threw the shells as he continued firing his weapon, driving the enemy back despite being severely wounded. He then made his way back to the company commander to file his report before seeking medical attention.

On Memorial Day 1946, Technical Sergeant Anderson received the Medal of Honor from President Harry S. Truman in a ceremony at the White House.

After the war, Anderson settled in California. He became active in local politics, serving two terms as mayor and two terms as a city councilman in Seaside, California, as well as two terms as a Monterey County supervisor and one as chairman of the board of supervisors. He also remained active in the U.S. Army Reserve until complications from his wounds forced him to retire. He died November 7, 1996.

The unassuming Anderson rarely discussed his Medal of Honor. Most of his friends and neighbors were surprised to hear after his death that he had received his nation's highest military honor. As a result, he was buried near his California home in a modest funeral ceremony. His wife died the next month and was buried next to him.

On December 15, 2000, a new 218-room dormitory of the Army Reserve Readiness Training Center was dedicated at Fort McCoy, Wisconsin. The facility was named Beauford T. Anderson Hall. It was at this ceremony that someone recognized that Anderson could have been buried at Arlington. The process was initiated, and on May 7, 2001, the urns containing the remains of Anderson and his wife, Phyllis, were reinterred in Arlington.

9-4: John H. Pruitt, Section 18, Grave 2453
38° 52.273' N, 77° 4.400' W

Corporal John Henry Pruitt was born in Fayetteville, Arkansas, on October 4, 1896. Serving with the Marine Corps in the Seventy-eighth Company, Sixth Regiment, Second Division, at Mont Blanc, France, in World War I, he single-handedly attacked two machine-gun positions, killing two German soldiers and capturing forty more. Later that same day, while serving on sniper duty, he was hit by a mortar shell and mortally wounded. He died the next day on his twenty-second birthday.

Military experts have said that Pruitt not only saved many American soldiers' lives but also that his heroic efforts greatly helped his unit accomplish its mission. For his actions, he was awarded two Medals of Honor, one from the army and one from the navy.

In addition, he was awarded the Croix de Guerre by France and the Croce di Guerra by Italy, those countries' equivalents of the Medal of Honor. He also received two Purple Hearts, four Silver Stars, four Bronze Stars, and several other combat and victory medals. He was the first person from Arkansas to earn a Medal of Honor.

9-5 and 9-6: William J. Hushka, Section 18, Grave 2262

38° 52.242' N, 77° 4.320' W

and Eric Carlson, Section 18, Grave 5217

38° 52.243' N, 77° 4.255' W

In 1924, the World War Adjusted Compensation Act awarded bonuses to World War I veterans, to be paid in 1945. President Calvin Coolidge vetoed the act on the grounds that patriotism should not have to be bought, only to see Congress override him. Veterans nationwide applauded the act and were willing to wait the two decades to get their money, which was to have interest compounded each year.

However, when the Great Depression hit, many veterans found themselves out of work and unable to support their families. They organized a group officially called the Bonus Expeditionary Force, also known as the Bonus Army. The veterans were referred to as "Bonus Marchers." In the spring of 1932, some forty-three thousand veterans gathered in Washington to demand early payment of their bonuses, setting up a well-organized campsite across the Anacostia River and naming it Hooverville, after unpopular president Herbert Hoover. In response, on June 15, 1932, Congress passed a bill to move the payment date up. Two days later, however, the Senate voted it down, and the

1945 payment date was maintained.

The angry Bonus Marchers failed to leave town after the defeat of the bill, prompting Attorney General William Mitchell to order the police to evict them from their camp. When the veterans ignored the order, a scuffle broke out that quickly escalated as police began shooting. Two veterans were killed—Eric Carlson, born in 1894 in Oakland, California, and William Hushka, a Lithuanian immigrant who had relocated to Missouri and joined the army when the war broke out. Hushka was killed instantly, while Carlson was mortally wounded. The incident was the final straw for American voters, who voted Hoover out of office in the next election.

Later on the day of the shootings, General Douglas MacArthur, under orders from President Hoover and assisted by Major Dwight Eisenhower, led infantry and cavalry regiments into the camp. These troops were supported by six tanks commanded by Major George S. Patton. Using fixed bayonets and tear gas, MacArthur's men entered the camp, drove out the veterans and their families, and burned their shelters and belongings. When the veterans fled across the river, Hoover ordered the assault stopped. MacArthur chose to ignore the president, however, and ordered a new attack, saying later that the Bonus Marchers were planning to overthrow the government. Fifty-five veterans were injured and 135 arrested.

Hushka was buried in Arlington with military honors on August 2, 1932, his casket borne by eight friends from the Bonus March. His pallbearers were visible reminders of why the marchers had come to Washington, their clothing best described as rags and mismatched reminders of old army uniforms. Not far away and about the same time Hushka was being lowered into his grave, Carlson drew his last breath. He was buried three days later.

A second demonstration was organized the following year. New president Franklin D. Roosevelt provided the marchers with a campsite in Virginia and gave them three meals a day. Eleanor Roosevelt visited the site, ate lunch with the veterans, and offered them positions in the newly created Civilian Conservation Corps. Roosevelt later issued an executive order waiving age and marital-status restrictions, which allowed the enrollment of twenty-five thousand veterans into the CCC.

The new Congress passed the Adjusted Compensation Payment Act in 1936, authorizing the immediate payment of $2 billion in World War I bonuses. As before, when the president vetoed the bill, Congress overrode it. This time, however, the senators agreed with their legislative colleagues and overwhelmingly approved the payment. Veterans across the country received their bonuses, which came too late for Eric Carlson and William Hushka. As a final show of power, the government deducted an average of $15 from each bonus check to pay for the food provided at the camp.

9-7: John McCloy, Section 8, Grave 5246
38° 52.198' N, 77° 4.212' W

Born in Kingston, New York, John McCloy felt the call of the sea from an early age, joining the merchant marine at age fifteen. Seven years later, he joined the navy. Over the next two years, he served on the USS *Columbia*, the USS *Monterey*, the schooner *Manila*, the gunboat USS *Gardoqui*, and the cruiser USS *Newark*.

In the summer of 1900, McCloy was a coxswain on the *Newark* during a relief expedition in China. There, he participated in the landing force at Peking, distinguishing himself in battle to the point where he was awarded the Medal of Honor "for distinguished conduct in the presence of the enemy in battles of the 13th, 20th, 21st, and 22nd of June."

In April 1901, McCloy reenlisted and was assigned

to the *Manila*. Over the next ten years, he served on six additional ships—the *Alliance*, the USS *Atlanta*, the USS *Galveston*, the USS *Hancock*, the receiving ship *Franklin*, and the collier *Lebanon*—before being assigned shore duty at the naval station at Key West, Florida.

Two years later, McCloy returned to sea aboard the USS *Florida* and participated as beach master for the landing force in the occupation at Veracruz, Mexico. He was wounded on April 21–22, 1914, when his detachment came under fire while unloading men and supplies at a pier. To determine the source of the fire, he took his boat away from the pier and directed fire at a building housing the Mexican Naval Academy. His action drew retaliatory fire that allowed nearby cruisers to locate and shell sniper positions, thus protecting the men on shore. McCloy, although wounded in the thigh, remained at his post for forty-eight hours until the brigade surgeon sent him to a hospital ship. This dedication to duty earned him his second Medal of Honor, making him a member of an exclusive group. Only nineteen men have twice received the Medal of Honor in our nation's history.

At the close of World War I, he commanded the

minesweeper USS *Curlew*, clearing mines in the North Sea. This assignment earned him the Navy Cross. He received three other navy decorations, one for service in the West Indies, one for the Philippines, and another for China. The state of New York also presented him a medal for an incident in 1898 when a navy tug under his command saved two men from drowning and rescued the entire crew of a schooner in a hurricane off the Florida Keys. Other honors accorded McCloy include the naming of a destroyer escort in his honor and his inclusion as one of the four best-known sailors of the twentieth century in a series of postage stamps.

On October 15, 1928, he retired from active duty as a lieutenant. He was promoted in retirement to lieutenant commander on February 23, 1942. McCloy died of an apparent heart attack on May 24, 1945.

9-8: William F. Friedman, Section 8, Grave 6379
38° 52.194' N, 77° 4.081' W

Wolfe Frederick Friedman was born September 24, 1891, in Kishinev, which was then part of imperial Russia. His father, an interpreter for the czar's postal service, became increasingly disenchanted with anti-Semitic Russian regulations. In 1892, the elder Friedman left his family and moved to the United States. The following year, the family followed him. Wolfe's name was changed to William in 1896 when his father attained American citizenship.

William Friedman graduated from Cornell University and eventually was hired by Riverbank Laboratories, near Chicago. At Riverbank, he became involved in the study of codes and ciphers. Deciding this would be his life's work, Friedman left Riverbank to become a cryptologic officer during World War I. When the war ended, he became known as an author, teacher, and cryptologist.

In 1939, the Japanese introduced a new cipher

machine for their most sensitive diplomatic traffic. To break the Japanese code, a joint army-navy effort known as Operation Magic was instituted. After several months of frustration, a team led by Friedman and Frank Rowlett decoded the Japanese machine, enabling American military commanders to read intercepts on Japanese military movements. Their work provided the U.S. military with much important intelligence throughout World War II.

One of the most important contributions of Operation Magic was the decoding of ciphers that revealed the Japanese attack plan for the Battle of Midway in mid-1942. Decoded information on Japanese objectives was passed on to Admiral Chester Nimitz, enabling him to fight off a superior Japanese force. It was at this battle that the plane of Japanese admiral Isoroku Yamamoto, planner of the attack on Pearl Harbor, was shot down, resulting in Yamamoto's death.

Friedman died in 1969 after pioneering security practices that are still in use by the National Security Agency.

9-9: Robert E. Peary, Section 8, Grave S-15
38° 52.233' N, 77° 4.108' W

Robert Edwin Peary was born in Cresson, Pennsylvania, and served in the U.S. Navy Civil Engineering Corps. Peary had a burning desire to secure a place in the history of exploration by being the first man to reach the North Pole. This was no easy feat, especially in the early 1900s. More than 750 explorers had already died attempting the same expedition by the time Peary launched his first effort.

Peary had made four voyages to the polar region between 1886 and 1896. These exploratory journeys earned him fame and convinced him he could reach the North Pole. In 1897, he undertook his first journey for the pole, returning four years later without reaching his goal. In 1905, he set out again, setting a new "farthest north" record but still coming 175 miles short of the pole when a critical shortage of supplies forced him back.

In February 1909, Peary, his assistant, Matthew Henson, and six sled teams launched a sixth and final effort to reach the North Pole. On April 6, they finally achieved their goal. Peary was fifty-two at the time.

In 1911, Peary's achievement was officially recognized by Congress. In March of that year, he was granted the rank of rear admiral. Peary died February 20, 1920, in Washington and was buried three days later at Arlington in Section 3, Grave 1853-B. President Warren G. Harding presided over the ceremonies.

In the late 1920s, a monument to Peary at Arlington was proposed, and the National Commission of Fine Arts initiated a study for a suitable location. The study concluded that Peary's original grave site would be too difficult to develop into a larger memorial because of its location on the side of a hill. An alternate area near the U.S. Coast Guard Memorial was selected as a better site. With the approval of Peary's family and

the National Geographic Society, his remains were dis-interred and relocated to his current grave.

The monument is a white Maine granite sphere with a carved map of the world. A three-inch bronze star representing the North Pole is positioned on the globe. The monument is oriented so this star points north. The design of the monument was in accord with suggestions Admiral Peary dictated to his wife shortly before his death. The monument bears the Latin inscription, "*Inveniam Viam Aut Facium*," meaning "I shall find a way or make one."

9-10: Matthew Alexander Henson, Section 8, Grave S-15-1

38° 52.236' N, 77° 4.107' W

Matthew Henson was born in Charles County, Maryland, and went to sea as a cabin boy on a sailing ship at age twelve. After the captain of his ship died, Henson took a job as a stock clerk in a hat store in Washington, where he met U.S. Navy commander Robert Peary. On the recommendation of the store's owner, Peary hired Henson as a valet. Over the next twenty-two years, Henson accompanied Peary on eight arctic expeditions, several of them in an attempt to become the first to reach the North Pole.

On April 6, 1909, Henson and Peary were nearly at the pole. On the final leg of their journey, Peary instructed Henson to take the lead but stop short of the pole so Peary, the expedition's leader, could reach it first. Somehow, by accident or by his own plan, Henson, an African-American, reached the pole first and planted the American flag before Peary arrived. Henson and two Eskimo assistants then waited nearly forty-five minutes for Peary, who was being pulled on a sled after suffering frostbite of both feet.

When Peary realized what had happened, he was said to be furious and did nothing to give credit to Henson in any way. The prejudices of the day caused the public to ignore Henson's role in the expedition, and Peary was credited with being the first to reach the North Pole.

After returning from the pole, Henson worked for many years in the U.S. Customs Bureau. In 1937, he finally received a semblance of recognition when he was elected to the International Explorers Club in New York. In 1945, the navy awarded him a medal. In 1954, he was a guest of President Dwight Eisenhower at the White House. In 1996, the USNS *Henson* was named for him. Four years later, the National Geographic Society gave him its highest honor, the Hubbard Medal, for distinction in exploration, discovery, and research.

Henson died in 1955 and was buried in a simple grave in Woodlawn Cemetery in New York City. In 1988, at the request of Dr. S. Allen Counter of Harvard University, President Ronald Reagan granted permis-

MATTHEW ALEXANDER HENSON

CO-DISCOVERER OF THE NORTH POLE

AUGUST 8, 1866 — MARCH 9, 1955

"THE LURE OF THE ARCTIC IS TUGGING AT MY HEART.
TO ME THE TRAIL IS CALLING! THE OLD TRAIL·
THE TRAIL THAT IS ALWAYS NEW."

AND HIS BELOVED WIFE

LUCY ROSS HENSON

sion for the bodies of Henson and his wife to be reinterred at Arlington.

9-11: U.S. Coast Guard Memorial, Section 4
38° 52.253' N, 77° 4.097' W

The men and women who have served in the U.S. Coast Guard are memorialized on this monument, which was inspired by two tragic events that occurred within a week and a half of one another in 1918. On September 16, eleven volunteers from the crew of the cutter *Seneca* were lost when an explosion took place on the British steamer *Wellington*, which had been torpedoed in the Bay of Biscay. The men from the *Seneca* were attempting a salvage operation when the explosion occurred. Eight members of the nineteen-man crew survived. Just ten days later, on September 26, the cutter *Tampa* was sunk by an enemy submarine in the British Channel. Tragically, all hands were lost. Both ships had been placed under the navy when the United States entered World War I.

The names of the crewmen of these vessels, as well as those of all Coast Guard personnel who lost their lives during World War I, are inscribed on the sides of the monument. Although the memorial was originally intended to honor those World War I vets, it has come to represent all who served or are serving in the Coast Guard.

The architect of the memorial was George Howe; the sculptor was Gaston Lachaise. The memorial features a bronze sea gull alighting below the Coast Guard motto, *Semper Paratus* ("Always Ready"). Together, the bird and motto symbolize the Coast Guard's role in maintaining security over the nation's maritime territory.

The memorial was dedicated May 23, 1928. Extensive restoration work was completed in 2013, and

U.S. Coast Guard Memorial

the memorial was rededicated May 23, 2013, exactly eighty-five years after the original dedication.

9-12: Don Carlos Faith Jr., Section 4, Grave 3016-RH

38° 52.294' N, 77° 4.087' W

Don Carlos Faith Jr. was born into a military family, his father being Brigadier General Don Carlos Faith Sr. Born August 26, 1918, Faith graduated from Georgetown University and served in the Eighty-second Airborne Division during World War II, taking part in all of the division's combat jumps in North Africa, Italy, France, and Germany. He was awarded two Bronze Stars and was promoted to lieutenant colonel on the staff of General Maxwell Taylor.

After World War II, Faith served in China and Japan. When the war in Korea broke out during the summer of 1950, he was sent with the Seventh Infantry. On November 27, 1950, he performed heroically against a fanatical attack near the Chosin Reservoir, leading several counterattacks and directing the removal of the wounded, despite himself suffering wounds from a fragmentation grenade and small-arms fire. Faith was ultimately killed in the action. He was awarded a Silver Star, later upgraded to the Medal of Honor.

Faith was classified as "Killed in Action, Body Not Recovered." When it became apparent to his family that his body would never be recovered, his father arranged to have his son memorialized on the back side of his own headstone. That headstone is adjacent to Don Car-

los Faith Jr.'s. His father died in 1963, never knowing the whereabouts of his son.

Lieutenant Colonel Faith remained classified as "Killed in Action, Body Not Recovered" for sixty-two years. Then, in 2012, the Joint Prisoners of War/Missing in Action Accounting Command recovered his remains and brought him home. He was buried in Arlington on April 17, 2013.

9-13: USS *Liberty* Memorial (William McGonagle), Section 34

38° 52.305' N, 77° 4.154' W

One of the most controversial events in U.S. military history, the attack on the USS *Liberty*, took place June 8, 1967.

Originally a World War II Victory ship, the *Liberty* had been reactivated and equipped with state-of-the-art electronic surveillance equipment. Armed with only a few .50-caliber machine guns and sailing in international waters, it was near Sinai, positioned to monitor electronic traffic taking place over most of the Arab-Israeli war zone during the Six-Day War. Captain William McGonagle had requested the protection of a destroyer, but his request was denied. That proved fatal about two o'clock that afternoon, when Israeli forces began an attack that would last more than two hours. It started when Israeli fighter jets fired rockets and dropped napalm on the *Liberty*. Three torpedo boats blasted a forty-foot-wide hole below decks, killing twenty-five men almost instantly. Finally, the ship was attacked by helicopters that machine-gunned the ship's life rafts.

Israeli officials quickly contacted Washington, saying the fighter pilots thought the *Liberty* was an Egyptian freighter. President Johnson accepted the explanation and an apology. Israel also paid more than $12 million in compensation. However, several high-ranking members of Johnson's administration and the

Mass grave of Liberty *victims*

military were not satisfied with the Israeli story. Crew members insisted that the *Liberty* was flying a large, brand-new American flag. They also said it carried navy markings and did not look like any Egyptian ship.

The incident has never been resolved, although a U.S. Naval Court of Inquiry determined that the *Liberty* was in international waters, that it was properly marked as to its identity and nationality, and that visibility was excellent in the calm, clear weather.

About a year after the attack, the *Liberty* was scrapped. The ship was awarded the Combat Action Ribbon and the Presidential Unit Citation. Members of the crew received a Navy Cross, several Silver Stars, and 205 Purple Hearts (34 of them posthumously).

In 1968, Captain McGonagle received the Medal of Honor. His citation reads in part,

> For conspicuous gallantry and intrepidity at the risk of his life above and beyond the call of duty. Sailing in international waters, the *Liberty* was attacked without warning by jet fighter aircraft and motor torpedo boats which inflicted many casualties among the crew and caused extreme damage to the ship. Although severely wounded during the first air attack, Capt. McGonagle remained at his battle station on the badly damaged bridge and, with full knowledge of the seriousness of his wounds, subordinated his own welfare to the safety and survival of his command. Steadfastly refusing any treatment which would take him away from his post, he calmly continued to exercise firm command of his ship. Despite continuous exposure to fire, he maneuvered his ship, directed its defense, supervised the control of flooding and fire, and saw to the care of the casualties. Capt. McGonagle's extraordinary valor under these conditions inspired the surviving members of the *Liberty*'s crew, many of them seriously wounded, to heroic efforts to overcome the battle damage and keep the ship afloat. Subsequent to the attack, although in great pain and weak from the loss of blood, Captain McGonagle remained at his battle station and continued to command his ship for more than 17 hours. It was only after rendezvous with a U.S. destroyer that he relinquished personal control of the *Liberty* and permitted himself to be removed from the bridge. Even then, he refused much needed medical attention until convinced that the seriously wounded among his crew had been treated. Capt. McGonagle's superb professionalism, courageous fighting spirit, and valiant leadership saved his ship and many lives. His actions sustain and enhance the finest traditions of the U.S. Naval Service.

A total of 821 rocket and machine-gun holes were later counted in the *Liberty*'s hull. Of the 294 men aboard the ship, 34 were killed and 171 wounded. Of the 34 killed, 15 are buried in Arlington, 6 in the mass grave indicated by the memorial stone on page 155. Captain McGonagle died in 1999 and is buried nearby in Section 34, Grave 208 (38° 52.283' N, 77° 4.193' W).

9-14: Keith C. Clark, Section 34, Grave 10
38° 52.290' N, 77° 4.196' W

He had done it hundreds of times, maybe thousands. In fact, Keith Clark, principal bugler with the U.S. Army Band, had played taps at Arlington's Veterans Day commemoration two weeks prior. President John F. Kennedy had been in attendance.

Clark was born November 21, 1927, in Grand Rapids, Michigan, where he played trumpet with the city's symphony orchestra before joining the army in 1946. He soon became the trumpet soloist with the army band, then was named principal bugler. Clark was based at Fort Myer, Virginia. His duties included sounding taps at military funerals held at Arlington.

Now, on a cold, rainy November 25, 1963, he was called on to play it again. Only this time, the entire world was watching and listening. This time, he was playing taps for the funeral of assassinated president John F. Kennedy.

As the ceremony drew to a close, it was up to the military to perform the time-honored rituals of honoring a fallen leader. A twenty-one-gun salute reverberated across the hills, and now it was time for Sergeant Keith Clark to sound taps. Clark solemnly raised his bugle, pointing it toward Mrs. Kennedy. He had often said he believed that taps should be played specifically for the grieving widow. And he began the mournful tune.

Taps is not a long song. It contains only twenty-four notes. Clark hit the first five of them perfectly. But on the sixth, the note cracked, somewhat akin to a sob. Clark continued flawlessly, brought the bugle down, and saluted the casket. Few thought ill of Clark for what happened. Instead, his mistake, if it could be called that, was viewed as capturing the grief of the American people. Some believed it was the perfect way for taps to be presented on that particular day. He would receive hundreds of letters of support in the weeks following the funeral, something that helped the perfectionist deal with the emotion of what he viewed as a missed note.

Clark refused to make excuses for what happened,

Bugle that Clark used at President Kennedy's funeral

although others quickly jumped to his defense. In addition to the pressure of performing on the world stage, he had been standing for several hours in a cold rain, unable to warm up his bugle because of the approaching funeral procession. He was further compromised by a television producer who insisted he stand directly in front of the firing party to improve the angle for the television cameras. The result was that the twenty-one-gun volley was still ringing in his ears when he was called on to play. Under the conditions, the result was understandable.

Clark retired from the army a few years later to write, teach music, and perform. He wrote *A Select Bibliography for the Study of Hymns* and went on to collect more than nine thousand volumes of hymns and books about hymns. His collection is now in the possession of Regent University in Virginia.

Fittingly, Keith Clark's death came shortly after he played a concert. He died of an aortic aneurysm on January 11, 2002, some thirty-nine years after capturing the mood and hearts of America on that cold, rainy day. His bugle, pictured on page 157, is now on display in the Arlington National Cemetery Welcome Center.

9-15: Ira Hamilton Hayes, Section 34, Grave 479A
38° 52.292' N, 77° 4.227' W

Ira Hamilton Hayes was a Pima Indian, born on the Gila River Indian Reservation in south-central Arizona on January 12, 1923. He left high school after completing two years of study, served in the Civilian Conservation Corps for two months, then took a job as a carpenter.

In August 1942, he enlisted in the Marine Corps Reserve. Following boot camp, he qualified as a parachutist and joined Company B, Third Parachute Battalion, Divisional Special Troops, Third Marine Division, at Camp Elliott, California. On March 14, 1943, he shipped out

to New Caledonia. A month later, his unit was redesignated Company K, Third Parachute Battalion, First Marine Parachute Regiment. In October, Hayes took part in the occupation of Vella Lavella, then moved north, where he fought at Bougainville.

Hayes returned home in February 1944. When the parachute units were disbanded, he was transferred to Company E, Second Battalion, Twenty-eighth Marines, Fifth Marine Division. After four months of training in Hawaii, he sailed with his unit to Iwo Jima.

On February 23, 1945, the fifth day of the Battle of Iwo Jima, Hayes and the marines were fighting on Mount Suribachi, an extinct volcano. The Japanese had honeycombed Mount Suribachi with tunnels and caves made into a series of gun emplacements, pillboxes, and storage depots. After hours of fierce fighting, the marines prevailed and raised a flag. However, the flag was deemed too small to be seen readily by troops on the beach, and a larger flag was dispatched to the summit.

Sergeant Michael Strank (see Chapter 12, site 12-

Hayes

8), Corporal Harlon Block, Private First Class Hayes, and Private First Class Franklin Sousley climbed Mount Suribachi, stringing communication wire as they went. Near the top, they met Corporal Rene Gagnon (see Chapter 2, site 2-9), who was carrying the flag that was to replace the smaller one. Shortly after reaching the summit, they were joined by a sixth man, initially thought to be navy corpsman John Bradley. However, in 2014, a controversy arose when two amateur historians provided compelling evidence that the sixth man may have been Private First Class Harold Schultz, who died in 1995. Further evidence was offered that Bradley's participation was limited to the raising of the earlier, smaller flag. As the six men raised the flag, Associated Press photographer Joe Rosenthal snapped one of

the most famous photos in history, one that brought him a Pulitzer Prize. Their mission accomplished, the six men resumed the fight. By the time the island was taken, Strank, Block, and Sousley were dead.

In April, Hayes returned to the United States, where he participated with Bradley, Gagnon, and a fourth marine, Technical Sergeant Keyes Beech, on a month-long promotional tour for war bonds. At the end of the tour, Hayes returned to his company in Hawaii. He was honorably discharged in December.

The list of Corporal Hayes's decorations and medals includes the Commendation Ribbon with "V" device, the Presidential Unit Citation with one star (for Iwo Jima), the Asiatic-Pacific Campaign Medal with four stars (for Vella Lavella, Bougainville, the consolidation of the northern Solomons, and Iwo Jima), the American Campaign Medal, and the World War II Victory Medal.

When the war ended, Hayes had difficulty adjusting. He turned to alcohol and lived a drifter's life. On January 24, 1955, he was found dead of exposure in an abandoned hut on the Pima reservation. He was thirty-two.

9-16: Frank W. Buckles, Section 34, Grave 579-A
38° 52.309' N, 77° 4.247' W

Frank Woodruff Buckles was born February 1, 1901, on a farm near Bethany, Missouri. When the United States entered World War I, he tried to enlist in the Marine Corps at age sixteen. The marines turned him down, saying he was too young and too short. He next tried the navy, which turned him down for flat feet. Determined to do his part in the war effort, he turned to the army. Having learned from his experience with the marines, he lied about his age, and the army accepted him in August 1917. He heard that the quickest route to France was to become an ambulance driver, so he immediately volunteered and was accepted.

In December 1917, Buckles set sail for England on the *Carpathia*, the ship that had gained fame in 1912 by helping save survivors of the *Titanic*. Although he never got closer than thirty miles from the trenches on the Western Front, he served in various locations in France, driving military vehicles and ambulances. At war's end, Buckles escorted German prisoners of war back to their homeland, then returned to the United States. Over the next several years, he worked for various steamship companies.

He was on business in Manila when the Japanese occupied that city after the attack on Pearl Harbor in December 1941. Buckles was taken prisoner and spent the next three and a half years in the Los Baños prison camp. Suffering from malnutrition from the poor diet in the camp, he saw his weight drop to less than a hundred pounds. Despite his frailty, and suffering from beriberi, Buckles was still able to lead his fellow prisoners in calisthenics. Allied forces finally liberated the camp on February 23, 1945.

After retiring from steamship work in the mid-1950s, Buckles ran a cattle ranch in Charles Town, West Virginia, where he was said to be riding his tractor at the age of 106. In one of his many interviews, he was asked about the secret of his long life. His answer was simple: "When you start to die, don't." On February 27, 2011, however, time caught up with Frank Buckles, and he died of natural causes at his home at 110. He had been the last living American veteran of World War I.

Buckles received the World War I Victory Medal and qualified for four Overseas Service Bars. In 1941, he received the Army of Occupation of Germany Medal for his postwar service in Europe during 1919.

Because he was a civilian when he was imprisoned by the Japanese, Buckles did not qualify under the criteria for the Prisoner of War Medal. In 1999, he was further honored when French president Jacques Chirac presented him with France's Legion of Honour.

Never having been in combat, Buckles did not meet the criteria for burial at Arlington. However, special permission was secured on March 19, 2008, three years before his death. When Buckles died, President Barack Obama issued a presidential order that the American flag be flown at half-staff on all government buildings, embassies, and the White House on March 15, the date of Buckles's funeral. He was buried in Arlington with full military honors after lying in state in the Memorial Amphitheater chapel. He lies near his former commander, General John J. Pershing.

9-17: John J. Pershing, Section 34, Grave S-19-LH
38° 52.315' N, 77° 4.228' W

Ask someone to name an American general from World War I and you will be hard pressed to get a name other than John Joseph "Black Jack" Pershing. Pershing was born September 13, 1860, on the eve of the Civil War in a shanty on the farm of Judge Meredith Brown near Laclede, Missouri. In 1879, he taught school at Prairie Mound, nine miles from Laclede. For the next three summers, he attended the state normal school at Kirksville, Missouri.

In the spring of 1882, Pershing saw an announcement for a competitive examination for an appointment to West Point. His sister suggested he try it. He took her advice and won the appointment, ultimately graduating thirtieth in a class of seventy-seven. He was elected president of the class of 1886 and each year held the highest possible rank in the Cadet Battalion.

After graduation, Pershing was assigned to active service against the last of the Apaches. In the early 1890s, he taught military science and tactics at the University of Nebraska while attending classes at the university's law school, from which he graduated in 1893. Over the next several years, he taught at West Point, served as regimental quartermaster of the Nineteenth Cavalry, directed the Division of Customs and Insular Affairs, fought against Moro insurrectionists in the Philippines, attended the Army War College, and patrolled the border with Mexico with the Eighth Brigade.

On March 15, 1915, Pershing led an expedition into Mexico to capture Pancho Villa. Despite a shortage of supplies and the Mexican government's refusal to allow American troops to use the railroads, Pershing and his ten thousand troops pushed 350 miles into Mexico and routed Villa's revolutionaries, severely wounding Villa in the process.

On August 27, 1915, tragedy visited Pershing when

a fire raged through his quarters at the Presidio, killing Mrs. Pershing and three of their four children. Only his son Warren survived. After the funerals, Pershing dealt with his sorrow by working excessively long hours, causing many to fear for his sanity.

When the United States declared war on Germany on April 3, 1917, Pershing assumed command of the American Expeditionary Forces. Starting with a regular army of only twenty-five thousand men, Pershing developed training programs that rapidly produced the finest, most far-flung army the world had ever seen. In the span of eighteen months, he produced a fighting force of two million men.

In the spring of 1918, when the Germans began their last, desperate drive on Allied positions, Pershing set aside any dreams of glory and placed the American troops under the command of General Ferdinand Foch of France, who had assumed the supreme command of Allied armies in Europe. This united front overwhelmed the Germans and was instrumental in bringing the war to a close.

In 1919, Congress recognized Pershing's achievements by creating and promoting him to the new rank of general of the armies of the United States. In 1921, he was appointed chief of staff of the U.S. Army. In 1922, he established the U.S. Army Band, known today as "Pershing's Own."

In 1924, at the age of sixty-four, he retired from active duty. Pershing passed away at Walter Reed Army Medical Center in Washington on July 15, 1948, at the age of eighty-seven. He was buried in a common grave site near his boys from World War I, according to his wishes. His two grandsons lie beside him.

9-18: Robert R. Scott, Section 34, Grave 3939
38° 52.388' N, 77° 4.138' W

Navy machinist's mate first class Robert Raymond

Scott was born July 13, 1915, in Massillon, Ohio. He had been in the service about three years when the Japanese attacked Pearl Harbor on December 7, 1941. Scott was aboard the USS *California* that day, a *Tennessee*-class battleship, where he was assigned to an air compressor that was vital to the ship's weapons-firing systems. Moored in Battleship Row, the *California* presented an easy target to the attackers. Struck by torpedoes and bombs, it was soon in danger of sinking. Scott's compartment was flooded by a torpedo hit, forcing an evacuation of the area. Scott helped with the evacuation and then remained behind in an effort to keep the weapons systems functioning. Refusing to abandon his position, he vowed to provide air as long as the guns kept firing.

When the action ended, a hundred of the *California*'s crew were lost and sixty-two wounded. Scott was one of the sailors who lost his life. He was posthumously awarded the Medal of Honor for his "conspicuous

devotion to duty, extraordinary courage and complete disregard of his own life."

On July 20, 1943, the navy named a destroyer escort the USS *Scott* in recognition of his heroism.

9-19: USS *Serpens* Memorial, Section 34
38° 52.442' N, 77° 4.120' W

On the night of January 29, 1945, the largest single disaster suffered by the U.S. Coast Guard in World War II occurred when the 14,250-ton ammunition ship USS *Serpens* exploded off Lunga Beach, Guadalcanal, British Solomon Islands. Servicemen had been loading

depth charges when the *Serpens* exploded, causing the deaths of 250 men, including 193 Coast Guard sailors, 56 army soldiers, and Dr. Harry M. Levin, a U.S. Public Health Service surgeon. Of the Coast Guardsmen, 17 were regular Coast Guard and 176 were reservists. None of the dead could be identified. Only two crewmen who were aboard survived the explosion: Seaman First Class Kelsie K. Kemp of Barren Springs, Virginia, and Seaman First Class George S. Kennedy of San Marcos, Texas. The lives of 2 officers and 6 additional crewmen were spared by being ashore on administrative business.

For the next two years, the Coast Guard believed an enemy attack had caused the blast. However, on

June 10, 1949, it was announced that the explosion was not the result of enemy action.

The 250 remains were originally buried at the army, navy, and marine cemetery on Guadalcanal with full military honors and religious services. In 1949, they were repatriated under the program for the return of World War II dead. They were placed in fifty-two caskets and buried in twenty-eight graves near the memorial in Arlington that is inscribed with their names. The memorial was dedicated November 16, 1950.

9-20: Henry Johnson, Section 25, Grave 64
38° 52.475' N, 77° 4.085' W

Born in poverty, Henry Johnson enlisted in the all-black Fifteenth New York National Guard Regiment, which was renamed the 369th Infantry Regiment when it shipped out to France during World War I. Known as the Harlem Hellfighters, the unit mostly performed menial labor there, unloading ships and digging latrines.

When the French Fourth Army found itself short on troops, Johnson's regiment was sent to assist. The French, unconcerned by the regiment's racial makeup, placed it on the western edge of the Argonne Forest, in France's Champagne region. There, Johnson and Needham Roberts were assigned sentry duty on the shift from midnight to four in the morning. Johnson would tell an American reporter later that he thought it was "crazy" to send untrained men out at the risk of the rest of the troops, but he nevertheless did as he was told.

He and Roberts weren't on duty long when German snipers began firing at them. The two American soldiers lined up a box of grenades in their dugout for use if a raiding party came near. A few hours after midnight, they heard the sound of wire cutters working on the perimeter fence. Johnson told Roberts to run back to camp to warn the rest of the troops. The apprehen-

sive Johnson then hurled a grenade toward the fence, bringing heavy gunfire and grenades from the Germans in response. Hearing the activity, Roberts returned to help Johnson fight, but he was immediately hit with a grenade and wounded too badly to hold his weapon. Johnson had him lie in the trench and hand him grenades, which Johnson threw at the Germans until the supply was exhausted.

Sensing that the Americans were now defenseless, the Germans advanced. Johnson was shot in the head and lip but continued to fire his rifle into the darkness. He was then shot in his side, then his hand, but he kept shooting until his French rifle jammed.

With the Germans now on top of him, Johnson

swung his rifle like a club until its stock splintered. Then he was felled by a blow to his head. Through his daze, he saw that the Germans were trying to take Roberts prisoner. Dizzily standing, he used his only remaining weapon, a bolo knife. Slashing at the Germans, he stabbed one in the stomach, felled a lieutenant, and was shot in his arm as he drove his knife into the side of a soldier who had climbed on his back. Fighting ferociously, Johnson managed to drag Roberts away from the Germans, who retreated when they heard French and American forces advancing.

When the reinforcements arrived, Johnson passed out and was taken to a field hospital. By daylight, an inspection of the area showed that he had killed four Germans and wounded an estimated ten more, despite suffering and surviving an amazing twenty-one wounds in hand-to-hand combat. The unassuming Johnson saw nothing special about what he did, saying he was only fighting for his life.

Both Johnson and Roberts were presented with the Croix de Guerre, France's highest military honor. Johnson's medal also contained the coveted gold palm for extraordinary valor.

On Johnson's return to the United States, former president Theodore Roosevelt called him one of the "five bravest Americans" to serve in the war. However, Johnson soon faded into history. His discharge records failed to mention his injuries, so Johnson never received a Purple Heart. With no records to support a claim, he was also denied a disability allowance. He took a job as a porter at the Albany, New York, train station but turned to alcohol and died, destitute, in 1929 at age thirty.

For decades, Henry Johnson was just another war veteran who died too young. He was thought to have been buried in a pauper's grave, but nobody knew for certain, nor did they care. Then historians presented his case to President William Clinton, who awarded Johnson the Purple Heart in 1996. Five years later, however, it was determined that Johnson had not been buried in a pauper's grave but was actually resting in Arlington. Upon this finding, the army awarded him the Distinguished Service Cross.

As welcome as the award was to Johnson's supporters, who were growing in number as his story became known, they felt he deserved more. Finally, a communiqué from the late general Black Jack Pershing praising Johnson's heroics was found. This final documentation was all that was needed. On June 2, 2015, President Barack Obama awarded Johnson the highest award America can bestow on a soldier, the Medal of Honor. Nearly a century after he had simply, as he put it, "fought for my life," Henry Johnson finally received the recognition he had so long deserved.

9-21: Bernard P. Bell, Section 25, Grave 3840
38° 52.435' N, 77° 3.999' W

Hailing from Calhoun County, West Virginia, Bernard Pious Bell served as a sergeant in the 142nd Infantry Regiment, Thirty-sixth Infantry Division, in World War II.

On December 18, 1944, Sergeant Bell and 8 other men of the regiment encountered 150 Germans in front of a schoolhouse in Mittelwihr, France. While his men covered him, Bell ran to the schoolhouse, where he surprised 2 guards at the door and took them prisoner without firing a shot. Cautiously entering the cellar, he found and captured 26 more Germans.

The next day, the Germans bombarded the house with artillery and mortar fire, heavily damaging Bell's communications. Under fire, he repaired the radio equipment and ran through crossfire to update his commander.

At dawn on the third morning, a German tank

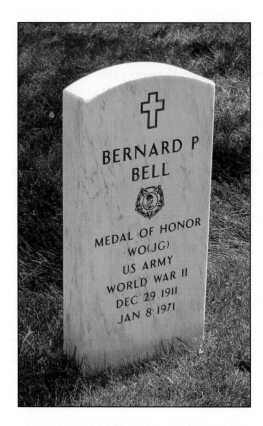

his eight-man squad to drive back approximately 150 of the enemy, killing at least 87 and capturing 42. Personally, he killed more than 20 and captured 33 prisoners."

Bell died January 8, 1971.

9-22: Marie Therese Rossi-Cayton, Section 8, Grave 9872

38° 52.302' N, 77° 3.957' W

Born in 1959 in New Jersey, Marie Therese Rossi-Cayton served as a pilot with the 101st Airborne Division. When the Gulf War began, she was deployed to

fired several rounds into the school, demolishing portions of the upper levels of the building. Despite the continuing assault by the tank, Bell climbed into the damaged second floor and directed artillery fire, causing the tank to withdraw. Later, he pointed out several Germans hidden behind a wall to an Allied tank, directing the tank's machine gunners to fire on the Germans as they ran for safety.

Eight months later, on August 23, 1945, the thirty-three-year-old Bell stepped forward to receive the Medal of Honor from President Harry S. Truman. Bell's citation stated in part, "By his intrepidity and bold, aggressive leadership, Technical Sergeant Bell enabled

Saudi Arabia, where she commanded Company B, Second Battalion, 159th Aviation Regiment, Eighteenth Aviation Brigade, a CH-47D Chinook helicopter company.

On the night of March 1, 1991, she led her squadron of Chinooks on a mission inside Iraq, delivering fuel and ammunition in the early stages of the ground assault known as Operation Desert Storm. With bad weather reducing visibility, she and her crew flew into an unlighted microwave tower while returning to their base, killing all on board.

Major Rossi-Cayton's death came at age thirty-two, just ten months after her marriage to Chief Warrant Officer John Anderson Cayton, also a pilot in the Gulf War. She was the first woman in American military history to serve as an aviation commander during combat and the first woman pilot to fly combat missions.

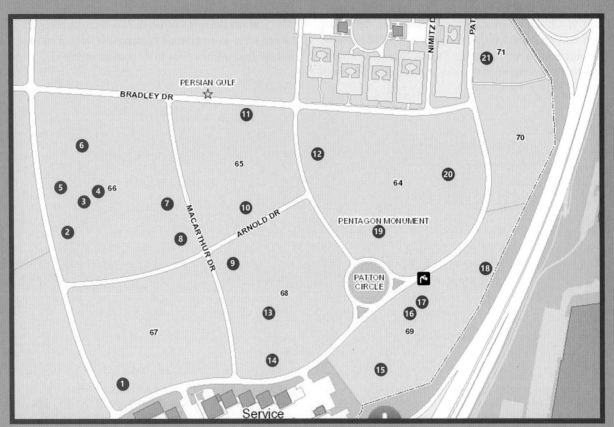

10-1: Rudolph B. Davila, Section 67, Grave 3457

38° 52.310' N, 77° 3.884' W

Rudolph Davila was born in El Paso, Texas, on April 27, 1916, to a Filipino mother and a Spanish father. He enlisted in the army in March 1941 and was placed in Company H, Seventh Infantry Regiment, Third Infantry Division.

On May 28, 1944, Davila, now a second lieutenant, and his men were in action outside Artena, Italy. Caught in an exposed position on a hillside, they were taking heavy enemy fire. Below them, a 130-man rifle company lay pinned down in tall grass. Just behind them, two dozen men from the platoon had taken refuge, afraid to move into position.

Davila crawled fifty yards to the nearest machine gun and opened fire as enemy bullets struck his tripod and passed between his legs. He emptied three 250-round ammunition chests into the German position before turning the gun over to one of his men. He then crawled forward and directed fire until two German machine guns were neutralized. Once Davila's three remaining machine guns were positioned, the enemy forces were pushed back two hundred yards to a rear position.

Ignoring a painful leg wound, Davila reached a burning tank and crawled onto the turret, where he engaged more enemy troops. Then, dodging bullets, he scampered toward a small house that had been taken by German troops. Crawling the last twenty yards, he entered the house and killed five enemy soldiers. With the downstairs cleared, he rushed to an upper floor, where he opened fire and destroyed two more machine-gun emplacements.

An officer in the company put Davila's name forward for the Medal of Honor, a recommendation that was downgraded to a Distinguished Service Cross.

A few months later, he was badly wounded again, struck in the chest by a tank shell that ricocheted off a tree. Thirteen surgeries saved his life but left him with a permanently shriveled and paralyzed right arm.

When the war ended, Davila returned home and settled into civilian life, working as a teacher in Los Angeles. Over the ensuing years, his wife, Harriet, fought to get her husband the Medal of Honor she believed he had earned. She researched records, wrote letters, and made phone calls to government officials. Then, in 1996, Congress directed the army to review the records of highly decorated servicemen of Asian and Hispanic descent to determine if they had been unfairly denied the military's highest award for valor. Four years later, in June 2000, the army announced that Davila and twenty-one others were to be awarded the Medal of Honor. Only seven of the recipients were still alive. Sadly, Davila's wife and biggest supporter had died just six months before, never knowing her husband would receive the medal.

On January 26, 2002, Rudolph Davila died of cancer at age eighty-five. He was cremated and laid to rest with full military honors in Arlington on March 29, 2002.

10-2: Francis Z. Lupo, Section 66, Grave 7489
38° 52.398' N, 77° 3.956' W

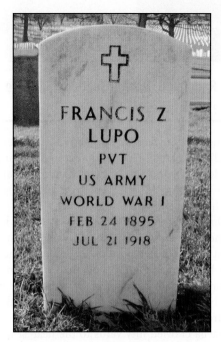

The First Infantry Division took 12,228 officers and enlisted soldiers into the Second Battle of the Marne as part of a combined French-American attack on German forces near Soissons, France, in 1918. Of those, 8,305 were killed, wounded, taken prisoner, or listed as missing. One of the missing was Francis Lupo, a member of Company E, Eighteenth Infantry Regiment.

Lupo was born in Cincinnati on February 24, 1895, and dropped out of school after the fifth grade. When World War I broke out, he was working as an eight-dollar-a-week "supply man" for the *Cincinnati Times-Star*, delivering papers to newsboys. Lupo never married and had no children.

He was drafted on October 3, 1917. Following training, he left with his regiment for Europe on March 14, 1918, and landed in France twelve days later. His personnel records indicate that he stood just five feet tall, weighed 120 pounds, and wore a size five and a half boot.

On June 2, 1918, he went into the line near the battered village of Cantigny. His Second Battalion was held in reserve on July 18 as two American divisions and tens of thousands of French troops began the at-

tack. On July 21, Lupo and the rest of Company E went into action. That was the last day anyone saw him.

That is, until 2003, some eighty-five years later. A construction project planned for the area brought an archaeological team in to comply with French law. While conducting its survey, the team discovered human remains. With the remains were scraps of clothing, some uniform buttons, bits of a gas mask, a rusted canteen cup handle, the stem of a pipe, a rusted straight razor, a warped No. 2 pencil, and a comb with seven teeth missing. Two other items were also found: a boot, size five and a half, and a wallet with what appeared to be the name *Francis Lupo* embossed on it. The French handed the items over to American officials for analysis.

In 2004, the bones and artifacts were delivered to the Defense Department's Joint POW/MIA Accounting Command in Hawaii, where the identification process began. The wallet and the boot provided excellent starting points, and it wasn't long until Francis Lupo's remains were identified. It was the first time the remains of a World War I service member had been recovered and identified since the Pentagon established an office in the 1960s with the specific mission of identifying war dead.

A second doughboy had been buried with Lupo, and their bones were mingled. The archaeologists speculated that the two had been placed in a bomb crater and hastily buried as the battle raged. Four days later, when the action ended, the battlefield grave was either forgotten or obliterated by the fighting. The second set of remains has yet to be identified.

The army searched for Lupo's next of kin. Genealogists worked out a family tree so army representatives could get in touch with his oldest living relative. After several months, a distant cousin was found in Kentucky; that relative made the funeral arrangements.

It was said that Francis Lupo's mother never accepted her son's death. She often wept and would open a window, calling out for him to come home. Although she had long since passed away, her son finally came home eighty-eight years after his death. The American service member longest missing in action had been found. He was buried in Arlington on September 26, 2006.

10-3: William J. Maddox Jr., Section 66, Grave 5829

38° 52.422' N, 77° 3.936' W

William J. Maddox Jr. was born in Newburgh, New York, on May 22, 1921. Raised in Washington, D.C., he earned his undergraduate degree from Michigan State University and a master's degree from George Washington University.

After receiving his commission in 1943, he served

in the Philippines and then in Japan in the latter stages of World War II. He was posted a second time to Japan and then to Germany. He was also a combat pilot in the Korean War and served three tours of duty in Vietnam, amassing 4,000 combat hours among his total of 10,600 flying hours. At various times in his tours in Vietnam, he commanded a battalion, brigade, or aviation group.

Maddox was one of the army's most highly decorated officers. His honors included the Distinguished Service Medal, four Purple Hearts, the Silver Star with three bronze oak leaf clusters, 127 Air Medals, eight Distinguished Flying Crosses, the Soldier's Medal, and five Legions of Merit. In 1976, he was inducted into the army's Aviation Hall of Fame.

He retired in 1977 as commander of the Army Aviation Center and School in Fort Rucker, Alabama. General William Maddox died of sepsis on January 5, 2001, at age seventy-nine.

10-4: John Joseph Tominac, Section 66, Grave 5141

38° 52.423' N, 77° 3.927' W

John Tominac was born April 29, 1922, in Conemaugh, Pennsylvania, a blue-collar community on the outskirts of Johnstown. He was a neighbor of Michael Strank (see Chapter 12, site 12-8), an Iwo Jima flag raiser. Tominac graduated from the University of Southern Mississippi and joined the army in November 1941, just weeks before the Japanese attack on Pearl Harbor. Assigned to Company I, Fifteenth Infantry Regiment, Third Infantry Division, he rose to the rank of first lieutenant by late 1944.

On September 12 of that year, his platoon, battered to less than 50 percent strength by five months of nearly daily fighting, was ordered to take control of the crossroads outside the French town of Saulx de Vesoul. The mission was expected to be an easy one, since intelligence indicated that German troops had pulled out. Tominac and his men quickly learned differently. They got within sight of the crossroads before walking into an ambush. Several of Tominac's men were wounded, three of them mortally. Unable to move his troops forward or back, Tominac took matters into his own hands. Ordering suppressing fire, he leaped from his position and raced toward the enemy, alone in his mission. Crouching, he covered the fifty yards of open terrain, firing his machine gun as he went. He killed the three-man crew of a German machine gun, providing temporary relief for his men. Gathering a squad, he then led an attack on a second group of Germans, killing thirty of them.

Now on the outskirts of town, Tominac led his troops toward a third group of Germans controlling the road. When one of his supporting tanks was hit by an enemy shell and burst into flames, Tominac was struck by shrapnel and suffered a painful shoulder wound.

With the tank rolling uncontrolled toward the enemy, Tominac jumped onto the turret and fired its .50-caliber machine gun at the roadblock. His actions forced the enemy troops to withdraw.

Just before the tank exploded, Tominac jumped to safety. Refusing to evacuate for treatment of his wound, he had his sergeant remove the shrapnel fragments from his shoulder with a pocketknife, then continued the attack. Rushing forward, he led his men in a hand-grenade assault on the enemy position, collecting thirty-two enemy prisoners. Altogether, Tominac was directly responsible for the capture of at least sixty enemy troops. For his actions, he was awarded the Medal of Honor on March 29, 1945.

Tominac remained in the army after the war, reaching the rank of colonel before retiring. He went on to serve in both Korea and Vietnam, earning the

Legion of Merit with oak leaf cluster, the Bronze Star with "V" device and oak leaf cluster, the Purple Heart, the French Fourragère, the Distinguished Unit Citation with oak leaf cluster, and the Combat Infantry Badge, in addition to numerous campaign and service medals. He died July 11, 1998, at age seventy-six. His hometown named a bridge in his honor.

10-5: John L. Levitow, Section 66, Grave 7107
38° 52.430' N, 77° 3.957' W

Born November 1, 1945, in Hartford, Connecticut, John Levitow joined the air force in June 1966. He was trained as a loadmaster, a job requiring him to set the ejection and ignition timer controls on Mark 24 magnesium flares and pass them to the gunner for deployment. These flares burned for about three minutes at four thousand degrees.

On February 24, 1969, Levitow was the loadmaster on an AC-47 gunship known as "Spooky 71" on a combat mission near Saigon. It was his 181st combat sortie. The aircraft had been airborne for four and a half hours when muzzle flashes became visible on the ground outside the Long Binh Army Base. The gunship's pilot banked his plane to engage the enemy below while Levitow and the gunner began deploying flares through the open cargo door.

As the gunner held a flare with his finger through the pull ring attached to the safety pin, the plane suffered a major hit. A North Vietnamese 82-millimeter round had landed on top of the right wing and exploded inside the wing frame. Shrapnel peppered the gunship, wounding all crew members in the back of the plane. Levitow had forty shrapnel wounds in his legs, side, and back, while the gunship itself had thirty-five hundred shrapnel holes, one of them three feet in diameter. As Levitow struggled to stand, he noticed that the man beside him was badly wounded and dangerously close to

the cargo door. He moved the man to safety, then observed a smoking flare on the floor in front of him. The flare had been knocked from the gunner's hand and was rolling amid cans that contained nineteen thousand rounds of live ammunition. The flare could burn through metal in less than twenty seconds if it ignited, turning the craft into an inferno.

Weak from loss of blood and partially paralyzed on his right side, Levitow realized he was closest to the flare. While the plane pitched as the pilot struggled to regain control, the fully armed flare rolled around the floor, eluding Levitow's grasp. He had no idea how much time remained on the flare's fuse, but he knew it would ignite in a matter of seconds. He threw himself onto the flare and, holding it close to his body, dragged himself back to the open cargo door, leaving a trail of blood behind him. At the instant he threw the flare through the door, it ignited in the air but was clear of the aircraft, saving the entire crew.

Seriously wounded, Levitow was flown to a hospital in Japan. After he recovered, he returned to Vietnam and flew twenty more combat missions before returning home.

On Armed Forces Day, May 14, 1970, President Richard Nixon presented Levitow with the Medal of Honor in recognition of his heroism. Levitow became the lowest-ranking airman in history to earn the honor.

After his air force service, Levitow worked on programs to benefit veterans. He died of cancer at age fifty-five at his home in Connecticut on November 8, 2000. In his honor, the Levitow Honor Graduate Award recognizes the top professional military education graduate from the air force's Airman Leadership School. In addition, the 737th Training Group Headquarters building at Lackland Air Force Base was named in his honor. And in 1998, the Air Mobility Command named a C-17 Globemaster III after him; the *Spirit of Sgt. John L. Levitow* was the first aircraft named for an enlisted person. Finally, Hurlburt Field in Florida honored Levitow in 1998 by making him part of its Walk of Fame, which honors Medal of Honor recipients.

10-6: David Mathieson Walker, Section 66, Grave 5191

38° 52.466' N, 77° 3.935' W

Born May 20, 1944, in Columbus, Georgia, David Mathieson Walker was raised in Eustis, Florida, and graduated from the U.S. Naval Academy in 1966. He then received flight training and was designated a naval aviator in December 1967. From there, he went to Naval Air Station Miramar in California for further assignment to fly F-4 Phantoms from the carriers USS *Enterprise* and USS *America*.

In January 1972, Walker served as an experimental and engineering test pilot in the flight test division at the Naval Air Test Center, Patuxent River, Maryland. While there, he participated in the navy's preliminary evaluation and Board of Inspection and Survey trials of the F-14 Tomcat. He also tested modifications to the F-4 Phantom. In 1975, Walker was assigned to Fighter

Squadron 142, stationed at Naval Air Station Oceana, Virginia, and was deployed to the Mediterranean Sea twice aboard the USS *America*. In 1978, he was selected by NASA to the first pool of astronauts hired to fly shuttle missions. Over his NASA career, he would fly four shuttle missions, three of them as mission commander.

His first space flight came in November 1984, when he served as pilot on STS 51-A, the second flight of the space shuttle *Discovery*. During that flight, which lasted nearly eight days, the crew deployed two communication satellites and conducted the first space salvage mission in history, retrieving two inoperable communication satellites for return to earth.

His second flight was his first as a shuttle commander, on *Atlantis*'s STS-30 mission in May 1989. Walker and his crew successfully deployed the Magellan spacecraft, the first planetary probe to be released from the space shuttle. Magellan arrived at Venus in August 1990 and successfully mapped 95 percent of the planet's surface.

The *Atlantis* mission was nearly his last for NASA. On Walker's return to earth, President George H. W. Bush invited him and his crew to the White House to be honored. While flying a T-38 jet trainer to those ceremonies, Walker came within a hundred feet of a Pan Am jetliner just outside Washington. This incident resulted in an investigation, during which he was grounded for flight-rule infractions. The investigation raised questions over what role air traffic controllers may have played in the incident, however, and Walker was reinstated to his astronaut duties in 1991.

In December 1992, he made his third space flight, this time in command of a five-member crew on STS-53 aboard *Discovery*. During the seven-day mission, the crew deployed a classified Department of Defense payload and performed several scientific experiments.

Walker's final mission came in September 1995 as shuttle commander on *Endeavour*. The STS-69 crew deployed and retrieved two payloads during the flight, which lasted nearly eleven days.

After logging more than 7,500 hours of flying time, including more than 6,500 in jet aircraft and approximately 725 in space, Walker retired from NASA in April 1996. Among his many awards were the Distinguished Flying Cross, the Legion of Merit, two Defense Meritorious Service Medals, six Navy Air Medals, two NASA Distinguished Service Medals, the NASA Outstanding Leadership Medal, and four NASA Space Flight Medals.

Walker died April 23, 2001, of cancer in Houston, Texas.

10-7: Charles E. Durning, Section 66, Grave 127
38° 52.423' N, 77° 3.846' W

Character actor Charles Durning was born February 28, 1923, in Highland Falls, New York. He was exposed to the military at an early age, since his mother worked as a laundress at the nearby U.S. Military Academy. Durning had five sisters and four brothers; all his sisters died in childhood from smallpox or scarlet fever.

Drafted into service in World War II, Durning landed at Normandy on D-Day, June 6, 1944. Nine days later, he was seriously wounded by a German mine, earning the first of his three Purple Hearts. Sent to England to recover, he returned to action just in time to take part in the Battle of the Bulge, where he earned his second Purple Heart, this time for bayonet wounds suffered in hand-to-hand combat. He earned his third Purple Heart in March 1945 when he suffered severe chest wounds. He spent the rest of the war recovering in the United States.

Following his discharge in January 1946, Durning took acting classes and bit parts in various New York stage productions. He got his break in 1973 with his role in *The Sting* and went on to perform in more than a hundred films. He also acted in live stage productions, did voice-overs, and played in several television movies and miniseries. He received two Academy Award nominations, six Emmy nominations, a Tony Award, and four Golden Globe nominations, including a win in 1991 for Best Supporting Actor. In January 2008, he received a Lifetime Achievement Award from the Screen Actors Guild and a star on the Hollywood Walk of Fame.

Durning was awarded the Silver and Bronze Stars for valor and the World War II Victory Medal. In 2008, the French consul presented him with the National Order of the Legion of Honor. Durning served a year as chairman of the U.S. National Salute to Hospitalized Veterans and for many years as guest speaker at the National Memorial Day Concert, held in Washington.

He died on Christmas Eve 2012 at age eighty-nine.

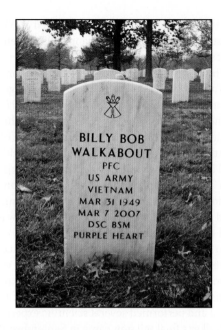

10-8: Billy Bob Walkabout, Section 66, Grave 59
38° 52.401' N, 77° 3.838' W

Billy Bob Walkabout, a Cherokee of the Blue Holly Clan, was born in Cherokee County, Oklahoma, on March 31, 1949. He graduated from high school in 1968 and joined the army soon after, serving in Company F, Fifty-eighth Infantry, 101st Airborne Division.

Walkabout was sent to Vietnam, where he would spend a total of twenty-three months. On November 20, 1968, he and twelve other soldiers went on a special mission into enemy territory. A firefight erupted that lasted several hours. All those with Walkabout were killed or wounded. Walkabout himself suffered severe wounds.

When extraction helicopters arrived, the lead man began moving toward the pickup zone, only to be struck by automatic weapon fire. Walkabout immediately stood and delivered steady suppressive fire on the attackers to allow other team members to pull the wounded man back. He then administered first aid to the soldier. As the wounded man was being loaded onto the evacuation helicopter, the enemy attacked again. Under heavy fire, Sergeant Walkabout positioned himself so he could place continuous rifle fire on the attackers. A command-detonated mine exploded, instantly killing three men and wounding others. The badly wounded Walkabout crawled from man to man administering first aid, reviving one man by heart massage. He then coordinated gunship and tactical air strikes on enemy positions. When evacuation helicopters arrived a second time, he worked single-handedly under fire to get his disabled men aboard. He refused to be extracted until all the casualties were evacuated and reinforcements arrived.

For his actions, Walkabout initially was awarded a Silver Star, which was upgraded to the Distinguished Service Cross. He also earned a Purple Heart, a Bronze Star, and the Army Commendation Medal. He is believed to be the most decorated Native American soldier of the Vietnam War.

Walkabout retired at the rank of second lieutenant. He experienced complications related to his exposure to the Agent Orange defoliant used in Vietnam and underwent dialysis three times a week. He was on a kidney transplant waiting list when he died of pneumonia and renal failure on March 7, 2007. He was fifty-seven years old. Following Cherokee tradition, Walkabout's family and friends tended a round-the-clock fire after his death as part of a four-day ceremony. The smoke was believed to carry prayers to heaven and spiritual messages around the world and to carry Walkabout's soul back to the creator, once the embers were cool.

10-9: Donald C. Alexander, Section 68, Grave 4652
38° 52.384′ N, 77° 3.802′ W

Donald Alexander was born May 22, 1921, in Pine Bluff, Arkansas, and served in the army as a forward artillery observer in World War II. Among his military awards were a Bronze Star and a Silver Star.

In 1942, Alexander graduated from Yale University. From there, he went to Harvard Law School, graduating in 1948. On passing the bar, he entered into private practice, concentrating on tax law. In 1973, he was appointed commissioner of the Internal Revenue Service by President Richard Nixon, a position he held until 1977. After only ten weeks on the job, he disbanded the Special Service Staff of the IRS, which had been investigating critics of Nixon and his Vietnam policies, including politically motivated tax audits of thousands of individuals. This act put him on a collision course with the president for his entire time as commissioner.

According to Alexander, Nixon tried to have him fired on numerous occasions. Unintimidated, Alexander continued to follow IRS policies and regulations to the letter, causing further rifts between himself and Nixon and friction with officials in the criminal investigation division.

Alexander's name became known to the public when he ordered an audit of Nixon's tax returns and learned that the president owed more than four hundred thousand dollars in back taxes and accrued interest and penalties. When this information became public, it signaled the beginning of the end of Nixon's presidency, which culminated with his resignation in 1974.

In 1975, Alexander received the Department of the Treasury's prestigious Alexander Hamilton Award. In 1987, he became director of the U.S. Chamber of Commerce, holding the position until 1989. He also served on the Martin Luther King Jr. Federal Holiday Commission from 1993 to 1996.

Alexander died of cancer on February 3, 2009.

10-10: Merlyn H. Dethlefsen, Section 65, Grave 1626

38° 52.422' N, 77° 3.775' W

Merlyn Hans Dethlefsen was born in Greenville, Iowa, on June 29, 1934. Following graduation from high school in 1951 at age sixteen, he enrolled at Iowa State University, leaving after two years to become a navigator in the air force. In 1958, he began pilot training.

Dethlefsen went on to serve two tours in Vietnam. On March 10, 1967, he was one of four F-105 pilots on a mission to destroy an antiaircraft complex containing surface-to-air missiles, artillery, and other automatic weapons. Two of the other planes, including that of the flight leader, were lost in the attack. Dethlefsen made seven passes at the target, flying low through heavy antiaircraft fire to avoid two enemy MiGs that were attacking him. Although his plane was hit several times by ground fire, he continued strafing for ten minutes, destroying the missiles. His effort was credited with disabling the defense system for a nearby steel plant, which was later destroyed by bombers that met minimal resistance. Dethlefsen's heroic actions that day earned him a Medal of Honor.

Eventually promoted to lieutenant colonel, Dethlefsen went on to serve as an instructor at the Army War College at Carlisle Barracks, Pennsylvania. While there, he was selected to fly the famed SR-71 Blackbird, a long-range, mach-three-plus strategic reconnaissance aircraft.

Dethlefsen retired from the air force in 1977 with the rank of lieutenant colonel. He died in Fort Worth, Texas, on December 14, 1987, of a heart attack and was interred in Arlington a week later with full military honors, including a squadron of airplanes flying overhead in a final salute.

10-11: Carlos C. Ogden Sr., Section 65, Grave 533

38° 52.479' N, 77° 3.758' W

Born May 9, 1917, at Borton, Illinois, Carlos Carnes Ogden was a graduate of Eastern Illinois State University. He entered the army in April 1941.

On June 25, 1944, Ogden was serving as a first lieutenant in Company K, 314th Infantry Regiment, Seventy-ninth Infantry Division, at the base of a hill outside Fort du Roule, France. During a firefight, Company K was pinned down by heavy enemy fire. Ignoring the danger, Ogden picked up an M-1 rifle, a grenade launcher, and several rifle and hand grenades. Alone, he moved up the slope toward the enemy emplacements. As he advanced, he was struck on the head and knocked down twice by machine-gun bullets. For several minutes, he lay unconscious with a live grenade

Governor Ronald Reagan to head the state's Selective Service operation in 1967.

Ogden died April 2, 2001, at age eighty-three at a VA hospital in Palo Alto, California.

10-12: William H. Mauldin, Section 64, Grave 6874
38° 52.458' N, 77° 3.707' W

William "Bill" Mauldin, born October 19, 1921, near Santa Fe, New Mexico, garnered fame as a Pulitzer Prize–winning cartoonist during World War II. Serving in the army's Forty-fifth Division, he created cartoon characters Willie and Joe for the division's newspaper. Willie and Joe became so popular that Mauldin was soon drawing for *Stars and Stripes*. By the end of the

in his hand. He slowly regained consciousness and, ignoring his wounds and dodging enemy fire from close range, continued up the hill, where he knocked out an 88-millimeter gun with a rifle grenade. He then moved toward two nearby machine-gun emplacements and used hand grenades to silence both. In the process, he was wounded a third time. His actions enabled Company K to advance and complete its mission.

On June 28, 1945, Ogden was awarded the Medal of Honor for his heroism. In addition, he received a Bronze Star and a Purple Heart with three oak leaf clusters.

Ogden reached the rank of major before leaving the army. He settled in San Jose, California, after the war, working as a counselor for the Veterans Administration. In 1950, the Republican Party tried to persuade him to run for Congress, but he refused, saying he didn't want to leave the VA. He was appointed by

war, he was syndicated by United Feature Syndicate.

The two fictional GIs, often cynical about army life, drew the ire of none other than spit-and-polish general George Patton, who objected to their scruffy appearance. Patton summoned Mauldin to his quarters in Luxembourg. There, he threatened to have Mauldin thrown in jail and, using the colorful language for which he was noted, told Mauldin that Willie and Joe were disrespectful to officers and that Mauldin should be given a medal by the Germans for interfering with discipline and spreading dissent. Mauldin took the dressing-down in stride, saying later that neither one convinced the other to change his mind.

In 1961, the National Cartoonists Society presented him the Reuben Award for Outstanding Cartoonist of the Year. In civilian life, he wrote sixteen books and worked as editorial cartoonist for the *St. Louis Post-Dispatch* and the *Chicago Sun-Times*. While at the *Times*, he drew the famous cartoon of the statue of Abraham Lincoln crying when President Kennedy was assassinated in 1963. By the time he retired in 1992, his cartoons were being syndicated in 250 newspapers.

Mauldin was also a soldier, earning a Purple Heart in late 1943 when he was struck in the shoulder by a fragment from a German mortar round. He protested that he didn't deserve the award because he had suffered more serious injuries sneaking through barbed-wire fences back home. His protest fell on deaf ears.

Sergeant Bill Mauldin died at age eighty-one on January 22, 2003, in a California nursing home after a long bout with Alzheimer's. When word got out that he was ill, thousands of veterans sent him cards and letters.

10-13: Tilman Klaus Bucher, Section 68, Grave 2903

38° 52.356' N, 77° 3.748' W

Tilman Bucher was born June 5, 1926, in Germany. He moved with his parents to New York City in 1928 and went on to serve more than thirty years for his adopted country. His service does not tell the whole story, however. A veteran of both World War II and Vietnam, Bucher achieved something most Americans never even consider: he served in four different branches of the military, wearing the uniforms of the army, navy, Marine Corps, and air force.

He graduated from high school in 1944 and immediately enlisted in the navy, becoming a corpsman and serving on the front lines with the First Marine Division in the Battle of Okinawa. He was still on Okinawa

when the atomic bomb was dropped on Hiroshima on August 6, 1945.

After his discharge in 1946, he attended the University of Southern California through the G.I. Bill and the army ROTC program, receiving a commission as a second lieutenant in the air force. His first assignment was to the Pentagon, where he served as a courier to the White House. This was followed by several assignments at various air force bases around the United States, including a stint with the Strategic Air Command (SAC).

In 1964, he served a tour in Vietnam, followed by an assignment as administrative officer for the air force's European headquarters in Wiesbaden, Germany. Subsequent assignments saw him back at the SAC and the Pentagon, where he served as an administrative officer to the Joint Chiefs of Staff. He retired in 1976 as a lieutenant colonel.

For his service in four separate military branches and his overall service record, Bucher received the Meritorious Service Medal for outstanding noncombat achievement. He died March 18, 2011.

10-14: Robert Benjamin Horner, Section 68, Grave 4912

38° 52.310' N, 77° 3.770' W

Robert Benjamin Horner was born on a farm in West Virginia on August 26, 1924, one of eight children. When World War II began, he joined the army and was assigned to Company H, 317th Infantry Regiment, Eightieth Infantry Division, better known as the Blue Ridge Division. In 1942, on his only home leave, Robert told his sister that he didn't think he would be coming back from the war. He was almost prophetic.

In September 1944, his company was positioned along the Moselle River near Millery, France, when

German artillery began firing. The next day, Horner was among the missing. He remained unaccounted for until April 27, 2001, when Michael Matheu discovered a helmet while digging in his garden at his home in southern France. Closer inspection revealed it was a World War II helmet, the type American soldiers wore. Further, it was accompanied by skeletal remains. Matheu contacted local authorities, who in turn notified U.S. Army officials. The army sent a representative to Matheu's home.

Excavation uncovered dog tags with Horner's name and serial number, clothing, rations, equipment, and a weapon of the type issued to American infantry troops in Europe in World War II. The remains were sent to the army's Central Identification Laboratory in Hawaii and were officially identified as Horner's. While there was some conjecture that he had been killed by friendly fire, the army concluded he most likely died from enemy artillery or mortar fire on or about September 19, 1945.

Horner was returned home and buried with full military honors on June 16, 2003, some fifty-eight years after his death.

10-15: Mark Matthews, Section 69, Grave 4215
38° 52.303' N, 77° 3.658' W

Mark Matthews was born August 7, 1894, in Greenville, Alabama, served in both World War I and World War II, and died of pneumonia September 6, 2005, at the age of 111.

He enlisted in the army at age sixteen and was assigned to the Tenth Cavalry, part of the famed Buffalo Soldiers, a name bestowed on African-American troops by Native Americans who fought them during the Indian Wars. Serving under General John J. "Black Jack" Pershing along the Mexican border, he partici-

pated in the pursuit of infamous bandit Pancho Villa.

Matthews remained in the military after serving in World War I. In 1931, he accepted an assignment to Fort Myer, where he helped tend the presidential stable for Franklin D. Roosevelt. He also trained recruits and played on the polo team. During World War II, he fought on the island of Saipan in the South Pacific despite being nearly fifty years of age.

Sergeant Matthews retired from the army in 1949 and worked as a security guard at the National Institutes of Health in Bethesda, Maryland. He rose to the position of chief of guards before retiring for good in 1970. In 1994, he was invited to the White House to meet President William Clinton in recognition of his service as a Buffalo Soldier. He was the last surviving member of that famed group.

At the time of his death in 2005, Matthews was believed to be the oldest man in Washington, D.C. Only one woman in the city was older.

10-16: Preston McDowell Burgess, Section 69, Grave 1710
38° 52.346' N, 77° 3.627' W

Born in Mercer, West Virginia, on November 12, 1913, Preston M. Burgess served as a sergeant in Battery B, Thirty-eighth Field Artillery Battalion, Second Infantry Division. On November 30, 1950, the Second Division, including the Thirty-eighth Battalion, was serving as rear guard for other units as they withdrew from the village of Kunu-ri in North Korea. The enemy occupied high ground on both sides of the narrow road, subjecting American troops to a deadly fire. Several roadblocks had also been set up. Burgess and the rest of his battalion pulled back, fighting their way through roadblock after roadblock along the route, which would become known as "the Gauntlet."

With casualties mounting rapidly and escape cut

off, Battery B found itself in an untenable position. Burgess was captured and is believed to have died a prisoner two weeks later, on December 15, 1950. His remains were not recovered until October 2004. On November 15, 2005, he was interred with full military honors in Arlington.

Sergeant Burgess was awarded the Purple Heart, the Prisoner of War Medal, the Korean Service Medal, the United Nations Service Medal, the National Defense Service Medal, the Korean Presidential Unit Citation, and the Republic of Korea War Service Medal.

10-17: John M. Connor, Section 69, Grave 1974
38° 52.352' N, 77° 3.614' W

John M. Connor was born June 25, 1916. Upon graduation from high school, he obtained a job as an apprentice printer in the Government Printing Office. He would be in this field his entire working life.

Connor was drafted in April 1941 and sent to the

Philippines six months later. On April 9, 1942, after a three-month battle against overwhelming odds, his men suffering greatly from hunger, disease, and heavy casualties, General Edward P. King Jr. surrendered his forces, including Corporal Connor, to the Japanese.

After stripping the prisoners of their weapons and personal effects, the Japanese ordered approximately seventy-five thousand Filipino and American troops to undertake a sixty-five-mile march in intense heat to prison camps farther north. Along the way, the troops were subjected to unspeakable conditions, marching with little food or water. The weak were bayoneted or shot. Others were simply left to die along the roadside or were run over with trucks in what would become known as the Bataan Death March.

Once the prisoners reached their destination, the overcrowded conditions and poor hygiene caused even more deaths from dysentery and other diseases. Little medical care was provided, and thousands of Americans died. Despite the hardships and cruelty, John

Connor survived. He spent more than three years as a prisoner and wrote a book after the war about his experiences in Japanese camps.

As Connor was regaining his health and putting his life back together, an American military tribunal tried Lieutenant General Masaharu Homma, commander of the Japanese invasion forces in the Philippines, for war crimes. Found guilty of allowing the death march, he was executed by firing squad on April 3, 1946.

Corporal John Connor died at age eighty-nine on December 16, 2005.

10-18: Robert Hopkins, Section 69, Grave 3420
38° 52.373' N, 77° 3.556' W

Born on April 26, 1919, Robert Hopkins served as chaplain of the Thirty-eighth Field Artillery Battalion, Second Infantry Division, during World War II. He was captured at Krinkelt, Belgium, in December 1944 during the Battle of the Bulge and was marched to Stalag VIII-A near Görlitz, Germany. In January 1945, he officiated the first formal military funeral service inside Germany, for American POW Bruce Schalm. Until that time, dead prisoners had been stripped and unceremoniously tossed into an open pit for burial, but German guards allowed Schalm to be buried in a crude casket covered with a homemade flag made from two sugar bags stolen by British soldiers. The red stripes were made from dye mixed with blood from wounded prisoners.

After the funeral, the flag was hidden. When Hopkins was transferred to another stalag, he smuggled it with him. Four months after transferring, Hopkins escaped. The flag went with him again. In all, he and other soldiers would carry it more than twenty-three hundred miles across Germany. It would be used at more than three hundred POW funerals during the war.

After his return to the United States, Hopkins be-

came a Methodist minister. In 1979, he donated the flag to the Second Infantry Museum at Camp Red Cloud, Korea. The Reverend Hopkins died on June 26, 2004, and was interred in Arlington on August 5, 2004. The homemade flag draped his casket.

10-19: Pentagon Group Memorial, Section 64
38° 52.408' N, 77° 3.656' W

On September 11, 2001, the al-Qaeda terrorist network launched an attack on the United States, flying two commercial jetliners into the World Trade Center in New York and another into the Pentagon in Arlington. A fourth plane crashed in a field in Shanksville, Pennsylvania, when passengers fought back against the hijackers.

The plane that struck the Pentagon was American Airlines Flight 77, flying from nearby Dulles International Airport to Los Angeles. At 9:37 A.M. local time, the terrorists crashed the plane into the western side of

The names on the memorial include:

ATTACK ON
- ◆ Steven D Jacoby
- Dennis M Johnson LTC USA
- ◆ Judith L Jones
- ◆ Ann C Judge
- Brenda Kegler
- ◆ Chandler R Keller
- ◆ Thomas F Kennedy AUSTRALIA
- ◆ Norma Cruz Khan
- ◆ Karen Ann Kincaid
- Michael S Lamana LT USN
- ◆ David W Laychak
- ◆ Dong Chul Lee
- ◆ Kenneth E Lewis & Jennifer Lewis
- Samantha L Lightbourn-Allen
- Stephen V Long MAJ USA
- ◆ Terence M Lynch
- Terence W Lynch JR
- Nehamon Lyons IV CPO USN
- Shelley A Marshall
- Teresa M Martin
- Robert J Maxwell
- Dean E Mattson SGM USA
- Timothy J Maude LTG USA
- Robert J Maxwell
- Molly L Mae
- ◆ Dora Marie Menchaca
- Priscilla E Mooreman
- Ronald D Milam MAJ USA
- Gerard M Moran JR
- Odessa V Morris
- Brian A Moss ETL USN
- Patrick J Murphy LT USN
- ◆ Christopher C Newton
- Khang Nguc Nguyen

THE PENTAGON
- Michael A North DM2 USN
- ◆ Barbara K Olson
- ◆ Ruben S Ornedo
- Diana B Padro
- Jonas M Panik LT USN
- Clifford L Patterson JR MAJ USA
- ◆ Robert Penninger
- ◆ Robert R Ploger III & Zandra F Ploger
- Darin H Pontell LT USN
- Scott Powell
- Jack D Punches CAPT USN RET
- Joseph J Pycior JR AW1 USN
- ◆ Lisa J Raines
- ◆ Deborah A Ramsaur
- ◆ Rhonda Sue Rasmussen
- Marsha D Ratchford IT1 USN
- Martha M Reszke
- ◆ Todd H Reuben
- Cecelia E (Lawson) Richard
- Edward V Rowenhorst
- Judy Rowlett
- Robert J Russell & Ruth CW4 USA
- William R Ruth SFC USA
- ◆ Charles E Salamone
- Marjorie C Salamone
- ◆ John F Sammartino
- David M Scales COL USN
- Robert C Scott CDR USN
- Janice M Scott USA RET
- Michael L Selves LTC USA RET
- Dan F Shanower CDR USN
- Antoinette Sherman
- Ronald D Sherman MAJ USA
- ◆ George W Simmons & Diane M Simmons
- Cheryle D Sincock

---

the Pentagon, killing 189 people—125 in the Pentagon and 64 aboard Flight 77.

The remains of 5 of the victims could not be identified. Those unidentified remains are buried as a group in a single casket under a five-sided memorial that sits within view of the Pentagon. The names of all 184 victims are listed on the memorial. Those who were on the plane are identified with a small diamond in front of their names. The 5 whose remains were not identified are shown with a star. Service members whose remains were identified are buried in the immediate area around the memorial.

The memorial was designed by Arlington National Cemetery superintendent John C. Metzler Jr.

10-20: John Cooper Jr., Section 64, Grave 1903
38° 52.435' N, 77° 3.602' W

John Cooper Jr., better known to the world as Jackie, was born September 15, 1922, in Los Angeles. One of the most famous child actors of all time, he became the youngest person nominated for an Oscar. He held that honor for fifty years. Best known for his roles in the *Our Gang* comedies and later for his work as an actor and director, Cooper also had a military career. He entered the navy in the V-12 program, initiated in 1943 to meet the country's needs for commissioned officers in World War II.

When *Hennessey*, his 1961 weekly television series, was credited with enhancing recruiting efforts, Cooper was offered and accepted a commission as a line officer

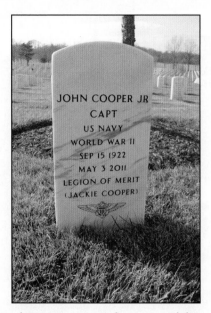

in the Naval Reserve. Among his responsibilities were recruitment, making training films, and public relations. Cooper also held a multiengine pilot's license and later copiloted jet planes for the navy, which made him an honorary aviator, authorized to wear wings of gold. At that time, he was only the third person so honored in naval aviation history.

By 1976, he reached the rank of captain. In 1980, the navy suggested he go on active duty at the Pentagon, an assignment that would have resulted in an eventual promotion to rear admiral. After some soul searching, Cooper declined the offer, fearing that his absence from the motion-picture industry would harm his chances of directing films. Despite this, Cooper holds letters of commendation from six secretaries of the navy and was honorary chairman of the U.S. Navy Memorial Foundation. He was also a charter member of VIVA, the effort to return POWs and MIAs from Vietnam.

When he retired from military service in 1982, he received the Legion of Merit from Secretary of the Navy John F. Lehman Jr. Except for actor Jimmy Stewart, who attained the rank of brigadier general in the Air Force Reserve, no other performer in his industry has achieved a higher uniformed rank in the U.S. military. Jackie Cooper died May 3, 2011.

10-21: Miguel A. Vera, Section 71, Grave 258
38° 52.523′ N, 77° 3.553′ W

Miguel Armando Vera was born October 11, 1932, in Puerto Rico, the youngest of five children. He joined the army in 1949 at age seventeen, mainly for the opportunity to further his education and to help his mother buy a home. He was assigned to Company F, Second Battalion, Thirty-eighth Infantry Regiment, Second Infantry Division.

On September 21, 1952, Vera, not yet healed from wounds suffered in a previous engagement, voluntarily left an aid station to rejoin his company in an assault on a well-entrenched enemy on the rocky slopes of a strategically important hill called Old Baldy, near Chorwon, Korea. Vera and his company got within twenty yards of the enemy when they were trapped by heavy fire from mortars, artillery, and small arms. As the company pulled back, Vera volunteered to stay behind and cover the withdrawal. Once most of the company was out of danger, the enemy concentrated its fire on Vera, who continued directing fire on its position.

Later that same morning, his company returned and found the twenty-year-old Vera's body, still facing the enemy position. His actions were credited with saving many lives, and he was awarded a Distinguished Service Cross.

Fifty years later, in 2002, Congress ordered the army to revisit the cases of Distinguished Service Crosses awarded to Jewish and Latino soldiers, to ensure that Medals of Honor were not improperly withheld. That review concluded that twenty-four Distinguished

Service Crosses should have been Medals of Honor. With the standard three-year limit for Medal of Honor awards waived, President Barack Obama awarded the medal to Vera and twenty-three others on March 18, 2014. Vera's nephew Joe Rodriguez accepted the award for his fallen uncle.

In addition to his Medal of Honor, Vera was awarded the Purple Heart, the Army Good Conduct Medal, the National Defense Service Medal, the Korean Service Medal with two bronze service stars, the Combat Infantry Badge, the United Nations Service Medal, the Republic of Korea–Korean War Service Medal, and the Wharang Distinguished Military Service Medal with silver star from Korea.

Private Miguel Vera was disinterred from his grave in Puerto Rico and reinterred in Arlington on November 20, 1914, fulfilling his nephew's dream. And indirectly, he did buy that house for his mother. She used the insurance money the government gave her to make the purchase.

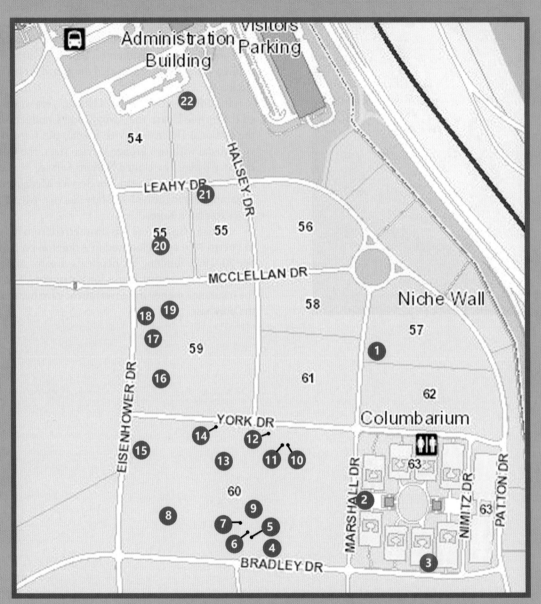

Courtesy of Arlington National Cemetery

11-1: Joseph Michael Snock Jr., Section 57, Grave 2974

38° 52.675' N, 77° 3.700' W

An estimated four hundred unidentified American servicemen were returned to the United States by North Korea between 1990 and 1994. Although many could not be identified at that time, the development of new technology has since allowed the Armed Forces DNA Identification Laboratory to identify some of those returned.

One such soldier was army sergeant Joseph Snock of Apollo, Pennsylvania, a member of the combat team of the Thirty-first Infantry Regiment, Seventh Infantry Division. Snock was twenty-one when he went missing

on November 29, 1950, east of the Chosin Reservoir and south of the reservoir's P'ungnyuri Inlet. Snock and his twin brother, John, were part of a contingent that had taken cover near the base of a snowy hill. John had already been wounded by shell fragments that went through his helmet and pierced his head. When the order came to launch an assault, John ignored the order and warned his brother not to go, saying, "They'll blow your brains out if you leave the side of this hill." Joseph chose to obey the order and less than twenty minutes later was carried back by fellow soldiers, badly wounded. John rushed to get a first-aid pack. When he returned, his brother was missing, taken prisoner by Chinese soldiers. John never saw his brother again.

Joseph Snock was listed as missing in action for three years. In 1953, returning American service members reported that he had been captured and died from malnutrition and lack of medical care in December 1950. His remains were not among those returned at the time.

Thanks to DNA collected from John and other family members, Joseph Snock's remains were finally identified in December 2014. He was buried in July 2015, more than sixty-five years after his death. John died in 2007, never knowing that his brother's remains would be identified.

11-2: Columbarium, Section 63

38° 52.553' N, 77° 3.718' W

Given the increased popularity of cremation, and faced with space limitations for ground burials, Arlington officials took steps in 1980 to provide for inurnments

by creating the Columbarium. Constructed in five phases, its first five-thousand-niche section opened that April 26. The completed Columbarium provides space for up to a hundred thousand cremated remains.

The criteria for the Columbarium are more liberal than for ground burials at Arlington and are extended to all honorably discharged veterans. Eligibility requirements for both methods can be found in Appendix B.

Each niche accommodates no more than two urns and is sealed with a marble plaque inscribed with the names, highest military grades, and years of birth and death of those inurned.

11-3: Ronald Scott Owens, Section 63, Court 5, Section M1, Column 2, Niche 5

38° 52.500' N, 77° 3.643' W

Born on October 31, 1975, Ronald Scott Owens lived in Vero Beach, Florida. When he graduated from high school, he took a job as a mechanic, then joined the navy in 1998, after which he planned to attend college to study computer science.

On August 8, 2000, he shipped out on the USS *Cole* from Norfolk, Virginia, for a six-month cruise. Electronic Warfare Technician Third Class Ronald Owens was embarking on his first trip to sea. On October 12, the *Cole* was taking on fuel in Aden, Yemen, when two suicide bombers approached in a small boat loaded with explosives. The terrorists approached the port side of the destroyer and detonated their deadly cargo. The blast ripped a forty-foot-wide hole near the water line of the *Cole*, killing seventeen American sailors and injuring thirty-nine. Owens was among those killed. He was twenty-five years old. His body was returned to the United States, where he was cremated. On June 22, 2001, his ashes were placed in Columbarium Court 5.

Three other victims of the attack were also interred

in Arlington, all in Section 60: Richard D. Costelow, Signalman Cherone L. Gunn, and Petty Officer Second Class Kenneth E. Clodfelter. For more information on these men, see site 11-9.

11-4: Robert G. Fenstermacher, Section 60, Grave 10353

38° 52.509' N, 77° 3.793' W

More than four hundred thousand American service members were killed during World War II. The remains of over seventy-three thousand were never recovered or identified. One of those was First Lieutenant Robert G. Fenstermacher of the U.S. Army Air Force, 506th Fighter Squadron, 404th Fighter Group, who was lost on December 26, 1944, near Petergensfeld, Belgium.

On that date, Allied and German ground troops were in their tenth day of fighting in the Ardennes Forest in what would become known as the Battle of the Bulge. Lieutenant Fenstermacher was piloting a P-47D Thunderbolt on armed reconnaissance against a train station near Roetgen, Germany. It was his fifty-seventh mission. Unfortunately, faulty intelligence had failed to determine that the station had already been captured by the Allies. As Fenstermacher approached his target, friendly forces on the ground are believed to have begun firing defensively. However it happened, Fenstermacher's plane was shot down. Fenstermacher was listed as missing in action. That classification was changed to killed in action on May 2, 1945.

Following the war, a local Belgian woman told the U.S. Army Graves Registration Service investigation team about an aircraft that had crashed into the side of her house. The team searched the surrounding area but was unsuccessful in locating the site.

In 2012, while excavating a private yard in Petergensfeld, a group of Belgian historians recovered aircraft wreckage consistent with a P-47D. Amidst it were human remains, which were turned over to the Joint POW/MIA Accounting Command. By means of forensic identification tests, the remains were identified as Fenstermacher's. On April 30, 2013, he was removed from the list of dead or missing. That October 18, Fenstermacher was laid to rest in Arlington, nearly sixty-nine years after being shot down.

11-5: Breaker Patrol, Section 60, Graves 8240–8242
38° 52.520' N, 77° 3.831' W

On May 9, 1967, the seven-man Marine Corps Reconnaissance Team Breaker set out on a mission to gather information on possible enemy infiltration routes just south of the Demilitarized Zone and northwest of the Khe Sanh Combat Base in Vietnam. Shortly after midnight, the patrol met enemy troops, and a furious firefight broke out. The battle lasted throughout the night and well into the next day. The patrol leader, Sergeant James Tycz, Second Lieutenant Heinz Ahlmeyer, Corporal Samuel Sharp, and Hospital Corpsman Malcolm Miller were killed or mortally wounded. The three remaining members of the patrol were wounded.

Although the wounded were extracted by helicopter, the dead could not be recovered due to heavy enemy activity in the area. It was not until 2003 that the remains of the four men of Breaker Patrol were recovered. That May 23, the remains were taken to Hawaii, where they were ultimately identified by DNA examination and dental comparisons.

On May 10, 2005, Tycz (Grave 8240, 38° 52.521' N, 77° 3.831' W), Miller (Grave 8241, 38° 52.521' N, 77° 3.831' W), and Ahlmeyer (Grave 8242, 38° 52.522' N, 77° 3.831' W) were laid to rest next to the memorial to the men of Breaker Patrol. Sharp was buried in his hometown of San Jose, California, but was included on the memorial inscription. The comingled unidentifiable remains representing all the dead from Breaker Patrol were placed under the memorial. On that day thirty-eight years after their deaths, the men of Breaker Patrol were home.

11-6: Larry Alan Thorne, Section 60, Grave 8136
38° 52.523' N, 77° 3.833' W

Larry Alan Thorne was born Lauri Allan Torni in Viipuri, Finland, on May 28, 1919. He enlisted in the Finnish army and rose to the rank of captain, training and commanding Finnish ski troops in the early part of World War II. His troops engaged regularly with the Soviet army, and Torni received every medal for bravery the Finnish army bestowed, including the Mannerheim Cross, the equivalent of the Medal of Honor.

When Finland fell to the Soviets in September 1944, Torni joined the German SS so he could continue fighting the communists. The Soviet Union tried to have him arrested as a Nazi collaborator, but Torni evaded capture and came to the United States, where he enlisted in the army, as was permitted under the Lodge-Philbin Act, which allowed the recruiting of foreign nationals into any forces under command of the United States. Those who served five years and obtained an honorable discharge were granted American citizenship. Having Americanized his name to Larry Thorne, he became part of the fledgling Special Forces program, eventually receiving a commission and serving a tour in Vietnam.

In February 1965, Thorne, now a captain, returned to Vietnam for a second tour. When the Viet Cong began using Laos as a sanctuary, American forces were granted permission by the U.S. government to pursue them as far as fifty kilometers across the border. In October 1965, a Special Operations team made its way into Laos in search of what was being called the Ho Chi Minh Trail. Thorne was aboard a helicopter charged with rescuing any crew members of other helicopters that went down during the insertion.

As the weather deteriorated after the successful insertion, the helicopter carrying Thorne began its return to base. Within a matter of minutes, radio contact was lost. A month-long search failed to locate the craft, and Thorne was declared missing in action. In December 1965, he was promoted to major.

Near the end of the war, the wreckage was found and a search-and-recovery team located the remains of the South Vietnamese air crew. No sign of Larry Thorne

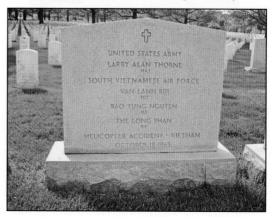

was found until 1999, when his remains were recovered. He was buried in Arlington on June 26, 2003.

Larry A. Thorne is the only American to fight communism under three flags—those of Finland, Germany, and the United States.

11-7: Kara Spears Hultgreen, Section 60, Grave 7710

38° 52.528' N, 77° 3.841' W

Kara Spears Hultgreen was born October 5, 1965, and graduated from high school in San Antonio, Texas. Always an overachiever, she graduated from the University of Texas with a degree in aeronautical engineering. She then attended naval aviation officer candidate school and qualified to fly an A-6 Intruder. Her long-range goal was to become an astronaut.

In 1993, Congress lifted a ban on female combat pilots, prompting Hultgreen to apply for and be accept-

ed at Naval Air Station Miramar to begin training in the F-14 Tomcat, the plane featured in the movie *Top Gun*. On July 24, 1994, she qualified in the F-14. Hultgreen became the first woman carrier-based fighter pilot when she successfully landed on the USS *Constitution*.

On October 25, 1994, she was making a final approach to the USS *Abraham Lincoln* about fifty miles off San Diego. As she neared the ship, her plane began to lose altitude. When it was apparent she was about to crash, Hultgreen and her radar intercept officer, Lieutenant Matthew Klemish, ejected. Klemish ejected first, suffering minor injuries. Hultgreen ejected shortly afterward, but by then the plane had rolled onto its back. When she ejected, she was thrown directly into the ocean. Her body was recovered on November 12, 1994, in thirty-seven hundred feet of water, still strapped into her ejection seat.

A four-month investigation determined that the left engine had stalled as the plane approached the ship, and that there had been no pilot error. Kara Spears Hultgreen was buried with full military honors on November 21, 1994. She was twenty-nine years old.

11-8: David McCampbell, Section 60, Grave 3150

38° 52.545' N, 77° 3.920' W

David McCampbell was born January 16, 1910, in Bessemer, Alabama, and graduated from the U.S. Naval Academy in June 1933. He began flight training in 1937 and was designated a naval aviator the following year.

On June 19, 1944, flying from the USS *Essex*, he led an attack against eighty Japanese fighter planes during the Battle of the Philippine Sea. He shot down seven enemy planes as the Americans routed the attackers and protected the fleet. Just four months later, on October 24, he shot down nine more enemy aircraft in the

Battle of Leyte Gulf. When he landed his Grumman Hellcat, his six machine guns had two rounds remaining, and the plane had only enough fuel to keep it aloft for ten more minutes.

For "conspicuous gallantry and intrepidity" on these occasions, McCampbell was awarded the Medal of Honor. During his tour with the *Essex*'s Air Group Fifteen, he became the navy's leading ace, downing a total of thirty-four Japanese aircraft. He also destroyed twenty-four planes on the ground. The third-highest-scoring American flying ace of World War II, he was the highest-scoring ace to survive the war. McCampbell also was awarded the Navy Cross, three Distinguished Flying Crosses, the Legion of Merit, the Silver Star, and the Air Medal.

McCampbell retired from active duty in 1964 and died June 30, 1996, in a nursing home in Riviera Beach, Florida, at age eighty-six. The terminal at Palm Beach International Airport is named in his honor,

and the navy christened an *Arleigh Burke*–class destroyer, the USS *McCampbell* (DDG-85), in his name on August 17, 2002.

11-9: USS *Cole* Victims, Section 60, Graves 7732, 7733, and 7734
38° 52.546' N, 77° 3.840' W

On October 12, 2000, the USS *Cole* (DDG 67) moored in the port of Aden, Yemen, for a scheduled refueling. A small boat carrying two suicide bombers approached the port side of the destroyer, where its explosives were detonated. The blast ripped a forty-foot-wide hole near the water line of the *Cole*, killing seventeen American sailors and injuring thirty-nine.

After the damage was controlled, salvage crews made the *Cole* seaworthy enough to be moved to deeper waters, where it was loaded onto the Norwegian-owned *Blue Marlin*. The Norwegian freighter was tasked with bringing the *Cole* back to the United States, where it would be rebuilt. An investigation determined that members of the al-Qaeda terrorist network planned and carried out the bombing.

Four of the dead were interred in Arlington. Richard D. Costelow (Grave 7732, 38° 52.546' N, 77° 3.840' W), Signalman Cherone L. Gunn (Grave 7733, 38° 52.546' N, 77° 3.840' W), and Petty Officer Second Class Kenneth E. Clodfelter (Grave 7734, 38° 52.547' N, 77° 3.840' W) were placed side by side in this section of the cemetery. The ashes of a fourth victim, Electronic Warfare Technician Third Class Ronald Scott Owens (see site 11-3), rest in the Columbarium.

Born on April 29, 1965, Chief Petty Officer Richard Costelow of New Florence, Pennsylvania, and Lexington Park, Maryland, had less than three weeks of sea duty left when the terrorists struck. From 1992 to 1995, he had worked as an electronics technician first class at

the White House, directing the engineering and installation of a new communications suite. For that work, he was awarded the Defense Meritorious Service Medal. Costelow left the White House for an opportunity at sea duty, a requirement for advancement.

Cherone Gunn was born February 14, 1978. He joined the navy because he wanted experience that would help him become a state trooper. His family requested that Gunn be buried next to any shipmate who also had been killed in the attack. That shipmate turned out to be Costelow, buried earlier on the day of Gunn's interment. Both were laid to rest October 20, 2000.

Kenneth Clodfelter of Mechanicsville, Virginia, was born December 26, 1978. He graduated in 1997 from Lee-Davis High School, where he was a good student who wrestled and played football. An Eagle Scout, he was planning to sign up for another tour of duty in January 2001. He was the father of a two-year-old son. One of the last of the victims to return to the United States, he was buried October 31, 2000.

11-10: Adam Lynn Dickmyer, Section 60, Grave 9396
38° 52.597' N, 77° 3.804' W

It had been forty-three years since the tomb sentinels had to bury one of their own, but on October 28, 2010, they had to do just that. Adam Dickmyer, badge

number 528, was only the twelfth sentinel interred at Arlington, and the third in the unit's history to be killed in combat.

Dickmyer was born February 2, 1984, in York, Pennsylvania, and grew up in Winston-Salem, North Carolina. Part of an ROTC drill team in high school, he enlisted in the army shortly after graduation. Following basic training, he attended the army's Airborne School, after which he was assigned to Company A, Third U.S. Infantry Regiment, the Old Guard.

He became a tomb sentinel in 2004 and served in that role for more than three years, advancing to specialist, sergeant, and then staff sergeant commander, in which role he served as the relief commander. He eventually was given the responsibility of assistant sergeant of the guard, the second-highest enlisted position in the platoon. He also served as the official "Voice of the Old Guard" in audio guided tours of Arlington. In 2007, Dickmyer became the casket team leader for the Joint Services State Funeral Team. He assumed the role of the lead pallbearer at the funeral for Senator Edward M. Kennedy in August 2009.

Shortly afterward, Dickmyer deployed to Afghanistan. On October 28, 2010, while acting as platoon sergeant, he was killed in action near Kandahar by an improvised explosive device. He was twenty-six years old.

In addition to his Tomb Guard Identification Badge, his numerous awards and decorations included the Bronze Star, the Purple Heart, the Meritorious Service Medal, the Army Commendation Medal, and the Army Achievement Medal with six oak leaf clusters.

11-11: Travis L. Manion, Section 60, Grave 9179
38° 52.597' N, 77° 3.808'

and Brendan Looney, Section 60, Grave 9180
38° 52.598' N, 77° 3.808' W

Travis Manion and Brendan Looney had never met before their plebe year at the U.S. Naval Academy.

By the time they graduated four years later, the roommates were best friends, so close that they joked they were brothers from different mothers.

Manion was born at Camp Lejeune, North Carolina, where his father was stationed in the Marine Corps. After many moves necessitated by his father's assignments as a colonel, the family settled in Doylestown, Pennsylvania. When he graduated from the U.S. Naval Academy in 2004, Manion was commissioned a Marine Corps officer and assigned to the First Reconnaissance Battalion, First Marine Division, First Marine Expeditionary Force Camp, located at Camp Pendleton, California. In 2005, he was deployed to Iraq. In September 2006, he became part of a military transition team attached to an Iraqi army battalion in Fallujah. The day after Christmas, he began his second tour in Iraq, serving as the company advisor for the Third Battalion, Second Brigade, First Iraqi Army Division Military Transition Team, Regimental Combat Team Six, Second Marine Expeditionary Force (Forward).

On April 29, 2007, during his final mission, Manion and his patrol were searching a suspected insurgent's house when they came under attack. As the fighting escalated, Manion and another marine left relatively safe cover to rescue a wounded corpsman. After

administering first aid to the injured man, Manion led his patrol in a counterattack that eliminated an enemy position. When another marine was wounded, Manion again deliberately exposed himself to enemy fire in an effort to recover the soldier. Taking fire from three sides, he was fatally wounded by an enemy sniper as he attempted to draw fire from the wounded marines.

Manion was posthumously awarded the Bronze Star with valor and the Silver Star for his heroic actions. The Iraqis named their new headquarters Combat Outpost Manion in his honor. He was laid to rest at Calvary Cemetery in West Conshohocken, Pennsylvania.

Looney, who lived in Owings, Maryland, took a slightly different path following his graduation from the U.S. Naval Academy. Commissioned as an intelligence officer, he became a navy SEAL in June 2008. In honor of his fallen former roommate and best friend, Looney wore a bracelet bearing Travis Manion's name.

Two days after his wedding, Looney was deployed to Iraq, then to Afghanistan, where he was assigned to Zabul Province, a Taliban stronghold. There, he went on fifty-eight successful missions. His fifty-ninth came on September 21, 2010, when he was sent to serve as an observer for an operation in the village of Ayatalah. On the way there, his helicopter crashed, killing him and eight other service members. He was awarded the Bronze Star.

Not long after Manion's burial, his family members learned he had once expressed a desire to be buried in Arlington if he died in combat. They had begun the process of having his body moved. Upon the news of her husband's death, and knowing that the Manion family was working to have Travis reinterred in Arlington, Looney's wife, Amy, decided that Brendan should be laid to rest next to his best friend. The two families worked with cemetery officials to make it happen.

On October 1, 2010, First Lieutenant Travis Manion's body was reinterred in Arlington. Three days later, Lieutenant Brendan Looney was laid to rest in the grave next to his best friend.

11-12: Ross Andrew McGinnis, Section 60, Grave 8544
38° 52.607' N, 77° 3.820' W

Ross McGinnis was born in Meadville, Pennsylvania, on June 14, 1987, and grew up in Knox in the northwest part of the state. His interest in being a soldier showed itself when he was still in kindergarten, when his teacher asked him to finish this sentence: "When I grow up, I want to be . . ." He quickly supplied three words: "an army man."

McGinnis joined the army through the Delayed Entry Program on his seventeenth birthday. Following graduation from high school in 2005, he left for basic training at Fort Benning, after which he was assigned to Company C, First Battalion, Twenty-sixth Infantry Regiment, which was attached to the Second Brigade Combat Team, Second Infantry Division. The youngest in his company, he planned to study automotive technology when he left the army.

In August 2006, he and the rest of his regiment

were deployed to Iraq. McGinnis served as a .50 caliber machine gunner in a HMMWV, better known as a Humvee. On December 4, he was at his position in the gunner's hatch while on patrol in Baghdad. Four other soldiers were in the vehicle with him when an insurgent tossed a grenade from above. Facing backward because his Humvee was in the rear of a six-vehicle convoy, McGinnis tried to deflect the grenade, but it fell through the hatch and lodged between the radios near his feet. Fighting his reflexes to leap from the vehicle, as he had been trained to do, he instead shouted a warning to his companions. From their positions, none could see where the grenade had landed. With little time to spare, McGinnis dropped down through the hatch and threw his back against the radio mount, covering the grenade with his body. The ensuing explosion killed him instantly. His four companions were all wounded, but their lives were spared by McGinnis's selfless action.

Nineteen-year-old Ross McGinnis was posthumously promoted from private first class to specialist and awarded a Silver Star for his bravery. In May 2008, that Silver Star was upgraded to a Medal of Honor. On June 2, 2008, just twelve days before what would have been McGinnis's twenty-first birthday, his Medal of Honor was presented to his mother and father.

11-13: Dieter Dengler, Section 60, Grave 6652
38° 52.596' N, 77° 3.856' W

Dieter Dengler was born in Germany on May 22, 1938. After his father was killed during World War II, he and his family fled Germany, arriving in the United States in 1957 and settling in the San Francisco area. There, he dabbled at a series of jobs until he graduated from college, became an American citizen, and earned his pilot's wings.

On February 1, 1966, Dengler, now a navy lieuten-

ant, took off from the deck of the aircraft carrier USS *Ranger* as part of a four-aircraft interdiction mission in Vietnam near the border of Laos. As he performed a normal recovery maneuver after rolling in on the target, the rest of the flight lost sight of him. It was learned later that heavy ground fire had damaged his plane and forced him to crash-land in Laos. A search was initiated that continued the rest of that day and part of the night, without success. The wreckage of his plane was spotted the following morning. A helicopter crew photographed it and reported that Dengler did not appear to be in the cockpit.

What nobody knew was that Dengler was alive and had actually seen the rescue aircraft. He had evaded capture but was unable to contact his would-be rescuers on his emergency radio. Later that day, he was tracked down and captured by Pathet Lao troops, who marched him through several villages, torturing him along the way. Eight days later, Dengler escaped but was recaptured within a short time.

Dengler was then taken to a POW camp in Laos, where he was held with other Americans. For the next several months, he suffered regular beatings, torture, harassment, hunger, and illness. Then, on June 29, 1966, after hearing the prisoners were to be killed, Dengler and several others made their escape. Gunfire erupted, and six guards were killed, angering his captors further. Most of the escapees were seriously ill; Dengler himself had jaundice. The men made their way through the dense jungle, foraging for fruits and berries to supplement the meager stash of rice they had managed to save during their captivity.

Eighteen days later, Dengler and one of his fellow escapees, Lieutenant Duane W. Martin, who was sick with malaria, stumbled onto a small village that appeared to be abandoned. There, they slept and ate some corn they found nearby. Unknown to the two, however, the village was indeed occupied. The men were attacked by an angry villager wielding a machete. Dengler managed to escape, but Martin was decapitated.

Dengler struggled along on his own. On the twenty-second day following his escape, with his strength nearly gone, he formed an SOS from rocks, desperately hoping someone friendly would find him. The next morning, an air force Skyraider passed overhead and spotted his SOS. The pilot contacted a rescue helicopter, bringing Dengler's ordeal to a close. He had weighed 157 pounds when he flew from the *Ranger*. His weight when he was rescued was 98 pounds. His feet were also badly swollen, his teeth were missing, and his hair was falling out, providing mute testimony to his time in enemy hands.

When Dengler returned home, he wrote a book about his experience as a POW. That book, *Escape from Laos*, became the basis for the movie *Rescue Dawn*.

Dengler was awarded the Navy Cross for his heroism in planning and leading his fellow prisoners in the escape. He also received the Prisoner of War Medal

and the Distinguished Flying Cross. Some might say he had an amazing run of good luck, despite his harrowing experience as a POW. Dengler probably wouldn't have disagreed, in light of the fact that he survived four plane crashes as a civilian pilot and in 1979 avoided drowning when his cabin cruiser sank in rough water off San Francisco Bay.

Dengler died of amyotrophic lateral sclerosis, or Lou Gehrig's disease, on February 7, 2001, and was buried in Arlington on March 16, 2001.

11-14: Paul Levern Bates, Section 60, Grave 6101
38° 52.611' N, 77° 3.865' W

Paul Bates was born March 4, 1908, in Los Angeles. He graduated in 1931 from Western Maryland College, where he played football. He then worked as a teacher and high-school football coach until he entered the army in 1941.

In January 1943, he took command of the 761st Tank Battalion, all of whose enlisted men were African-Americans. The 761st did so well in boot camp that Bates refused a promotion because he would have had to separate from what he considered one of the army's best battalions. He eventually received that promotion to full colonel. At Fort Hood, Texas, a black officer was arrested when he refused to move to the back of a bus. Bates was ordered to court-martial the man for insubordination but refused. The man, Jackie Robinson, went on to a Hall of Fame career after breaking major-league baseball's color barrier when he signed with the Brooklyn Dodgers.

In November 1944, the 761st saw its first combat. Fighting as part of Patton's Third Army, the unit received a Presidential Unit Citation for extraordinary heroism after capturing, destroying, or liberating more than thirty major towns, thirty-four tanks, four air-

at the end of World War II, he left military service and attended New York University, earning his bachelor's degree in electrical engineering. He returned to duty during the Korean War, followed by an assignment to Edwards Air Force Base, where he graduated in 1954 from what is now the U.S. Air Force Test Pilot School. He soon became the first lead air force project pilot for the X-15 flight research program, launched by NASA, the air force, and the navy. The X-15 was the forerunner of the space shuttle.

In March 1961, White extended his string of "firsts," flying a plane at 2,905 miles per hour to become the first pilot to exceed Mach 4. In June 1961, he became the first pilot to exceed Mach 5, recording a speed of 3,603 miles per hour. That November, he flew his X-15 at 4,094 miles per hour, making him the first pilot to exceed Mach 6. Seven months later, in July 1962, White flew the X-15 to an altitude of 314,750 feet, 59.6 miles above earth and nearly 10 miles above the atmosphere.

fields, three ammunition dumps, 461 wheeled vehicles, 113 large guns, and a radio station. It also aided in the liberation of Gunskirchen, a subcamp of the Mauthausen concentration camp complex.

Bates had the dubious distinction of being the first member of the 761st to be wounded. Over the course of the war, he received a Purple Heart, a Silver Star, two Bronze Stars, and the Legion of Merit. Colonel Paul Bates died of cancer on February 21, 1995, at age eighty-six.

11-15: Robert Michael White, Section 60, Grave 540
38° 52.591' N, 77° 3.962' W

Born in New York City on July 6, 1924, Robert Michael White entered military service in 1942. In February 1945, after flying more than fifty missions, he was shot down over Germany and taken prisoner. Released

By piloting an airplane in space, White became the first man to earn a winged astronaut rating. Later that year, at a ceremony on the White House South Lawn, Major White was awarded the Collier Trophy for Aviation from President John F. Kennedy.

When the war in Vietnam heated up, the unassuming White returned to combat, flying seventy missions over North Vietnam. In 1967, he led an attack on targets around Hanoi, for which he earned the Air Force Cross.

White never was considered a celebrity on the level of the Mercury 7 astronauts. But without his efforts, the Mercury program would likely not have been so successful so early. It was White's accomplishments that enabled NASA to learn the effects of heat on aircraft surfaces at extremely high speeds and altitudes, as well as the physiological impact on fliers.

White also earned the Distinguished Service Medal with oak leaf cluster, the Silver Star with three oak leaf clusters, the Distinguished Flying Cross with four oak leaf clusters, and the Prisoner of War Medal. He retired from military service in 1981 as a major general and died March 17, 2010, at age eighty-five.

11-16: Grace M. Hopper, Section 59, Grave 973
38° 52.651' N, 77° 3.931' W

To many, Grace Murray Hopper is a household name. And although others may not have heard of her, their lives have been influenced by what she did.

Hopper was born in New York City on December 9, 1906. She graduated from Vassar College in 1928 and six years later received a PhD in mathematics from Yale. She was also a member of the Vassar faculty. In 1943, she joined the Naval Reserve, where she was assigned to the Bureau of Ordnance. For the next forty years, she was a pioneer in the development of the computer and programming language, gaining the

nickname "Amazing Grace." Her ideas in the field of data processing led to the development of COBOL, one of the first modern computer programming languages.

At the end of World War II, Hopper joined the Harvard faculty, retaining her Naval Reserve affiliation and reaching the rank of commander before her retirement in 1966. In less than a year, she was recalled to active duty and assigned to the staff of the chief of naval operations. She gained regular promotions, attaining the rank of rear admiral in 1985, becoming the first woman to reach that status. She retired a year later.

Among all her achievements, she may best be remembered for an innocent comment she made in 1945 while at Harvard. The Mark II computer had stopped working. When she began investigating, she determined that a moth had become stuck in a relay. She remarked to her colleagues that she had found a bug in the computer. The incident was noted in the operation log, along with the remains of the moth, which were taped to the page. Today's popular phrase "debugging a computer" originated from Grace's explanation of the problem.

Admiral Hopper remained active in industry and education until her death on January 1, 1992. The USS *Hopper* (DDG-70) is named in her honor. In addition, the navy named its data automation center in San Diego after her.

11-17: Beirut Barracks Bombing, Section 59
38° 52.687' N, 77° 3.944' W

At 6:22 A.M. on October 23, 1983, a truck bomb struck a four-story building housing 300 U.S. military personnel in Beirut, Lebanon. The troops were serving as part of a multinational peacekeeping mission. The attack killed 241 American servicemen, including 220 marines, 18 sailors, and three soldiers. Another 128 Americans were wounded, 13 of whom eventually succumbed to their injuries; those 13 are included in the death total. The bombing marked the deadliest single attack on marines overseas since World War II.

The Beirut Barracks Memorial honors those killed in the bombing. It consists of a marker placed in front of a Cedar of Lebanon tree. The inscription reads,

LET PEACE TAKE ROOT
THIS CEDAR OF LEBANON TREE GROWS IN
LIVING MEMORY OF THE AMERICANS KILLED
IN THE BEIRUT TERRORIST ATTACK AND ALL
VICTIMS OF TERRORISM THROUGHOUT THE
WORLD.
DEDICATED DURING THE FIRST MEMORIAL
CEREMONY FOR THESE VICTIMS.

GIVEN BY NO GREATER LOVE
OCTOBER 23, 1984
A TIME OF REMEMBRANCE

Some of the victims are buried in the same section of the cemetery not far from the memorial.

The bombing was traced to Hezbollah, a militant

and political group that originated in Lebanon in 1982. Terrorists from Iran and Syria were also suspected of being involved. U.S. courts ultimately ruled that Iran should pay $1.75 million to the victims' families.

At about the same time as the attack on the American barracks, a similar truck bomb explosion occurred at a building in Beirut housing French military forces, killing fifty-eight paratroopers and wounding fifteen more.

11-18: Edward A. Carter Jr., Section 59, Grave 451

38° 52.697' N, 77° 3.946' W

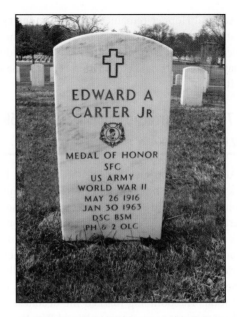

Edward "Eddie" Carter Jr. was born May 26, 1916, in Los Angeles. In 1921, his missionary parents left the United States to go to Calcutta, then to China, taking young Edward with them. Educated in a Chinese military school, Carter joined the Chinese army until it learned he was underage. He then left China and moved to Spain, where he fought in the Spanish Civil War. His time in the two foreign armies would come back to haunt him.

After serving in Spain's war, Carter returned to the United States. On September 26, 1941, he enlisted in the army, where he quickly rose to staff sergeant. However, in America's segregated forces at the time, African-American troops such as Carter were thought to be unreliable in combat. Despite his previous service, he was assigned as a mess sergeant in the 3535th Quartermaster Truck Company.

On November 13, 1944, Carter and his truck company deployed to Europe, where they transported supplies to the fighting troops. Each day for three months, he unsuccessfully volunteered for combat. After the Battle of the Bulge, however, the army needed reinforcements, and the appeal went out for volunteers among the black troops. Carter was among the twenty-six hundred volunteers, even though he was informed he would have to give up his rank and become a private. He became part of the First Provisional Company, assigned to the Twelfth Armored Division, then was assigned to the Fifty-sixth Armored Infantry Battalion. Seeing his potential, the commanders gave Carter his staff sergeant stripes back and made him an infantry squad leader.

On March 23, 1945, the Twelfth Armored was moving toward the city of Speyer, Germany. Carter and others were riding on a Sherman tank when they came under heavy antitank and machine-gun fire. Carter and his squad took cover, noticing that the rocket fire was coming from a warehouse 150 yards in front. Carter immediately volunteered to lead a three-man patrol to neutralize the attack. As the four left cover, one of Carter's men was cut down immediately. Carter ordered the other two to turn back. Before they could reach safety, one was killed and the other wounded. Carter continued alone. By the time he reached the warehouse, he was hit by five bullets and three pieces of shrapnel. He crawled the last few yards, blood and dirt staining his fatigues. Then he waited until an eight-man patrol came out of the warehouse to make sure Carter was dead. When they got close enough, Carter fired his .45-caliber Thompson submachine gun, killing six of the Germans. He then took the other two prisoner and used them as human shields as he returned to his company.

Despite being severely wounded and suffering from loss of blood, Carter refused medical treatment. Instead, he went to the observation post, where he pointed out several German machine-gun nests before turning over his prisoners for interrogation. The intelligence he provided, coupled with information obtained from the prisoners, enabled the army to clear the road and capture Speyer.

In July 1945, Carter's commanding officer signed a recommendation that Carter be awarded the Distinguished Service Cross. The award was approved, making him one of only nine black soldiers so recognized for heroism during the war.

At war's end, Carter returned to Los Angeles and went into business. When his venture failed, however, he reenlisted in the army, keeping his old rank. He soon was promoted to sergeant first class. At the end of his three-year enlistment, he tried to reenlist again. This time, he was turned down under suspicion of being a communist. Unknown to Carter, he had been under surveillance. His time in the Chinese and Spanish armies had raised suspicions about his loyalty. Shortly after his return from the war, he had attended a dinner at which Frank Sinatra, Ingrid Bergman, and Harpo Marx were headliners. The dinner was organized by the American Youth for Democracy, a left-wing political group.

A stunned Carter sent letters and telegrams to army officials, congressmen, the defense secretary, and anyone else he thought may be able to help. He even traveled to Washington to plead his case with the Adjutant General's Office. All his efforts were unsuccessful.

Finally, by May 1950, Carter had enough. He had already lost two jobs because of the accusation that he was a communist. He felt that the country he had fought for had turned its back on him. He sent a letter to an attorney who had represented him. Enclosed was his Distinguished Service Cross. The letter asked the attorney to return it to President Harry S. Truman.

Carter died from lung cancer January 30, 1963, at age forty-six and was buried in Sawtelle National Cemetery in Los Angeles. His Distinguished Service Cross was returned to his family by the attorney, who chose not to send it to the White House.

In 1995, the army undertook a study to determine why no black soldiers in World War II had received a Medal of Honor. The study focused on the nine blacks who had earned the Distinguished Service Cross. A special Army Awards Board panel determined that seven of those DSC recipients, including Eddie Carter, should have their awards upgraded to the nation's highest combat award, the Medal of Honor. On January 13, 1997, President William Clinton presented the award to Carter's family. When the announcement was made that Carter was to be awarded the Medal of Honor, his family requested he be moved to Arlington. Carter was reinterred here the day after his family received his medal.

In November 1999, the army formally apologized for unfairly branding Carter as a suspected communist. At the same time, it also presented the family with three military awards that a review of his personnel file showed he qualified for but had never received. Those were the Army Good Conduct Medal, the Army of Occupation Medal, and the American Campaign Medal.

11-19: Walter J. Sabalauski, Section 59, Grave 929

38° 52.698' N, 77° 3.930' W

Walter Sabalauski was born in 1910 in Lithuania but grew up in Chicago after his family immigrated to the United States. He became a professional boxer, losing only two of his thirty-three bouts. His boxing career ended abruptly as a result of injuries sustained in an automobile accident.

He entered the army in 1941, serving in World War II in the Pacific theater. He also served in the Korean War with the 187th Regimental Combat Team (Airborne) and the Twenty-fifth Infantry. In 1963, Sabalauski went to Vietnam for the first of his three tours. He then served in the Dominican Republic in 1965. The following year, he returned to Vietnam for his second tour.

While on patrol in June 1966, Sabalauski's Charlie Company made contact with an enemy battalion near Dak To. Under heavy enemy fire and unable to maneuver, Sabalauski dashed from position to position, repeatedly exposing himself to muster his unit and quell the hostile fire. As the Viet Cong attacked the perimeter, Sabalauski organized an assault line and delivered suppressive fire. Although artillery was called in as close as twenty-five meters from the friendly force and air strikes devastated the jungle around the perimeter, the enemy continued to advance. When the company commander called in air strikes on his own position as a last resort, Sabalauski remained on his feet to control the beleaguered paratroopers. Already wounded, he suffered napalm burns.

For the next thirty hours, he raced from one side of the perimeter to the other to direct and encourage his men. Ignoring his own pain, Sabalauski aided his wounded comrades, comforted the dying, and continued to direct his men. When reinforcements arrived, he went beyond the perimeter and retrieved a dead comrade. After moving a thousand meters to an evacuation point, Sabalauski personally supervised the extraction of the wounded and dead.

For his extraordinary heroism in defending his wounded men against the enemy and in evacuating causalities, he received both the Distinguished Service Cross and the Silver Star. At the end of his tour, he returned to the United States, only to go back to Vietnam for a third tour in 1968.

Sabalauski retired in 1971 at the age of sixty-one. His awards included the Legion of Merit, eight Bronze Stars, three Air Medals, six Army Commendation Medals, four Purple Hearts, three Combat Infantry Badges, the Master Parachutist Badge, and campaign medals for service in World War II, Korea, the Dominican Republic, and Vietnam. Fort Campbell's air assault school is named in his honor.

Command Sergeant Major Sabalauski died in 1993.

11-20: Cecil E. Harris, Section 55, Grave 938

38° 52.769' N, 77° 3.940' W

Cecil Edwin Harris was born March 4, 1925, in Shelbyville, Tennessee. He left home at age nineteen to fight in World War II, leaving behind a wife who was pregnant with a son he would never live to see.

Harris served in a rifle platoon with Company D, 179th Infantry Regiment, Forty-fifth Infantry Division. On January 2, 1945, he and his platoon came under attack in Dambach, France. The fighting was so intense that the platoon became scattered in the confusion of battle. When the men regrouped, Harris was missing.

He would remain so for seventy years, until French hikers found his remains in 2013 in a shallow grave near the France-Germany border. He finally returned home in the summer of 2014. That October 22, Harris was laid to rest in Arlington. Several family members, including his son, were present.

Private First Class Cecil Harris's military awards included the Combat Infantry Badge, the European–African–Middle Eastern Campaign Medal, the World War II Victory Medal, the Bronze Star, and the Purple Heart.

11-21: James H. Patterson, Section 55, Grave 3820

38° 52.799' N, 77° 3.882' W

James H. "Jim" Patterson was born in Canton, Ohio, on March 15, 1931, graduated from the University of Massachusetts, and earned an MBA from Auburn University. In 1952, he joined the army, attending Officer Candidate School.

In 1960, he served in Korea. Then, in 1966, deciding to make the military a career, he deployed to Vietnam. That October 22, after he had been in country three months, his helicopter was hit by enemy fire and crash-landed as it maneuvered to rescue the crew of another downed aircraft. As the crew exited Patterson's helicopter, one man was wounded in the neck. Patterson, ignoring the intense fire, leaped from the craft and dragged the man to safety behind a rice-paddy dike. He then raced back to his helicopter and obtained a machine gun, which he used to repel the enemy, even though he had no protective cover. Patterson spent the night hiding in the rice paddy with several other American troops. Repeatedly, he exposed himself to enemy fire to rescue and treat the wounded.

When a rescue helicopter was shot down seventy-five meters away, Patterson crawled and swam through the rice paddies, consolidating the crews of the downed craft. His effort was credited with being a critical factor in the troops' eventual evacuation. When a medical evacuation aircraft arrived, he dragged the wounded across the rice-paddy dikes and loaded them aboard.

After a fourth helicopter crashed, he extended his perimeter to protect those men. The next morning, he led a small patrol to the original downed ship, strengthened the perimeter, treated three wounded men, and directed their medical evacuation.

For risking his life that night while pulling wounded men to safety, Patterson was awarded the Distinguished Service Cross. His citation stated, in part, "His courageous actions saved four aircraft, their crews and infantrymen. Major Patterson's extraordinary heroism and devotion to duty were in keeping with the highest traditions of the military service and reflect great credit upon himself, his unit, and the United States Army."

Patterson was shot down two more times on his first tour of Vietnam. On his second tour, having been promoted to lieutenant colonel, he fell into a foxhole and broke his ankle badly enough that his deployment was cut short after only seven weeks. Following his recovery, he volunteered to return to Vietnam for a third tour but was turned down because of the injury. Unable to serve in a war zone, Patterson accepted a position at the Pentagon. He retired from the army in 1987 with the rank of major general.

Patterson received more than thirty awards for valor, including the Distinguished Service Medal, the Distinguished Flying Cross, two Legions of Merit, two Bronze Stars for valor, twenty-one Air Medals, and the Purple Heart.

He died October 21, 2009, at age seventy-eight.

11-22: Martin Conboy, Section 54, Grave 3841
38° 52.876' N, 77° 3.907' W

On August 2, 1861, when the Civil War was in its fourth month, Martin Conboy enlisted at the age of thirty-four in New York City. He was assigned to the Thirty-seventh New York Volunteers as a private in Company K. By December 9, he transferred to Company B, where he was promoted to sergeant, then to first sergeant.

On May 5, 1862, the Thirty-seventh was in Williamsburg, Virginia, where it encountered the Confederate army's rear guard as it retreated from Yorktown. The Union troops, under General Joseph Hooker, made an unsuccessful assault on Fort Magruder along the Williamsburg Road. In the heavy fighting, Company B's captain was wounded. Since all the other commissioned officers were in other areas, Conboy took command of the company and led it for the rest of the fight.

On Christmas Eve 1862, he was made a second lieutenant, retroactive to October 20, 1862. He mustered out on June 22, 1863, at New York City.

On October 11, 1893, Conboy was awarded the Medal of Honor for his actions. His citation reads, "Took command of the company in action, the captain having been wounded, the other commissioned officers being absent, and handled it with skill and bravery."

Conboy died December 21, 1909, and was buried in Holy Sepulchre Cemetery in East Orange, New Jersey. On July 31, 2001, he was reinterred in Arlington at the request of his family. Since the older sections of the cemetery were filled, he had to be reinterred in Section 54, making him the only Civil War soldier in that part of the property.

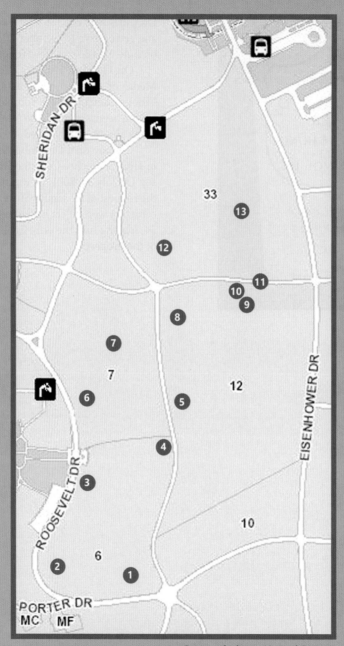

Courtesy of Arlington National Cemetery

12-1: Elizabeth P. Hoisington, Section 6, Grave 9239-A-B

38° 52.473' N, 77° 4.188' W

Elizabeth Paschel Hoisington was born into a military family on November 3, 1918. Her grandfather was one of the organizers of the Kansas Army National Guard, and her father was an army colonel and a marksman. She enlisted in the Women's Army Auxiliary Corps in 1942 and quickly gained the admiration and respect of those around her for her organizational and leadership skills.

In 1944, Hoisington was assigned to Europe, becoming one of the first American women to step onto French soil after the D-Day invasion. Following the German surrender, she put her organizational abilities to the test, helping organize the telephone system used at the Potsdam Conference. She served as executive officer of a WAC battalion in Tokyo from 1948 to 1950, then returned stateside to assignments at the Pentagon

and the San Francisco area until 1964. Following a stint as commandant of the Women's Army Corps School at Fort McClellan, Alabama, she was named director of the corps in 1966.

On June 11, 1970, Hoisington became one of the first two women in the United States to be named brigadier generals, the other being Anna Mae Hays of the Army Nurse Corps, who was promoted at the same time. Hoisington's older brother, Perry, was a major general at the time, making the two the first brother-sister combination to serve as generals.

Upon her retirement in 1971, Hoisington was only the third WAC to receive the Distinguished Service Medal. Among her other awards were the Legion of Merit (twice), the Bronze Star, and the Army Commendation Medal. She died August 21, 2007, at age eighty-eight. Her father, Colonel Gregory Hoisington, and her youngest brother, First Lieutenant Gregory Hoisington Jr., are also interred in Arlington.

12-2: Lee Andrew Archer Jr., Section 6, Grave 9215-RH

38° 52.474' N, 77° 4.257' W

Born on September 6, 1919, in Yonkers and raised in Harlem, Lee Archer left New York University to enlist in the U.S. Army Air Corps in 1941 but was rejected for pilot training because of his race. He then applied and was accepted into Tuskegee Institute as a fighter pilot in 1942 as a member of the 302nd Fighter Squadron under the 332nd Fighter Group. He graduated from pilot training in July 1943. Archer went on to fly 196 missions during World War II with the famous Tuskegee Airmen. In October 1944, he became one of four

men who "tripled," destroying three German Me 109s on a single mission. Three months earlier, he had been credited with destroying six aircraft on the ground during a strafing mission, along with several locomotives, motor transports, and barges. He was officially credited with four planes shot down during his career and shared a fifth with another pilot. Investigation revealed that it was Archer's shots that caused the enemy plane to go down, giving him five kills and making him the only African-American air ace in history.

After the war, he served with distinction for twenty-nine years in the air force, retiring in 1970 with numerous honors including citations from three presidents. Among his many awards were the Air Force Distinguished Service Medal, the Distinguished Flying Cross, the Air Medal with eighteen clusters, and a Distinguished Unit Citation. In 2008, he and his fellow Tuskegee Airmen were each awarded a Congressional Gold Medal. The following year, he served as an advisor for the feature film *Red Tails*.

Archer died January 27, 2010, and was buried in Arlington two weeks later.

12-3: John Archer Lejeune, Section 6, Grave 5682
38° 52.560' N, 77° 4.228' W

John Archer Lejeune graduated from Louisiana State University, then from the U.S. Naval Academy in 1888. Often referred to as "the greatest of all Leathernecks," he served more than forty years with the Marine Corps. He led the army's famed Second Division in World War I from July 28, 1918, through August 1919, becoming the first marine officer to hold an army divisional command. He proudly led the division into Germany following the armistice.

The French government was so impressed with his performance that it awarded him the Legion of Merit and the Croix de Guerre. General John J. Pershing

presented him with the Army Distinguished Service Medal. He was then awarded the Navy Distinguished Service Medal on his return to the United States. He also received the Marine Corps Expeditionary Medal with three stars, the Spanish Campaign Medal, the West Indies Naval Campaign Medal, the Mexican Service Medal, the Nicaraguan Campaign Medal, and the World War Victory Medal with three clasps.

Lejeune served in the Spanish-American War, the Philippine-American War, and the occupation of Veracruz. He also participated in campaigns in Cuba and Panama and served two stints as commander of the Marine Barracks, Quantico, Virginia. In 1920, he became the thirteenth commandant of the Marine Corps, serving in that capacity until 1929. He is credited with founding the Marine Corps League, the only congressionally chartered Marine Corps–related veterans' organization in the United States.

General Lejeune retired from service on November 10, 1929, to become the fifth superintendent of the Virginia Military Institute, a position from which he retired for reasons of health in October 1937. He died November 20, 1942, and was buried in Arlington with full military honors.

Camp Lejeune, North Carolina, and the navy transport ship USS *Lejeune* (AP-74) are named in his honor.

12-4: Barbara Allen Rainey, Section 6, Grave 5813-A-7
38° 52.584' N, 77° 4.132' W

Barbara Rainey was destined to become part of the navy when she was born on August 20, 1948, at Bethesda Naval Hospital, the daughter of a career naval officer. Following graduation from Whittier College in California, she was commissioned in the U.S. Naval Reserve. Not long afterward, she applied to and was accepted into U.S. Naval Flight Training School. On February 22, 1974, she became the first female naval aviator in history.

She resigned her commission in November 1977 to devote time to her family. But when the navy experienced a shortage of flight instructors in 1981, she was recalled to active duty. On July 13, 1982, she was conducting a training flight at Middleton Field, Alabama, with Ensign Donald Bruce Knowlton, who is believed

to have been at the controls, although that was never proven. While flying touch-and-go exercises, the plane appeared to turn left prematurely, placing it on a potential collision path with another plane. Two other pilots immediately called out warnings via their radios, leading Rainey's plane to bank sharply right. As it did, it rapidly lost altitude, crashed, and burned. Both Rainey and Knowlton were killed. Lieutenant Commander Rainey was buried in Arlington a week after her death, on July 20, 1982.

Although the accident was eventually attributed to pilot error, the engine had been operating at reduced power, and the plane may have experienced an uncommanded engine response or an uncommanded deceleration known as a "rollback." Refusing to accept the finding of pilot error, and believing the accident had been caused by an equipment malfunction, the families of Knowlton and Rainey brought a product-liability lawsuit against Beech Aircraft Corporation, manufacturer of the plane. The lawsuit eventually made its way to the U.S. Supreme Court, which ruled in favor of the families.

12-5: John Basilone, Section 12, Grave 384
38° 52.617' N, 77° 4.125' W

Born into an Italian-American family of ten children on November 4, 1916, in Buffalo, New York, John Basilone spent his formative years in Raritan, New Jersey, where he gained a modicum of local fame as a light-heavyweight boxer. At age eighteen, he enlisted in the army and served in the Philippines, where he picked up the nickname "Manila John." He was honorably discharged in 1937. However, seeing the war clouds of World War II gathering, he enlisted in the marines in July 1940.

On the night of October 24–25, 1942, Sergeant Basilone was on Guadalcanal, where his two sections of heavy machine guns were defending a narrow pass to Henderson Airfield. One gun crew was knocked out of service by a fierce Japanese frontal assault, leaving only two men to continue the fight. Basilone grabbed a machine gun and its tripod and raced with his ninety-pound load more than two hundred yards under heavy fire to the silenced gun pit, where he took over firing. When enemy soldiers worked their way around to Basilone's rear, he fought them off with his pistol. Low on ammunition, he sprinted another two hundred yards to an ammunition dump, then returned with an armload of ammunition.

In the darkness, the light from flares revealed one wave after another of attackers. Basilone fired until the heat from his weapon burned his hands so badly that blisters formed. He continued shooting, pausing only long enough to crawl forward and move the enemy bodies out of his field of fire. By the time the attackers were finally driven off, thirty-eight enemy bodies lay at the edge of the gun pit. For his actions, Basilone was awarded the Medal of Honor.

He was sent back to the United States, where he appeared around the country at war-bond rallies. His appearances helped raise $1.4 million in pledges. His picture appeared on the cover of *Life* magazine. Still, he was restless in his new role and asked to return to his men.

On February 19, 1945, he was back in action, this time on Iwo Jima. There, he single-handedly took out an enemy blockhouse. Minutes later, an enemy mortar round exploded in the midst of his platoon, killing and wounding several. Basilone was among the wounded. He died an hour and a half later. He was twenty-seven years old.

Gunnery Sergeant Basilone was posthumously awarded the Navy Cross and a Purple Heart in addition to his Medal of Honor, making him the only enlisted marine in World War II to receive all three.

12-6: George Catlett Marshall, Section 7, Grave 8198
38° 52.619' N, 77° 4.221' W

General George Catlett Marshall, called by Winston Churchill "the true architect of victory" in Western Europe in World War II, was born December 31, 1880, in Uniontown, Pennsylvania. He graduated from the Virginia Military Institute in 1901. On September 1, 1939, he was promoted to chief of staff with the rank of general and was named general of the army on December 16, 1944.

Marshall served as secretary of state from 1947 to 1949, during which time he developed his economic program known as the Marshall Plan, which pushed for economic recovery and stability to ensure a successful rebuilding of Europe after World War II. He believed America's security and economic health depended on a healthy Europe. While his plan included the So-

viet Union and Eastern Europe, the Soviets rejected it, which resulted in Western Europe's economic recovery being much more rapid than that of the east. When that gap widened to a point where it posed a threat to the security of the West, Marshall joined with other world leaders to form the North Atlantic Treaty Organization to counter that threat.

His last official position for the United States was as secretary of defense from 1950 to 1951. In that position, Marshall oversaw the formation of an international force that turned back the North Korean invasion of South Korea. His efforts to achieve world peace were recognized in 1953 when he was awarded the Nobel Peace Prize.

General Marshall died October 16, 1959, and was buried with full military honors.

12-7: Jeremiah A. Denton Jr., Section 7, Grave 8011-B

38° 52.665' N, 77° 4.190' W

The title of *hero* is often applied more generously than is justified, but such is not the case with Jeremiah Denton Jr. Denton graduated from the U.S. Naval Academy with honors in 1947 and became a test pilot. He also graduated from the Armed Forces Staff College and the Naval War College, where his thesis on international affairs earned him the prestigious President's Award. In 1957, he was credited with developing "the Haystack Concept," a strategy calling for avoiding typical naval formations and concealing aircraft carriers from radar by intermingling them with commercial shipping. The plan completely changed the navy's strategy and tactics in the event of a nuclear war.

In June 1965, Denton began flying combat missions in Vietnam. When his navy A-6A Intruder jet was shot down on a bombing mission over North Vietnam later that year, he was captured and suffered greatly at the hands of his captors, as did most POWs in that war. Subjected to brutal interrogations and suffering from starvation, he defied his tormentors to the point where he and ten other rebellious POWs were placed in solitary confinement in a special prison in Hanoi. The POWs referred to it as "Alcatraz" and to themselves as "the Alcatraz Eleven."

Denton repeatedly defied his captors, leading to additional harsh punishment. In 1966, the North Vietnamese forced him to appear in a propaganda interview on live television. Denton's answers to his captors' questions were defiant, but it was his actions that were most noteworthy. While answering a question in a manner he knew would bring him a beating when the cameras were turned off, he repeatedly blinked the letters *T-O-R-T-U-R-E* in Morse code. The North Vietnamese did not immediately notice it, and Denton's message got through to the world that he and his fellow prisoners were undergoing significant mental and physical suffering, in violation of the Geneva Convention.

He was finally released in 1973 after more than seven years in captivity. In January 1974, he assumed command of the Armed Forces Staff College, now the Joint Forces Staff College. Denton retired from the navy on November 1, 1977, with the rank of rear admiral. Just before his retirement, he wrote a book describing his experiences as a prisoner of war. The book, *When Hell Was in Session*, was turned into a television movie. In 1980, he became the first Alabama Republican elected to the U.S. Senate since Reconstruction. He served until 1986.

Denton counted among his many military awards the Navy Cross, the Defense Distinguished Service Medal, the Navy Distinguished Service Medal, three Silver Stars, the Distinguished Flying Cross, the Bronze Star with combat "V," the Air Medal, the Navy Commendation Medal with combat "V," the Purple Heart, the Combat Action Ribbon, and the Prisoner of War Medal.

He died at age eighty-nine in March 2014. The

navy's POW Survival, Evasion, Resistance, and Escape School was named in his honor.

12-8: Michael Strank, Section 12, Grave 7179
38° 52.685' N, 77° 4.110' W

Michael Strank was born in Jarabenia, Czechoslovakia, on November 10, 1919. He and his family came to the United States in 1922, settling in Conemaugh, Pennsylvania, a working-class suburb of Johnstown. He became a citizen when his father was naturalized in 1935 but never received a certificate of his own naturalization. Still, he enlisted in the Marine Corps following graduation from high school in 1937 and short stints with the Civilian Conservation Corps and the state highway department.

Strank served on various bases in the United States

and at Guantanamo Bay, Cuba, before sailing for combat in the Pacific in 1942. On February 19, 1945, he was leading his men in the battle for Iwo Jima. The Japanese troops had dug in with a labyrinth of fortified bunkers, artillery, and underground tunnels, all protected by minefields.

On the fourth day of fighting, a patrol of marines reached the summit of Mount Suribachi, an extinct volcano that overlooked the landing beaches. Shortly afterward, a small American flag appeared as the marines below cheered. When it was determined that the flag was too small to be seen by the troops on the eastern end of the island, a larger flag was sent up. Meanwhile, Strank and three of his men—Corporal Harlon Block, Private First Class Ira Hayes (see Chapter 9, site 9-15), and Private First Class Franklin Sousley—were in the process of running communication wire up the mountain when they were joined by Rene Gagnon (see Chapter 2, site 2-9), the man carrying the flag to the top. The five were joined at the summit by a sixth man, initially believed to have been navy corpsman John Bradley but later thought to be Private First Class Harold Schultz. As the second flag was raised, Associated Press photographer Joe Rosenthal took the iconic photo that would win the Pulitzer Prize that year. Strank is difficult to see in the photo but is easily witnessed on the Marine Corps War Memorial, which sits just outside the north end of the cemetery.

A week after the famous flag raising, Strank's outfit, Easy Company, Second Battalion, Twenty-eighth Marines, joined an assault on another heavily fortified part of the island. Coming under heavy sniper fire, Strank, said by his men to be the ultimate "marine's marine," led them to cover under a rocky outcropping. There, Strank was killed by what is believed to have been a shell from an American ship moored offshore. He was the first person in the famous photograph to be killed. Soon, Block and Sousley joined him. By battle's end, nearly seven thousand American military personnel, mostly marines, lay dead and nearly twenty thousand were wounded, making it one of the war's bloodiest fights.

Strank was buried in the Fifth Marine Division Cemetery. On January 13, 1949, his remains were reinterred in Arlington. It was after his funeral that his family members learned he was one of the famous flag raisers. They recalled seeing the photo in the local newspaper but had no idea Strank was in it.

After Strank's remains were placed in Arlington, his story seemingly ended. But until 2008, the Marine Corps was unaware of his immigrant background, believing he was born in Pennsylvania. A marine security guard at the U.S. embassy in the Slovak Republic who was researching Strank's background found no record of his being an American citizen. Surprised, he filed an application for posthumous naturalization for Strank. Only then did a subsequent investigation reveal that Strank actually was a citizen but had never received his certificate of naturalization. That oversight was corrected when his sister was presented with his certificate in a ceremony in front of the Marine Corps War Memorial in July 2008.

12-9: Wataru Nakashima, Section 12, Grave 5125
38° 52.689' N, 77° 4.053' W;

and Raito Nakashima, Section 12, Grave 5124
38° 52.690' N, 77° 4.053' W

The Japanese attacked Pearl Harbor on December 7, 1941. Two months later, on February 19, 1942, President Franklin D. Roosevelt signed Executive Order 9066. Demonstrating fear of potential sabo-

tage and more than a hint of wartime hysteria, the order authorized the secretary of war to set up areas known as military zones. Ten such zones were established throughout the United States. The action also ordered all Japanese-Americans to evacuate the West Coast and report to one of the ten zones. These zones, or internment camps, quickly became the new homes for 120,000 people, more than half of them American citizens.

Eventually, the government allowed some of these Japanese-Americans to serve in the armed forces, fighting for the country that had placed them under lock and key. Some four thousand signed up, including brothers Raito and Wataru Nakashima, both of whom became part of the famed 442nd Regimental Combat Team. Raito served as a private in Company B, while Wataru was a sergeant in Company M. The 442nd

Regimental Combat Team, made up almost entirely of Japanese-Americans, became one of the most decorated infantry regiments in the history of the U.S. Army. The unit was awarded eight Presidential Unit Citations and 9,486 Purple Hearts. Twenty-one of its members received the Medal of Honor.

Raito was killed on April 14, 1945, in action near Castelpoggio, Italy. When he observed four of the enemy attempting to infiltrate his company's position, he stood up and threw a hand grenade, killing two and wounding one. As he attempted to throw a second grenade, he was wounded twice. Fighting off intense pain, he continued firing until he collapsed, mortally wounded. His actions gained him a posthumous Silver Star. Wataru died just a short time later, on January 9, 1946. The two brothers were buried side by side in Arlington on November 19, 1948.

12-10: Curtis C. Morris, Section 12, Grave 8055
38° 52.708' N, 77° 4.068' W

Curtis Morris was born in Lake Charles, Louisiana, on September 18, 1917. Three months before the United States was drawn into World War II, he enlisted in the army, eventually becoming a paratrooper with Easy Company, 504th Parachute Infantry Regiment, Eighty-second Airborne Division. He made his first combat jump in July 1943 in Sicily. After recovering from wounds suffered in Salerno when he was struck by shrapnel from mortar grenades, he rejoined his unit and took part in the Battle of Anzio.

On September 17, 1944, Morris jumped into Holland with the Eighty-second Airborne as part of Operation Market Garden. The objective was to seize the Maas Bridge. Unfortunately, Morris's parachute malfunctioned, causing him to plummet into the farmyard

of Dutch citizen Jan Van Den Hoogen. Morris's companions carried him into Van Den Hoogen's barn and quickly summoned a priest from a nearby Jesuit monastery, who baptized Morris and gave him last rites. Approximately two hours later, he died, one day before his twenty-seventh birthday. Morris was buried September 21, 1944, in Molenhoek, a temporary American military cemetery near Nijmegen. On February 9, 1949, he was reburied in Arlington.

Shortly after the initial burial in Holland, Van Den Hoogen found Morris's helmet liner as he worked on his farm. He kept it for sixty years as a memory of the day Holland was liberated by the Allies. Then, thinking it may be better for Morris's family to have it, he turned it over to the U.S. Embassy. Fortunately, the serial number in the helmet liner was still legible, and the embassy contacted the Pentagon to determine the owner's name. Once it was discovered that the liner had belonged to Morris, the search began for any remaining family members. A nephew saw an article in a military magazine and contacted Morris's daughter, who was put in touch with Van Den Hoogen.

The Dutch farmer was reluctant to mail the liner to Morris's daughter, fearing it could be lost or stolen in transit, so arrangements were made for a military attaché to deliver it to the Pentagon. Pentagon officials in turn presented the helmet liner to Morris's daughter in a special ceremony in January 2006.

12-11: McClellan Gate, Section 33
38° 52.727' N, 77° 4.027' W

When Arlington National Cemetery was established, its eastern boundary lay where Eisenhower Drive is located today. In 1871, U.S. Army quartermaster general Montgomery C. Meigs ordered that a main ceremonial gate be constructed. Meigs named it

the McClellan Gate after Major General George B. Mc-Clellan, who organized the Army of the Potomac and served from November 1861 to March 1862 as general in chief of the Union army. The main entrance was located where the McClellan Arch currently towers thirty feet above the roadway. As part of the design, Meigs ordered McClellan's name to be inscribed at the top of the gate's face in gilt letters. Never accused of being shy, Meigs then had his own name inscribed in the left main column as a tribute to himself.

The use of the McClellan Gate as the main entrance became impractical when the land east of Eisenhower Drive was returned to the cemetery's possession in 1932 from the Department of Agriculture, which had been using it as an experimental farm. At that time, the current main entrance at the Women in Military Service to America Memorial was established.

Of the 315,555 citizens who died in defense of the country from 1861 to 1865, some 15,585 are buried in Arlington. They are recognized in a tribute appearing beneath McClellan's name above the arch. The inscribed lines from Theodore O'Hara's poem "Bivouac of the Dead" are as follows:

ON FAME'S ETERNAL CAMPING GROUND
THEIR SILENT TENTS ARE SPREAD,
AND GLORY GUARDS, WITH SOLEMN ROUND,
THE BIVOUAC OF THE DEAD.

The rear of the arch contains another inscription from O'Hara's poem:

REST ON EMBALMED AND SAINTED DEAD,
DEAR AS THE BLOOD YE GAVE,
NO IMPIOUS FOOTSTEP HERE SHALL TREAD
THE HERBAGE OF YOUR GRAVE.

The McClellan Gate is the only survivor among the original public entrances to the cemetery.

12-12: John W. Boutwell, Section 33, Grave 2937
38° 52.747′ N, 77° 4.136′ W

Born at Hanover, New Hampshire, on August 3, 1845, John Boutwell joined Company B of the Eighteenth New Hampshire Volunteer Infantry when it mustered in on September 13, 1864. The length of service for the Eighteenth New Hampshire was ten months.

On April 2, 1865, the regiment launched an assault on Confederate lines at Petersburg, Virginia. In that action, Boutwell came across a member of the regiment who had been wounded in both legs. He ran through a storm of enemy fire, picked the man up, and carried him to safety. He was awarded the Medal of Honor for this action.

Fighting was so heavy at Petersburg that day that fifty-four Medals of Honor were awarded. Boutwell's citation reads, "The President of the United States of America, in the name of Congress, takes pleasure in presenting the Medal of Honor to Private John W. Boutwell, United States Army, for extraordinary heroism on

2 April 1865, while serving with Company B, 18th New Hampshire Infantry, in action at Petersburg, Virginia. Private Boutwell brought off from the picket line, under heavy fire, a comrade who had been shot through both legs."

Boutwell survived the war and lived until December 11, 1920.

12-13: Francis C. Hammond, Section 33, Grave 9011

38° 52.781' N, 77° 4.067' W

Francis Colton Hammond was born in Alexandria, Virginia, on November 9, 1931. Following his high-school graduation, he enlisted in the navy in 1951. Trained as a hospitalman, he was sent to Korea in February 1953, attached to the Fifth Marines.

During the night of March 26–27, 1953, near Sanae-dong, his platoon came under a ferocious attack. Following a deadly barrage of mortar and artillery fire, the North Koreans launched an infantry assault. As several marines fell under the onslaught, Hammond coolly moved from one wounded man to the next, treating their injuries despite being badly hurt himself. The attack continued for four brutal hours, during which time Hammond continued to care for his injured comrades. When his platoon was directed to withdraw, he guided the evacuation of the wounded. Still ignoring the danger, he then remained behind to assist the corpsmen attached to the relieving unit until he was struck by an enemy mortar round. That wound proved fatal.

For his actions, Hammond was awarded the Medal of Honor and the Purple Heart. In late December 1953, his widow and son accepted his Medal of Honor.

In 1956, a new school was named for Hammond in his hometown of Alexandria. On July 25, 1970, the navy commissioned the destroyer USS *Francis Hammond* (FF-1067) in his honor. His name also adorns a medical clinic at Camp Pendleton, California.

One note: Since the photograph above of Hammond's grave was taken, a new tombstone that shows his date of death as March 26 has been installed.

Medal of Honor Recipients Buried in Arlington National Cemetery

Three versions of the Medal of Honor are currently awarded: the army, navy, and air force. The present design for the army version was adopted in 1904. The current navy design, presented to members of the U.S. Navy, Marine Corps, and Coast Guard, was adopted in 1913. Because the navy version was awarded to noncombatants as well as combatants, the navy in 1919 opted for a second design, known as the Tiffany Cross, for noncombatants. The Tiffany Cross never caught on, and the navy returned to the original design for all recipients in 1942. The air force designed its own version of the Medal of Honor in 1965. Prior to that, honorees from the Army Air Corps and its predecessor, the Army Air Service, were presented with the army's version.

Since the first Medal of Honor was awarded to Jacob Parrott in 1863, more than 3,400 individuals have been so honored. Of these, 406 are interred in Arlington as of this writing and are listed below. In addition, Medals of Honor have been awarded to each of the unknowns interred in the Tomb of the Unknowns, one each for World War I, World War II, Korea, and Vietnam. Although the occupant of the Vietnam crypt was ultimately identified, the medal itself remains in the Arlington National Cemetery archives.

Nineteen individuals have been awarded the honor twice, and four of these rest in Arlington. Recipients of the Medal of Honor who received the award for heroic actions during peacetime are shown as "Interim" recipients in the list.

Name	Branch	Action	Section[1]	Grave No.
Albee, George Emerson	Army	Indian Wars	2	850-ES
Anderson, Beauford Theodore	Army	WW II	44	292
Anderson, Edwin Alexander	Navy	Mexican War	2	3798
Anderson, Marion T.	Army	Civil War	1	512
Antrim, Richard Nott	Navy	WW II	35	2613
Badger, Oscar Charles	Navy	Mexican War	2	3760-WS
Baird, Absalom	Army	Civil War	1	55
Baker, John Franklin	Army	Vietnam	34	687
Baker, Vernon Joseph	Army	WW II	59	4408
Baldonado, Joe R.	Army	Korea	MH	644
Baldwin, Frank Dwight[2]	Army	Civil War, Indian Wars	3	1894
Barber, William Earl	Marines	Korea	66	6904
Barnes, Will Croft	Army	Indian Wars	6	9754
Basilone, John	Marines	WW II	12	384
Batchelder, Richard Napoleon	Army	Civil War	2	998
Batson, Matthew A.	Army	Philippine-American War	2	3604-WS
Beaufort, Jean J.	Army	Civil War	13	13784

Name	Branch	Action	Section[1]	Grave No.
Bell, Bernard Pious	Army	WW II	25	3840
Bell, Dennis	Army	Spanish-American War	31	349
Bell, James Franklin	Army	Philippine-American War	3	1735-4
Bennett, Floyd	Navy	Interim	3	1852-B
Berkeley, Randolph Carter	Marines	Mexican War	3	1767-SH
Birdsall, Horatio Latin	Army	Civil War	13	6935
Birkhimer, William Edward	Army	Philippine-American War	1	339-WD
Bliss, Zenas Randall	Army	Civil War	1	8-B
Blume, Robert	Navy	Spanish-American War	6	9752-SS
Boehm, Peter Martin	Army	Civil War	2	3674
Boone, Joel Thompson	Navy	WW I	11	137-2
Bourke, John Gregory	Army	Civil War	1	32-A
Boutwell, John W.	Army	Civil War	33	2937
Boyington, Gregory "Pappy"	Marines	WW II	7A	150
Boynton, Henry Van Ness	Army	Civil War	2	1096
Bradbury, Sanford	Army	Indian Wars	3	2162-WS
Brannigan, Felix	Army	Civil War	3	1642
Breeman, George Adrian	Navy	Interim	6	9743-SH
Brett, Lloyd Milton	Army	Indian Wars	6	8367
Brewster, Andre Walker	Army	Boxer Rebellion	2	1130
Bronson, Deming	Army	WW I	30	500-2
Brown, Bobbie Evan, Jr.	Army	WW II	46	1021-17
Brown, John Harties	Army	Civil War	3	1486 1/2
Brown, William H.	Navy	Civil War	27	565-A
Buchanan, Allen	Navy	Mexican War	9	845
Buckingham, David Eastburn	Army	Civil War	2	3677
Bulkeley, John Duncan	Navy	WW II	5	129-9-RH
Burke, Daniel Webster	Army	Civil War	2	3739
Burke, Lloyd Leslie "Scooter"	Army	Korea	7A	155
Burnett, George Ritter	Army	Indian Wars	3	2193-WS
Byrd, Richard Evelyn, Jr.	Navy	Interim	2	4969-1
Byrne, Bernard Albert	Army	Philippine-American War	1	707
Cahey, Thomas	Navy	Interim	6	8667
Calvert, James Spencer	Army	Indian Wars	3	2490
Campbell, James A.	Army	Civil War	3	1468-55
Cann, Tedford Harris	Navy	WW I	7	10118-SS
Capehart, Charles E.	Army	Civil War	3	2033-WS
Capehart, Henry	Army	Civil War	1	140-A-B
Caron, Wayne Maurice	Navy	Vietnam	51	2600
Carter, Edward Allen, Jr.	Army	WW II	59	451
Carter, Joseph Edward	Navy	Spanish-American War	34	2631-1

Name	Branch	Action	Section[1]	Grave No.
Carter, Joseph Franklin	Army	Civil War	3	1550
Carter, Robert Goldthwaite	Army	Indian Wars	1	106A
Carter, William Harding	Army	Indian Wars	1	443WS
Cary, Robert Webster	Navy	Interim	6	5695-G
Castle, Guy Wilkinson Stuart	Navy	Mexican War	3	4345
Catlin, Albertus Wright	Marines	Mexican War	7	10038
Catlin, Isaac Swartwood	Army	Civil War	2	3397
Cavaiani, Jon Robert	Army	Vietnam	60	10590
Cecil, Joseph Samuel	Army	Philippine-American War	6	5718
Chambers, Justice Marion	Marines	WW II	6	5813-A9
Charlton, Cornelius H.	Army	Korea	40	300
Charrette, George	Navy	Spanish-American War	7	10222
Cheever, Benjamin Harrison, Jr.	Army	Indian Wars	1	421
Christiancy, James Isaac	Army	Civil War	1	580
Church, James Robb	Army	Spanish-American War	3	1409A
Clancy, Joseph	Navy	Boxer Rebellion	7	8145
Clay, Cecil	Army	Civil War	2	1012
Collier, John Walton	Army	Korea	12	4637
Conboy, Martin	Army	Civil War	54	3841
Condon, Clarence Milville	Army	Philippine-American War	2	3834
Cook, Donald Gilbert[3]	Marines	Vietnam	MI	110
Cook, John	Army	Civil War	17	18613
Coughlin, John	Army	Civil War	2	936-WS
Courts, George McCall	Navy	Mexican War	7	9874
Crandall, Orson Leon	Navy	Interim	48	2004
Cregan, George	Navy	Mexican War	46	10666
Crescenz, Michael Joseph	Army	Vietnam	59	3226
Crilley, Frank William	Navy	Interim	8	6430
Cruse, Thomas	Army	Indian Wars	3	1763
Cukela, Louis[4]	Marines	WW I	1	427-A
Cutts, James Madison	Army	Civil War	3	1371-SS
Davila, Rudolph B.	Army	WW II	67	3457
Davis, Charles Willis	Army	WW II	7A	170
Davis, John	Navy	Spanish-American War	11	639-SS
Decker, Percy A.	Navy	Mexican War	7	10302
Delaney, John Carroll	Army	Civil War	3	2170-WS
Dethlefsen, Merlyn Hans	Air Force	Vietnam	65	1626
Diggins, Bartholomew	Navy	Civil War	13	5400-15
Dilboy, George	Army	WW I	18	4574
Dillon, Michael A.	Army	Civil War	13	14660
Doane, Stephen Holden	Army	Vietnam	59	1617

Name	Branch	Action	Section[1]	Grave No.
Dodge, Francis Safford	Army	Indian Wars	3	1874
Dolby, David Charles	Army	Vietnam	59	498
Donahue, John L.	Army	Indian Wars	13	14045
Donovan, William Joseph	Army	WW I	2	4874
Doolittle, James Harold	Army	WW II	7A	110
Drexler, Henry Clay	Navy	Interim	4	3051
Drustrup, Niels	Navy	Mexican War	3	4378-RH
Durham, James R.	Army	Civil War	3	1435
Edson, Merritt Austin	Marines	WW II	2	4960-1-2
Edwards, Walter Atlee	Navy	Interim	4	3183
Eggers, Alan Louis	Army	WW I	2	3389-A
Eglit, John[5]	Navy	Spanish-American War	MI	306A
Ellis, Michael B.	Army	WW I	6	9520
Elrod, Henry Talmage	Marines	WW II	12	3246
Engle, James Edgar	Army	Civil War	1	569
Estes, Lewellyn Garrish	Army	Civil War	3	1437
Everhart, Forrest Eugene, Sr.	Army	WW II	60	7516
Faith, Don Carlos, Jr.	Army	Korea	4	3016
Ferguson, Arthur Medworth	Army	Philippine-American War	3	4016
Fisher, Almond Edward	Army	WW II	6	8751-2
Fletcher, Frank Friday	Navy	Mexican War	3	1933
Fletcher, Frank Jack	Navy	Mexican War	2	4736-E
Forsterer, Bruno Albert	Marines	Samoa	53	2757
Foss, Joseph Jacob	Marines	WW II	7A	162
Foster, Paul Frederick	Navy	Mexican War	5	106
Frazer, Hugh Carroll	Navy	Mexican War	46	282
Freeman, Henry Blanchard	Army	Civil War	2	937
Fryer, Eli Thompson	Marines	Mexican War	34	102-A
Fuger, Frederick W.	Army	Civil War	1	511
Funk, Leonard Alfred, Jr.	Army	WW II	35	2373-4
Fuqua, Samuel Glenn	Navy	WW II	59	485
Garlington, Ernest Albert	Army	Indian Wars	3	1735-B
Gaujot, Julien Edmund	Army	Mexican War	6	8423-NH
Gause, Isaac	Army	Civil War	17	19595
Gere, Thomas Parke	Army	Civil War	1	361
Gerstung, Robert E.	Army	WW II	66	6152
Gilmore, John Curtis	Army	Civil War	1	270
Godfrey, Edward Settle	Army	Indian Wars	3	4175-E
Grace, Peter	Army	Civil War	3	2556-EH
Grady, John	Navy	Mexican War	4	2723-2-RH
Graham, James Albert	Marines	Vietnam	13	8576-F

Name	Branch	Action	Section[1]	Grave No.
Grant, Joseph Xavier	Army	Vietnam	30	1648-2
Greely, Adolphus Washington	Army	Interim	1	129
Greer, Allen James	Army	Philippine-American War	1	701-B
Hagen, Loren Douglas	Army	Vietnam	28	1204
Hall, William Preble	Army	Indian Wars	1	653
Hamberger, William Francis	Navy	Boxer Rebellion	6	9164
Hammond, Francis Colton	Navy	Korea	33	9011
Hansen, Hans Anton	Navy	Boxer Rebellion	17	18576
Hardaway, Benjamin Franklin	Army	Spanish-American War	2	1044-1
Harner, Joseph Gabriel	Navy	Mexican War	17	21199-B2
Harrington, David	Navy	Interim	17	23162-D
Harris, James H.	Army	Civil War	27	985-H
Harrison, William Kelly	Navy	Mexican War	2	1080
Hartigan, Charles Conway	Navy	Mexican War	3	2194-B
Harvey, Raymond	Army	Korea	6	830-B-LH
Hatch, John Porter	Army	Civil War	1	333-C
Hawthorne, Harry Leroy	Army	Indian Wars	3	1952
Hayden, David Ephraim	Navy	WW I	36	1864
Hays, George Price	Army	WW I	11	540-2
Henderson, Joseph	Army	Philippine-American War	20	50042
Henry, Guy Vernor	Army	Civil War	2	990
Heyl, Charles Pettit Heath	Army	Indian Wars	1	135-B-WH
Hill, Walter Newell	Marines	Mexican War	6	9646-BC
Hobson, Richmond Pearson	Navy	Spanish-American War	6	5014
Holland, Milton Murray	Army	Civil War	23	21713
Hooper, Joe Ronnie	Army	Vietnam	46	656-17
Horner, Freeman Victor	Army	WW II	11	338-2
Houghton, Charles H.	Army	Civil War	3	2411
Howard, James Howell	Army	WW II	34	2571
Howard, Robert Lewis	Army	Vietnam	7A	138
Hughes, John Arthur	Marines	Mexican War	8	5264
Hulbert, Henry Lewis	Marines	Samoa	3	4309
Humphrey, Charles Frederick	Army	Indian Wars	4	3115
Huse, Henry McLaren Pinckney	Navy	Mexican War	2	4889
Ingram, Jonas Howard	Navy	Mexican War	30	643-RH
Izac, Edouard Victor Michel	Navy	WW I	3	4222-16
Jacobson, Douglas Thomas	Marines	WW II	Court 5, Stack 17, Sec. H, Niche 3	
Jardine, Alexander	Navy	Interim	12	4280
Jennings, Delbert Owen	Army	Vietnam	7A	157
Joel, Lawrence	Army	Vietnam	46	15-1
Johanson, John Peter	Navy	Spanish-American War	6	9768

Name	Branch	Action	Section[1]	Grave No.
Johansson, Johan J.	Navy	Spanish-American War	13	720
Johnson, Dwight Hal	Army	Vietnam	31	471
Johnson, Henry	Army	Indian Wars	23	16547
Johnson, Henry	Army	WW I	25	64
Johnson, James Edmund	Marines	Korea	MH	451
Johnson, Joseph Esrey	Army	Civil War	3	2278
Johnson, Leon William	Army	WW II	7A	209
Johnson, William	Navy	Interim	23	16648-32
Johnston, Gordon	Navy	Philippine-American War	7	10092
Johnston, Rufus Zenas, Jr.	Navy	Mexican War	2	3645-RH
Jones, Claud Ashton	Navy	Interim	11	546-SS
Kane, John Riley	Army	WW II	7A	47
Keefer, Philip Bogan	Navy	Spanish-American War	11	527-SH
Keller, Leonard Bert	Army	Vietnam	60	9197
Kelley, Leverett Mansfield	Army	Civil War	2	3756
Kelly, Thomas Joseph	Army	WW II	7A	125
Kennedy, John Thomas	Army	Philippine-American War	7	10076
Kerr, John Brown	Army	Indian Wars	3	1950-SH
Kerr, Thomas R.	Army	Civil War	3	1623
Kilbourne, Charles Evans, Jr.	Army	Philippine-American War	3	1705
Kingsley, David Richard	Army	WW II	34	4786
Kirby, Dennis Thomas	Army	Civil War	1	334
Knappenberger, Alton W.	Army	WW II	59	3193
Koelsch, John Kelvin	Navy	Korea	30	1123-RH
Langhorne, Cary DeVall	Navy	Mexican War	11	868
Lannon, James Patrick	Navy	Mexican War	8	6410-B
Latham, John Cridland	Army	WW I	35	1127
Lawson, Gaines	Army	Civil War	1	37-A
Lawton, Henry Ware	Army	Civil War	2	841
Leims, John Harold	Marines	WW II	2	1132-2
Levitow, John Lee	Air Force	Vietnam	66	7107
Libby, George Dalton	Army	Korea	34	1317
Lipscomb, Harry	Navy	Interim	3	2481-WS
Loman, Berger Holton	Army	WW I	37	4909
Loring, Charles Joseph, Jr.	Air Force	Korea	MK	89
Lower, Cyrus B.	Army	Civil War	17	19971
Ludgate, William	Army	Civil War	3	1488
Lyle, Alexander Gordon, Jr.	Navy	WW I	2	1114-1
MacArthur, Arthur, Jr.	Army	Civil War	2	856-A
MacGillivary, Charles Andrew	Army	WW II	48	568
Maclay, William Palmer	Army	Philippine-American War	7	9008-F

Name	Branch	Action	Section[1]	Grave No.
Mathias, Clarence Edward	Marines	Boxer Rebellion	6	8681
Maus, Marion Perry	Army	Indian Wars	3	3886-B
Mausert, Frederick William, III	Marines	Korea	12	5559
Mays, Isaiah	Army	Indian Wars	1	630-B
McBryar, William	Army	Indian Wars	4	2738-B
McCampbell, David	Navy	WW II	60	3150
McCarthy, Joseph Jeremiah	Marines	WW II	30	1716
McClernand, Edward John	Army	Indian Wars	3	1931-SW
McCloy, John[6]	Navy	Boxer Rebellion, Mexican War	8	5246
McConnell, James	Army	Philippine-American War	7	8317
McDonnell, Edward Orrick	Navy	Mexican War	2	4955-4
McGinnis, Ross Andrew	Army	Iraq	60	8544
McGonagle, William Loren	Navy	International Waters	34	208
McGovern, Robert Milton	Army	Korea	3	1312-BC
McGrath, Hugh Jocelyn	Army	Philippine-American War	1	315-ES
McGuire, Thomas Buchanan, Jr.	Army	WW II	11	426-SH
McGunigal, Patrick	Navy	WW I	6	8674
McMahon, Martin Thomas	Army	Civil War	2	1101
Meagher, John William	Army	WW II	64	1701
Merriam, Henry Clay	Army	Civil War	1	114-B
Miles, Nelson Appleton	Army	Civil War	3	1873
Miller, Archie	Army	Philippine-American War	1	300-A
Miller, Willard D.	Navy	Spanish-American War	46	15
Mindil, George Washington	Army	Civil War	3	1568
Mitchell, Alexander H.	Army	Civil War	3	2515
Moffett ,William Adger	Navy	Mexican War	3	1655-A
Monegan, Walter Carleton, Jr.	Marines	Korea	34	4513
Morelock, Sterling Lewis	Army	WW I	35	1824
Morgan, George Horace	Army	Indian Wars	3	2053
Morgan, John Cary	Army	WW II	59	351
Muller, Frederick	Army	Spanish-American War	8	6035
Murphy, Audie Leon	Army	WW II	46	366-11
Murphy, Robinson Barr	Army	Civil War	6	9749
Murray, Charles P., Jr.	Army	WW II	60	9725
Myers, Fred	Army	Indian Wars	13	14034
Myers, Reginald Rodney	Marines	Korea	60	884
Neville, Wendell Cushing	Marines	Mexican War	6	8409
Nininger, Alexander R., Jr.	Army	WW II	MK	139
Nordsiek, Charles Luers	Navy	Mexican War	7	10230-SS
Nordstrom, Isidor A.	Navy	Interim	7	8273
Novosel, Michael Joseph	Army	Vietnam	7A	178-C

Name	Branch	Action	Section[1]	Grave No.
O'Connor, Timothy	Army	Civil War	MF	10-3
Ogden, Carlos Carnes, Sr.	Army	WW II	65	533
O'Kane, Richard Hetherington	Navy	WW II	59	874
Osborne, John	Navy	Interim	17	19689
Ostermann, Edward Albert	Marines	Haiti	46	521
Page, John Upshur Dennis	Army	Korea	4	2743-AB
Palmer, George Henry	Army	Civil War	3	2104
Parks, Henry Jeremiah	Army	Civil War	2	1200-SS
Peters, Alexander	Navy	Interim	8	5300-A
Pharris, Jackson Charles	Navy	WW II	13	16281
Pipes, James Milton	Army	Civil War	3	1332-A
Plowman, George H.	Army	Civil War	3	4417-EH
Pope, Everett Parker	Marines	WW II	59	3800
Pope, Thomas A.	Army	WW I	35	3157
Port, William David	Army	Vietnam	7	8120-B
Porter, David Dixon	Marines	Philippine-American War	2	3479
Porter, Donn F.	Army	Korea	33	4357
Preston, Arthur Murray	Navy	WW II	3	1847-A1
Pruitt, John Henry[7]	Marines	WW I	18	2453
Purman, James Jackson	Army	Civil War	1	615
Quinn, Peter H.	Army	Philippine-American War	6	9749-SH
Rabel, Laszlo	Army	Vietnam	52	1326
Ramage, Lawson Paterson "Red"	Navy	WW II	7A	184
Rand, Charles Franklin	Army	Civil War	1	125-B
Raub, Jacob F.	Army	Civil War	3	1469
Raymond, William H.	Army	Civil War	2	4853
Reem, Robert Dale	Marines	Korea	6	9376-B
Reid, George Croghan	Marines	Mexican War	2	1096-A
Rice, Edmund	Army	Civil War	3	1875
Richmond, James	Army	Civil War	27	886
Roach, Hampton Mitchell	Army	Indian Wars	3	2393-WS
Roberts, Charles DuVal	Army	Spanish-American War	2	3671
Robinson, Robert Guy	Marines	WW I	46	390
Roeder, Robert E.	Army	WW II	12	6116
Rogers, Charles Calvin	Army	Vietnam	7A	99
Romeyn, Henry	Army	Indian Wars	3	1750
Rose, George Harry	Navy	Boxer Rebellion	7	9978-ES
Rush, John[8]	Navy	Civil War	17	18768
Rush, William Rees	Navy	Mexican War	3	3977
Russell, Henry Peter	Navy	Spanish-American War	31	6377
Ryan, Francis Thomas	Navy	Boxer Rebellion	17	21008

Name	Branch	Action	Section[1]	Grave No.
Ryan, Thomas John	Navy	Interim	34	80-A-1
Sage, William Hampden	Army	Philippine-American War	2	913
Saxton, Rufus, Jr.	Army	Civil War	1	20-A
Schilt, Christian Franklin	Marines	Nicaragua	2	E-151-2
Schmidt, Oscar Nate, Jr.	Navy	WW I	11	116-LH
Schnepel, Fred Jurgen	Navy	Mexican War	11	825
Schofield, John McAllister	Army	Civil War	2	1108
Schonland, Herbert Emery	Navy	WW II	7A	168
Schou, Julius Alexis	Army	Indian Wars	17	21482
Schwan, Theodore	Army	Civil War	2	860
Schwenk, Martin[9]	Army	Civil War	17	20472
Scott, Alexander	Army	Civil War	17	18563
Scott, Robert Raymond	Navy	WW II	34	3939
Seach, William	Navy	Boxer Rebellion	11	334-2
Shacklette, William Sidney	Navy	Interim	10	10295
Shanahan, Patrick	Navy	Interim	7	10295
Shaw, George Clymer	Army	Philippine-American War	3	4247
Shaw, Thomas	Army	Indian Wars	27	952-B
Shoup, David Monroe	Marines	WW II	7A	189
Sickles, Daniel Edgar	Army	Civil War	3	1906
Sidman, George Dallas	Army	Civil War	3	2492
Sigler, Franklin Earl	Marines	WW II	12	2799
Silk, Edward A.	Army	WW II	30	1045-C
Sitter, Carl Leonard	Marines	Korea	7A	57-A
Skaggs, Luther, Jr.	Marines	WW II	46	1066-B
Skinner, John Oscar	Army	Indian Wars	3	1662
Skinner, Sherrod Emerson, Jr.	Army	Korea	3	2032
Slack, Clayton Kirk	Army	WW I	34	59
Smedley, Larry Eugene	Marines	Vietnam	31	6485
Smith, Charles Henry	Army	Civil War	1	128-A
Smith, Fred E.	Army	WW I	1	305-A
Smith, John Lucian	Marines	WW II	3	2503-H-2
Smith, Joseph Sewall	Army	Civil War	2	996
Smith, Maynard Harrison	Army	WW II	66	7375
Smith, Paul Ray	Army	Iraq	MD	67
Snyder, William Ellsworth	Navy	Interim	10	10636
Stahel, Julius H.	Army	Civil War	2	998
Stanley, Robert Henry	Navy	Boxer Rebellion	7	8348
Staton, Adolphus	Navy	Mexican War	4	280-A
Stewart, George Evans	Army	Philippine-American War	2	3408-A-RH
Stickney, Herman Osman	Navy	Mexican War	3	1821

Name	Branch	Action	Section[1]	Grave No.
Stokes, John S.	Navy	Interim	17	20184
Street, George Levick, III	Navy	WW II	7A	130-B
Sullivan, Daniel Augustus Joseph	Navy	WW I	8	5327-A
Sundquist, Gustav Adolf[10]	Navy	Spanish-American War	MK	192
Sutton, Clarence Edwin	Marines	Boxer Rebellion	17	18847
Svehla, Henry	Army	Korea	MG	27
Swanson, Jon E.	Army	Vietnam	30	7755
Swayne, Wager	Army	Civil War	3	1406
Thomason, Clyde A.	Marines	WW II	60	8036
Thordsen, William George	Navy	Philippine-American War	1	69-W
Thorn, Walter	Army	Civil War	2	3689-WH
Tilton, Henry Remsen	Army	Indian Wars	1	392
Tominac, John Joseph	Army	WW II	66	5141
Torgerson, Martin Torinus	Navy	Boxer Rebellion	6	8680
Townsend, Julius Curtis	Navy	Mexican War	6	8590
Truell, Edwin M.	Army	Civil War	13	5274-C
Turner, Charles William	Army	Korea	12	7762
Turner, George Benton	Army	WW II	71	589
Tweedale, John	Army	Civil War	1	470-WS
Upton, Frank Monroe	Navy	WW I	8	55-A
Urban, Matt Louis	Army	WW II	7A	40
Urell, Michael Emmet	Army	Civil War	1	51-D
Van Iersel, Ludovicus M. M.	Army	WW I	42	1770
Van Voorhis, Bruce Avery	Navy	WW II	MI	86
Vance, Wilson J.	Army	Civil War	3	2360-WS
Vandergrift, Alexander Archer	Marines	WW II	2	4965-B-RH
Veazey, Wheelock Graves	Army	Civil War	2	1026
Vera, Miguel Armando	Army	Korea	71	258
Versace, Humbert Roque	Army	Vietnam	MG	108
Vosler, Forrest Lee	Army	WW II	60	4924
Wainwright, John	Army	Civil War	2	1061
Wainwright, Jonathan M., IV	Army	WW II	1	358-B
Walker, Kenneth Newton	Army	WW II	MC	36-M
Walmsley, John Springer, Jr.	Air Force	Korea	MF	46-3
Walsh, Kenneth Ambrose	Marines	WW II	65	2996
Walsh, William Gary	Marines	WW II	12	487
Wanton, George Henry	Army	Spanish-American War	4	2749
Ware, Keith Lincoln	Army	WW II	30	258-3
Watters, Charles Joseph	Army	Vietnam	2	E-186-A
West, Frank	Army	Indian Wars	1	549
Westa, Karl	Navy	Interim	11	83-SH

Name	Branch	Action	Section[1]	Grave No.
Weston, John Francis	Army	Civil War	2	856
Wheeler, George Huber	Navy	Interim	7	10040-EH
Wheeler, Henry W.	Army	Civil War	3	1496
Whitaker, Edward Washburn	Army	Civil War	3	1324
Whittington, Hulon Brooke	Army	WW II	13	8-W
Wigle, Thomas W.	Army	WW II	34	3307
Wilkinson, Theodore Stark, Jr.	Navy	Mexican War	2	3645
Willcox, Orlando Bolivar	Army	Civil War	1	18
Williams, Charles Quincy	Army	Vietnam	65	1471
Williston, Edward Bancroft	Army	Civil War	1	422
Wilson., Louis Hugh, Jr.	Marines	WW II	7A	103-B
Windrich, William Gordon	Marines	Korea	31	4856
Wood, Henry Clay	Army	Civil War	1	80-A
Wood, Leonard	Army	Indian Wars	21	S-10
Woodall, Zachariah Taylor	Army	Indian Wars	22	15788
Woodfill, Samuel	Army	WW I	34	642-A
Young, Frank Albert	Marines	Boxer Rebellion	17	18979-D
Young, Gerald Orren	Air Force	Vietnam	7A	87
Zeamer, Jay, Jr.	Army	WW II	34	809-4

Courtesy of the Medal of Honor Historical Society of the United States and the Congressional Medal of Honor Society

[1] Sections beginning with the letter *M* are memorial sections
[2] Double recipient
[3] Remains never recovered
[4] Double recipient
[5] Remains never recovered
[6] Double recipient
[7] Double recipient
[8] Buried as Israel W. Little
[9] Buried as George Martin
[10] First name shown as *Gustaf* in cemetery records

I am a veteran. Does this mean I automatically qualify to be buried in Arlington?

Not necessarily. Because of the prestige of Arlington and the dwindling number of available spaces, qualifications for burial are more stringent than at most national cemeteries. Also, qualifications for in-ground burials are not the same as for above-ground inurnment at Arlington.

Those eligible for in-ground burial at Arlington National Cemetery include any service member of the armed forces killed in active duty; any retired veteran of the armed forces who made a career out of military service and is entitled to receive retirement pay; recipients of high honors such as the Medal of Honor, the Distinguished Service Cross, the Navy Cross, the Air Force Cross, the Distinguished Service Medal, the Silver Star, or the Purple Heart; any former prisoner of war whose service terminated honorably and who served on or after November 30, 1993; anyone who has held elected office in the U.S. government or served as a Supreme Court justice, provided they also served in the military and were discharged honorably; and the spouses and dependent children of anyone qualified to be buried at ANC.

Those qualified to be buried at Arlington also qualify for above-ground inurnment. In addition, above-ground inurnment is available to any former member of the armed forces whose service terminated honorably; members of the national reserves, the National Guard, or the Air National Guard who were killed in active duty or who are retired and qualify to receive retirement pay (assuming they served as least one day on active duty); and the spouses and dependent children of those qualified for inurnment at Arlington.

Eligibility information is current at the time of publication and is summarized from http://www.arlingtoncemetery.mil/Funerals/Scheduling-a-Funeral/Establishing-Eligibility. Consult that site for detailed information or before making final application for burial or inurnment.

What documents will my family need to schedule my funeral service, or a service for an eligible next of kin?

Before a service can be scheduled, all documentation must be submitted and reviewed by Arlington staff to establish and confirm eligibility. At the minimum, those documents include the deceased's DD214 or equivalent service documentation showing honorable discharge and active-duty service (mandatory for a veteran, though second interment of a spouse does not require this if ANC can verify the veteran's eligibility from archived records); death certificate; cremation certificate, if applicable; and succession documents for the person authorized to direct disposition (PADD) to act on behalf of the primary next of kin (PNOK).

Unmarried adult dependents must have two additional documents. The first is a notarized statement from an individual who has direct knowledge as to the marital status, degree of dependency of the deceased child, the name of that child's parent, and the military service upon which the burial is being requested. Also required is a certificate from the attending physician regarding the nature and duration of the physical and/or mental disability.

For inurnments, Arlington National Cemetery requires certification of 100 percent of cremated remains and a cremated remains certificate. It is important to note that Arlington does not accept cremated remains by mail.

I qualify for an Arlington burial but prefer to be buried in a national cemetery closer to my home. May I choose the national cemetery in which I want to be buried?

Qualified personnel may be buried in any national cemetery that has available space.

I qualify for burial in Arlington but am concerned that space may no longer be available when I die. May I reserve a plot now to be sure I have a space?

Arlington does not permit reserving burial plots in advance. If you wish to be buried in another national cemetery, contact that facility for its policy on advance reservations.

How many national cemeteries exist in the United States?

There are currently 134 national cemeteries. Of these,

only Arlington and the U.S. Soldiers' and Airmen's Home National Cemetery are maintained by the Department of the Army, with the National Park Service responsible for Arlington House. The remaining 132 national cemeteries are maintained by the Veterans Administration.

I've seen funerals at Arlington that had a band and a horse-drawn caisson, while others seemed far less formal. Why the difference?

The less formal funerals are available to any qualified enlisted service member or officer. This type of funeral includes a chaplain, a six-man burial detail, a firing detail, and a bugler. The more formal ceremonies, known as "full military honors" funerals, are available at the family's request if the deceased was a commissioned officer or a warrant officer or held the pay grade of E-9 or higher. Any enlisted service members killed on active duty also qualify for full military honors.

A funeral with full military honors includes a procession to the grave site with a horse-drawn caisson, a marching band, a marching escort, and a four-man color guard. A chaplain walks in front of the caisson but behind the escort, band, and color guard.

Services for both types of funerals are identical except that in the full military honors ceremony the band plays while the casket is taken to the grave and while the flag is folded.

Spouses and dependent children receive the services of a casket team and a military chaplain.

Some funerals with full military honors have a riderless horse, while others do not. Is that an option for any burial with full military honors?

Not all burials with full military honors qualify. The riderless horse, symbolizing that the deceased fell as a warrior and will not ride again, is reserved for those who served as an army or Marine Corps colonel or above.

What will burial in Arlington National Cemetery cost my family?

Qualified personnel do not have to pay for burials. Their veterans' benefits include the cost of opening and closing the grave, perpetual care, a government headstone, a burial flag, and a Presidential Memorial Certificate. Customized headstones or private vaults, however, are at the family's expense. If a family elects to pay to have a private monument erected, then the deceased must be buried in an older section of the cemetery where such monuments are permitted, providing space is available.

All costs associated with the preparation of the remains, the casket or urn, and the shipping of the remains to the Washington area are at the expense of the estate unless the deceased was on active duty with a branch of the armed forces. Interested persons should check with their local VA and Social Security offices to determine if any benefits are available from either or both agencies.

What is said to the family when the folded flag is presented at the end of the service?

"On behalf of the president of the United States and a grateful nation, please accept this flag as a token of the honorable and faithful service of your loved one."

I am eligible for burial in Arlington and would like to have the symbol of my religion on my headstone. Is that allowed?

It depends. Only approved graphics are permitted on government-issued headstones. As of this writing, emblems of sixty belief systems have been approved for inclusion on headstones at Arlington. A listing of currently approved symbols may be viewed at http://www.cem.va.gov/cem/docs/emblems.pdf. If yours is not included, contact the cemetery for the procedure to request a new symbol. The available emblems for use on military headstones are not limited to religious symbols, nor is it a requirement that a symbol be included.

Index